A THEOLOGY OF
TRANSITION

A THEOLOGY OF TRANSITION

TRANSITION

H. R. MACKINTOSH AS
AN APPROACH TO BARTH

By

JAMES W. LEITCH
M.A., B.D., D.Theol.

WITH A FOREWORD BY
PROFESSOR KARL BARTH

LONDON: NISBET & CO., LTD.
22 BERNERS STREET, W.1

First published 1952

Made and printed in Great Britain

FOREWORD

THIS examination and presentation of the theology of H. R. Mackintosh originated in Basle and was accepted by our Faculty as a dissertation for the Doctorate of Theology. I am glad to say a word about it here.

H. R. Mackintosh and I actually met only once—it must have been in the summer of 1930. I remember that it was in the station in Edinburgh, where I was waiting for my train to London, and there, with a very earnest face, he asked me about my conception of the Atoning Death of Christ. My answer then must have been a very poor one. His personality made an unforgettable impression on me. It was not until later that I also came to know his books. I had reason to admire him for both of the things which are now brought so clearly to light in this dissertation: the thoroughness with which this man had penetrated and made himself familiar with the positions of nineteenth-century German theology, of the school of Schleiermacher and particularly Albrecht Ritschl and his followers, *and* the honest unrest and refreshing frankness in which, because the Scottish Calvinist tradition was still as live in him as ever, he strained beyond these positions. His work filled me with interest because, for one thing, I found him engaged quite independently in a movement which, in its general direction, was very like my own. But he was older than I. He was more deeply rooted in the old school than I could ever have been. He had no doubt gained in harder struggles than I the insight into its relative rightness. And so it obviously cost him more trouble than me to recognise its limits and to break out beyond them at the decisive points. But I lacked also such a sharp imprint of the Calvinist heritage as the one which first of all led him *to* Ritschl and his followers and then just as strongly away from them.

v

So I could, and still can, think of this man only with sincere respect. And when Mr. Leitch came to Basle and thought of writing a dissertation, it was very natural for me to suggest that he should make precisely this compatriot of his the object of his study. I think he has done so in a manner which is worthy of this great teacher of the Scottish Church and which, for the understanding of her more recent theology, but also for the understanding of the relation between continental and British theology and their effect upon each other in the period of crisis which both have entered, is illuminating and worthy of all consideration.

Time does not stand still. And the question of the relevant form of theology cannot stand still either. The Holy Spirit too, fortunately enough, does not cease to urge us all to ever new reflection. Mackintosh, if he were still with us, would certainly be surprised—or perhaps he would *not* be surprised—to learn that in Germany the problems presented by Schleiermacher and Ritschl and Herrmann have meanwhile risen again in a new form: in the discussion of the work of Rudolf Bultmann they have already received once more a new—a much greater reality and urgency than some had supposed twenty-five years ago. They must be surmounted. We cannot return to the flesh-pots of Egypt. But Israel's journey from Egypt to the land of Canaan was, as we know, a very weary, winding and often interrupted journey. It should be clearly realised everywhere that the entry into that land is on no account to be had cheaply. God preserve us from all ready-made formulae and prescriptions. Is it not the case that in all ages proper theology has existed only as "Theology of Transition"—in Latin, *theologia viatorum?* As such may it find also in the second half of our century, on both sides of the Channel, some representatives as earnest as the man to whose work this book is dedicated. Then there need be no fears for its future.

KARL BARTH.

BASLE, *March 1952.*

CONTENTS

CHAPTER I

INTRODUCTORY

CHAPTER II

THE FUNDAMENTAL PRINCIPLES OF DOGMATIC

CHAPTER III

THE CONCEPT OF GOD

vii

Chapter IV

PREFACE

SOMEONE has pointed out that "theology" is simply the Greek for "thinking about God"—in which sense we are all called to be theologians. It is for all who are ready to answer this call, not just for the technical theologian, that this book is intended. For the movement it seeks to trace in H. R. Mackintosh's thought is not only significant for the understanding of his own work: it is also of very great importance to any to-day who care to think seriously about their faith. Mackintosh, indeed, has a certain universality, in so far as his teaching is likely to command fairly wide assent: we may feel difficulties at many points, as he did, but comparatively few are likely to be conscious of any very thorough-going disagreement with the positions he adopts. Yet the obvious difficulties are often only the symptoms of deeper and much graver problems involved in these positions, and largely inherited from the " enlightened " thought of the nineteenth century.

The extraordinary thing about Mackintosh was his increasing awareness of the nature of these problems, and the solution he eventually found to them. It is at this point that his thought becomes not so much representative as in a sense prophetic. And it is above all here that he has so much to teach us to-day. I cannot expect that the study now offered should have for its readers the same thrill and value which its preparation has had for me personally. But I do hope it may help both to stimulate new interest in one of our finest teachers, and also to cast fresh light on our still extensive legacy from the nineteenth century and indicate how we may find relief from the burdens it so often imposes on our thought.

It may seem a little strange that no special account is here given of Mackintosh's Christology or his doctrine of the

Atonement, although these were two of his prime interests. I had, at first, intended to include them, but for a number of reasons this turned out scarcely practicable, and in the end it seemed best to limit the discussion meantime to the fundamentals and the general concept of God. This has at least had the advantage of allowing the movement of thought to be traced at these points more clearly and in greater detail than would have been possible in the shorter chapters which would otherwise have been necessary. I hope to be able to treat the doctrines of the Person and Work of Christ more adequately later.

I should like to record here my gratitude to the Rev. Harry Whitley, whose encouragement and affection have so long meant so much to me. My debts to my teachers both in New College and in Basle are too many and varied for individual mention, but I want to thank especially Professor Karl Barth for his inspiring guidance and for all the many tokens of a kindly interest extending far beyond the mere supervision of my studies. I am indebted to the Basel Mission for allowing me to share the fellowship and comfort of the Missionshaus, and especially to the Matron, Frl. Veronika Müller, whose care and efficiency made it such a pleasant place to stay. My thanks are also due to Dr. Lex van Wyk of Johannesburg for many a fruitful discussion; to Pfarrer Werner Simpfendörfer of Korntal and Pfarrer Eugen Stöffler of Kircheim for, among other things, their invaluable help with the preparation of the type-script; to the Carnegie Trust for a grant towards publication; and to Messrs. James Nisbet & Co. for the patience and understanding with which they have handled a not always easy task.

JAMES W. LEITCH.

Rothiemurchus Manse,
 Aviemore,
  May 1952.

Chapter I

INTRODUCTORY

1. LIFE AND WORK

IN a tribute to his admired and beloved teacher, Pringle-Pattison, H. R. Mackintosh once wrote: "In his works the best elements of British and German philosophy enter into a uniquely convincing and fruitful combination". Had Mackintosh written " British and Continental theology ", he would have aptly characterised the aspect of his own work in which it is likely to make its most immediate claim on our interest and attention. For not only had he a wide knowledge of the writings of the Church Fathers and especially of the great Reformers, but he is said to have studied every work of the slightest theological importance published in English, French or German during the nineteenth and twentieth centuries. And he combined with this knowledge not only a remarkable critical and selective insight but also a simplicity and lucidity of style which is all too seldom a feature of theological writing.

That in itself would be enough to recommend the study of his work. Yet it still leaves untouched another feature of it which is no less important for being perhaps a little less immediately obvious—namely the way in which, as he recognises in an ever-recurring tone of wonder, the things he wished to express repeatedly broke through the terms of the day in which he sought to express them and which continually proved inadequate to the purpose. It was this, surely, which led him to the conviction that theological statements call for constant revision; and part at least of his greatness is shown by the fidelity with which he held to this principle—he was constantly revising his college lectures, and even in the last year of his life completely rewrote some of them, while after a whole life-time devoted to the study of the Atonement he was still marvelling at the incomprehensibility of it and asking what it really means. It is this feature of his work which makes it so peculiarly intriguing and valuable: for it imparts to it a certain fluidity and a freely acknowledged lack of finality which must be an example to his successors and, at the same time, a constant inspiration and challenge to renewed theological effort. His aim was to formulate in terms of human language and thought the convictions and implications of his faith ; but because his faith was a living faith in the living God his work could never be static, and because the Reality with which he was concerned is infinitely richer than either human language or human thought, the task of interpretation was for him, as it must be for every true theologian, one which can never be finished but must constantly be begun again " in the faith and fear of the Lord ".

Thus his work is, like his life, that of a humble seeker and pilgrim. Indeed, the two cannot be separated : he was not one of those thinkers whose life and work are independent of each other, so that either can be completely luminous apart from the other. No doubt he was both a great scholar and a great saint ; but his scholarship depended as much on personal friendships and influences as on book learning, and his faith was proved and tested not only in the study but throughout a life of devoted Christian service and warm personal relationships. So it will help us to understand his work, if we glance for a moment at some of the significant facts of his life.

He was born in Paisley on 31st October 1870, the son of a Gaelic-speaking minister of the Free Church ; and it may well be the Celtic spirit thus inherited which accounts for the touch of fire and of more than half-prophetic insight so often found in his work, as well as for that other quality of which it has been said that its importance in a theologian is as great as its presence is rare—a powerful sense of humour. Both his parents died in his early childhood, and he was brought up by an uncle and aunt in Ross-shire. But his uncle was also a minister of the Free Church, who gave him the traditional Scottish upbringing with its thorough grounding in the knowledge of Scripture and the Catechism which was to mean so much for his later work.

If, indeed, there was one thing which was more formative of his thought than any other, then it was surely the Calvinist influence which surrounded his earliest years. For the continual and reverent searching of the Scriptures thereby became almost a second nature with him, while the recognition of the sovereign supremacy of God set in the forefront of the Catechism was a veritable pillar of cloud and of fire to him in his theological journey through the wilderness of nineteenth century thought. From first to last it was his intention to be guided by nothing else but the Word of God as made known in Scripture through the inner witness of the Holy Spirit, and if at times he may have wandered from the way, he never wandered really far and soon came back to it again. While if his earlier works show signs of a certain antipathy towards the subordinate standards of his Church, it was for the most part only the barren and sterile " orthodoxy " sometimes built upon them that he was attacking: they themselves not only remained virtually unassailed as far as their fundamental principles were concerned, but also rendered him good service through-out his struggle with Liberalism in all its forms. And it is not too much to say that they came out the stronger in the end. For it is reported that in his last years, if there were any among his students whom he was predisposed to favour, they were the few who still knew their Catechism by heart. But however that may be, in a series of lectures on the West-minster Confession and Catechisms, written shortly before his death in 1936, but never published, he expresses a deep respect for them: he was far from wishing to canonise them or to turn a blind eye to their short-comings, but he speaks in the highest terms of the Confession itself and stoutly defends the Larger Catechism against the charge that it was obviously composed by "tolerably hard-hearted people, without a gleam of tenderness or sensitive insight", while of the Shorter Catechism he not only insists that in parts it is "superlatively good" but also says: "It is all in all a masterly performance. No Catechism can be placed on the same level for strength, lucidity, and happy arrangement."

A second extremely important element in his thought derives from his student days. By the time he entered the Arts Faculty of Edinburgh University in 1888 he had already been well grounded in classical studies, but here he developed alongside his abiding love of the Classics a new and even greater interest in philosophy. This was due to the powerful influence of Professor Pringle-Pattison, for whom he conceived a profound admiration and affection. And it would probably be difficult to over-estimate the significance of Pringle-Pattison's work especially for the attitude he adopted towards Hegelianism and for the place he came to assign to philosophy in relation to theology. In some ways it was rather a baneful influence; for it inclined him to turn aside at times into what, for the theologian, are surely forbidden or at least perilous paths, and one soon learns to regard the name of Pringle-Pattison in the argument as often something in the nature of a danger signal. Yet on the whole it was much more of a blessing than a curse; for it led him to such a familiarity with philosophical opinions of all descriptions as probably went a long way both to convince him of the limitations of philosophy and to fortify him against the theological positivism which denounces speculative thought of any and every kind.

During his theological studies at New College he learned much from the New Testament scholarship of Marcus

Dods ; and doubtless most of all from that remarkable figure
A. B. Davidson—in many ways so far ahead of his time—
who gave him a profound insight into the theology of the
Old Testament which, especially in regard to its view of the
Divine holiness, was later to stand him in such good stead.
But probably the most decisive factor in his student days
was the three semesters in Freiburg, Halle and Marburg
which brought them to a close. For Freiburg laid the
foundations of his first-class knowledge of German language
and literature, while Halle and Marburg brought him into
immediate contact with some of the leading continental
theologians of the day. His studies under Reischle formed
an introduction to the Ritschlian theology, for which he soon
developed a respect somewhat deeper, one feels, than was its
due ; and he describes the lectures of Herrmann the following year as an unforgettable experience. Yet his interest was
not confined to the Ritschlians : he was also open to influences from many other quarters, and found above all in the
lectures of Kähler a valuable antidote to Ritschl which he
was not slow to accept. Nor, of course, was it only to the
Continent that he looked for stimulus and guidance : he
took over much from the singularly arresting writings of
P. T. Forsyth, as well as from lesser men too numerous to
mention, while he maintained exceedingly fruitful friendships with James Denney and H. A. A. Kennedy, both of
whom (especially the latter) helped him enormously towards
the understanding of Pauline theology which was one of
the chief weapons in his armoury. Yet it is the German, and
more particularly the Ritschlian, influence which is the most
marked, at least on the surface, of his early works. And it
is one of the ironies of fate that although he did more than
most to bring Continental thought to Britain, he himself
remains little more than a name to most of those on the
Continent who know him at all.

Last, but by no means least, among the things which went
to mould his thought was the Scot's intense interest in

practical affairs. His life in the pastoral ministry of the Church was extremely short, for in 1904 he was called to the Chair of Systematic Theology (now Christian Dogmatics) in New College, which he held until his death. Yet he was not by any means the traditional professorial figure, ensconced upon the heights of academic learning remote from the world, but took a thoroughly active part in the work of the Church and a lively interest in all that went on in the College outside as well as inside the lecture-room. If, in fact, he had little sympathy with those whose chief desire is to get on with the job and leave the theory to any who care for such things, he had just as little with a conception of theology which would suggest that it is theorising merely for the fun of it: doctrine and life, he kept insisting, must answer to each other, and the less they in fact do so the falser both must be.

It was largely this, no doubt, which attracted him at first to the Ritschlians, who laid such stress on the practical side of religion. And probably it was largely this, too, which brought him back to Calvin in the end, whom he cannot praise highly enough in a late (unpublished) lecture for the vital and indissoluble inter-relation in which he sets Dogmatics and Christian Ethics almost as a matter of course—he himself, indeed, was somewhat dissatisfied with the unnatural separation of the two disciplines which confined his own Chair to the former. Yet his interest was not in any vague or undefined practical activity ; for he held that *the* practical task laid upon the Church is the proclamation of the Word. Thus he maintained that although dogmatic theology must have a vital bearing upon the whole range of Christian life and practice, it is first and foremost to serve the preacher that it exists. And for his own part he sought to give concrete expression to this intimate relation between dogmatic and preaching in two main ways. On the one hand, in spite of all the demands of his Professorship he was to be found on most Sundays in the pulpit of one church or another. And on the other hand, he had a special arrangement made whereby he was allowed to conduct the weekly College class in homiletics, although it fell outwith the scope of his own Chair.

2. *THE BRITISH HEGELIAN MOVEMENT*

If there are aspects of Mackintosh's thought which cannot be understood entirely apart from his life, there are others which are best seen in relation to the background of British thought in the latter part of the nineteenth century. We cannot, of course, attempt to disentangle all the threads of a quarter of a century of thought, but fortunately there is no need to do so: for there is one movement which was so predominant that almost every writer was influenced by it and compelled to take up a position either for, or in a few cases, against it. This was the movement of British Hegelianism. It would be impossible to give a complete survey of this movement within the scope of a few pages, but we may note its salient features.

The movement came as a reaction against the sensual Individualism and Utilitarianism of J. S. Mill and the equally sensual Agnosticism and Evolutionism of Spencer, as also against the much less poverty-stricken Scottish Common Sense Philosophy of Reid, developed by Stewart, Hamilton and Cousin. A few writers had already in the first half of the century turned their attention to Continental thought—for example, the Scots philosopher Sir William Hamilton, who had devoted a large part of his work to a criticism of Kant, and other writers such as Coleridge, Emerson in America, and above all Carlyle with his tremendous admiration for Goethe. The interest thus aroused is witnessed by the appearance in the 30's and 40's of the first critical translations of the works of Kant and the ethical works of Fichte ; while Hegel himself was known and studied at Oxford in the 50's, notably by Jowett. But it is not until 1865 that the movement properly begins*—with the publication of Hutchison Stirling's *The Secret of Hegel*. From then on it rapidly gained complete dominance. A few real connoisseurs of Kant pled his cause, some even arguing that the path of German philosophy after Kant should be ignored as one which must inevitably be retraced. But they remained a minority: Kant's theoretical teaching has practically never met with anything but criticism and even rejection in Britain, and though his ethical teaching caused certain modifications in the Hegelian position and was later to find still greater acceptance, yet Kant never attained anything like the dominance which Hegel had in the last quarter of the century and a little later.

The speed and completeness of the new movement's dominance had doubtless its ground in the peculiarly satisfactory answer it appeared to give to the needs of the period. We may notice four of the main ones:—

(*a*) One was the need for a principle of distinction between sacred and secular on which the whole universe could be spiritually discerned—the need felt by a romantic culture which rebelled against the arbitrary distinction of rigid orthodoxy, yet was not at heart materialist. And this seemed to be admirably provided by the fundamental Hegelian principle of identity mediated by difference. For it meant that there do not exist in actual fact two opposed and mutually exclusive worlds—a higher spiritual world of religious truths and a lower, material world of every-day sense experience. Rather is there but one single rational or spiritual reality manifesting itself alike through the material

* By this time, of course, Hegelianism was a thing of the past in Germany. But if one is tempted to quote the saying that " German philosophies when they die go to Oxford ", it is well to remember that at this time Mill and Spencer, whom we were abandoning, and above all Darwin were beginning to have a powerful influence on the continent. We had, in fact, made a complete exchange. For as someone has pointed out, there never was a widespread Hegelianism in Germany as there was in Britain, and there never was a thoroughgoing Darwinism in Britain but there was one in Germany.

and through the spiritual world, in all history, all experience and all thought, in a series of necessarily contrasted forms.

(b) Moreover, Hegel's Idealism was rigorously immanental: the Finite and the Infinite are relatively opposite but ultimately identical. This means that the spiritual world is to be sought *within*, instead of *above* or *beyond*, the natural ; and thus the movement allied itself consciously or unconsciously to the contemporary trend of thought which was becoming increasingly more immanentist.

(c) But the Hegelian essential unity of absolute reality was not a static, but a moving or living unity, such that the form in which it manifests itself *must* immediately produce its opposite, the two contrasted forms then being brought together in a higher union, in which the contradiction is not removed but " conserved ", so that the whole process must begin again ; and not only thought, but being—all life and all history—advances in this great spiral through the stages of thesis, antithesis and synthesis. Here, then, was a principle in the light of which real development could be ascribed to evolutionary forms (as it could not be on Spencer's principles), and which gave meaning and direction to the new historical interest aroused by the discoveries of biology and anthropology.

(d) Applied in the sphere of ethics, Hegel's dialectic method had found in the relations of family, community and state, the highest expression of moral life. Thus his thought linked itself also to the new emphasis on society which followed the discoveries of science and the experiences of the Industrial Revolution, with the consequent sense of the comparative insignificance of the individual. It is true that modifications were to be introduced into Hegel's thought in this sphere, that the influence of other thinkers besides him was to make itself felt, and that the British writers as a whole were to show a greater interest in ethics than Hegel had done. But at least the basis for this development was provided by Hegel himself.

Yet the British Hegelians are not mere imitators of Hegel, but work over his principles, each in his own way, applying them to the problems of British culture and giving them a British dress. Alongside the thought of Hegel there are almost always ethical elements from Kant and Fichte to be found. John Caird, for example, emphasises the ethical side of religion much more than Hegel had done: he sees religion as the surrender of the finite, self-centred will to the Infinite, and finds in the religious union of the human and Divine the true solution of the problem of ethics, the only possible means of attaining moral ends. Again, the British Hegelians are on the whole less esoteric than Hegel, in the sense that they are rather less inclined than the continental Hegelians to distinguish between the ordinarily accepted meanings of religious doctrines and the true interpretation of them known only to the philosophical initiate. And the characteristic empirical turn of the British mind makes itself specially clear in the fact that they are not interested in the Hegelian system solely as a system, but only as it is translated into terms of concrete human values. Hegel had applied his dialectical method throughout every realm of thought and being and built up one great comprehensive system, but the British Hegelians have little desire to see the system in all its detail. They are content to show that it exists—that the very existence of the worlds of science, art, morality and religion proves that reality is a Divine order and not merely a " concatenation of facts, perceived by the senses or inferred from what is so perceived, and considered in abstraction from all reference to the mind for which alone they constitute a world at all "[2]—and that there is thus a justification for the teachings of religion.

It is, indeed, in religion that they are chiefly interested: the earlier writers at least seek to express their Idealism in values which are predominantly and definitely religious (perhaps less definitely so in Wallace and Nettleship); and even with later writers like Bradley and Bosanquet, whose outlook is somewhat wider, or McTaggart, whose attitude to religion is chiefly critical, religious thought still occupies a high place. It is, in any case, with their attitude to religion that we are here concerned ; and here they stand, or understood themselves to stand, very close to Hegel. For Stirling, the " Secret of Hegel " is, that he had "no object but to restore Faith—Faith in God—Faith in the Immortality of the Soul and the Freedom of the Will—nay, Faith in Christianity as the Revealed Religion—and that, too, in perfect harmony with the Right of Private Judgment ";[3] and this he endeavours to show from a translation and study of the second part of the *Science of Logic*. John Caird, in his *Introduction to the Philosophy of Religion* (1880), lays down three stages of religious knowledge—Imagination, which is sensual, Understanding, which causes an abstract separation or deflection into (for it) irreconcilable opposites, and Reason, which unites the contradictions of the Understanding in a higher synthesis. And in *Fundamental Ideas of Christianity* (1899) he proceeds to apply these principles to the chief Christian doctrines and seeks to show that each is the expression of a rational truth. His brother, Edward Caird, takes up fundamentally the same position—only, as a layman, he is a little freer in his handling of Christian doctrines. And even Bosanquet later attempts a similar speculative idealisation of such Christian doctrines as those of Incarnation, Reconciliation, and Justification by Faith.

It is clear that in these and kindred writers, in spite of all variations of detail which they show from Hegel as a school and from each other as individuals, the *spirit* of Hegel is yet unmistakable throughout. This must be the justification of the fact that, although this was the completely dominant trend of thought in the period immediately before Mackintosh, so that he could scarcely have failed to be influenced either positively or at least negatively by it, he nevertheless scarcely ever refers expressly to the writers of this school: he confines his attention and criticism to Hegel himself, and for

Hegelian theology "at its best", to Biedermann, only noting in passing that the position of such writers as the Cairds is "very much the same" as that of the latter.[4]

3. MACKINTOSH'S RELATION TO HEGELIANISM

Mackintosh's attitude to the movement, which, as we have just seen, is included by implication in what he has to say of Hegel and the Continental Hegelians, is uniformly one of almost complete rejection. He objected to its fundamental principles chiefly on the ground of the difference between the religious teaching built upon them and that of New Testament Christianity. His primary objections were thus made from the standpoint of faith, on the ground of the conclusions to which the principles led in this realm. But he also added, for a reason that will presently appear, objections to the principles themselves from the side of philosophy.

One of the chief issues on which he crosses swords with Hegel is his insistence upon the ultimate identity of God and man. He grants, indeed, that to speak of "unity" or "identity" is for Hegel only to assert the existence of an essential relation, which obtains quite independently of actual harmony or disharmony;[5] and he is then prepared to allow a certain value to the Hegelian principle over against the habit of speaking of God and man solely in mutually exclusive and contradictory terms, which he holds must make the Incarnation not only a wonder but a "mere absurdity".[6] But whatever difference might be found room for on Hegel's terms alongside the identity, it remains true that such difference is seen as in the last resort only relative; and whatever the service of Hegelianism in calling attention to the kinship between God and man, he finds that it has, in actual fact, done so only at the cost of complete neglect of the Divine "otherness". And while the biblical doctrine of the Divine Image in man demands that we be mindful of a certain kinship, the thought of the "otherness" of God is the more important for faith: for on it depends the recognition of His transcendent Holiness, of His Wrath and of His sovereign creative Grace. That the Hegelians' insistence upon their principle of identity caused them to remain blind to these aspects of the Divine Being, he regarded as a fatal objection from the side of faith. And from the side of philosophy itself he adds the objection that they are wrong to disregard the distinction that " God's thought is creative, man's only reflective "—and this to such an extent that "eventually they turn human reason into part creator of the world ".[7]

But if he took exception to this principle, he rebelled even more strongly against the Hegelian dialectic according to which all reality, including the Absolute, continually advances by "evoking antagonism to its own imperfection, then capturing this antagonism for a richer combination inclusive of, and completing, both terms in the former contrast ".[8] On this principle, Hegel found room for religious teaching formally resembling that of Christianity, and held that Christian doctrine was but an imaginative or pictorial representation of such speculative truth. But Mackintosh had no delusions as to the fact that the resemblance was one of form alone, and that to remove from Christianity those elements which were for Hegel imaginative symbols meant to empty it of the content which was vital for faith.

For example, there is indeed for Hegel a Divine Trinity: "As pure abstract idea God is Father ; as going forth eternally into finite being, the element of change and variety, God is Son ; as once more sublating or cancelling this distinction, and turning again home enriched by this out-going in so-called self-manifestation or incarnation, God is Holy Spirit ".[9] But this, Mackintosh observes, " really represents that which is in no sense eternal but only coming to be ; it has no meaning, or even existence, apart from the finite world. It is a dialectical triad, not Father, Son and Spirit in any sense in which Christian faith has ever pronounced the threefold Name ".[10] Or again, the uniqueness of Christ is also emphasised. But He is unique only as the first to recognise the great speculative idea of the unity of God and man, which must by logical necessity emerge in the course of history and whose rise apparently coincided with that of Christianity: through Christ men learned to perceive that " the life of man is God's life in the form of time, and the Divine and human natures, being related as universal and particular, realise themselves only in organic unity with each other ",[11] and with the story of His death, resurrection and exaltation, came a priceless symbol of the truth that " finite man, construed merely as finite, is inevitably the prey of negation and decay; yet view him in the light of his unity with the Infinite, and straightway he rises and mounts to a lofty and positive participation in the pantheistic world-process ".[12]   For the uniqueness of Christ, not merely as the first subject and example of faith, but as its proper Object and the Person in whom the eternal Word entered history and wrought once for all the redemption of men, Hegel's philosophy has no place: " He is interested in the God-man solely as a logical construction, not as a living Person ".[13]   The reality of sin is also recognised—but only as an obstruction through which the Spirit, by the logical necessity of the dialectical process, must inevitably work its way.   It is a necessary point between innocence and virtue: " Hegel's teaching is definitely to the effect that sin *must* lead to virtue and that there is no virtue which is not based on sin ".[14]   By thus losing its irrationality, Mackintosh finds that sin " loses much more than half its evil ".[15]   But whether it can be rationally explained or is, as he himself holds, essentially irrational, he points out that the Hegelian teaching here neither finds any echo in the leading conviction of the penitent sinner as he stands before the transcendent holiness of God—the conviction of the terrible enormity of his sin and of his personal responsibility for it—nor can it give him any assurance that his guilt has been removed.   Much the same must be said of redemption: it, too, is given a place in Hegel's system—but it, likewise, is only a necessary element in the dialectical process and not, as for Christian faith, an act of the free sovereign grace of God. Lastly, we may notice a point of a slightly different nature: the Hegelian dialectic involves an insistence on the point that it is in the consciousness of man that God first reaches self-consciousness. The difference here is, that to this Christianity neither can nor does offer any parallel, formal or otherwise: for it means that God exists only in a state of becoming and makes the world as necessary to Him as He is to it. The Hegelian emphasis on this point Mackintosh regarded as " perhaps from the standpoint of Christian faith the most sinister feature in the entire construction ". [16] Such objections from the side of faith he again held to be fatal. And again he added an objection from the side of philosophy itself: for he held it to be philosophically unsound to transfer to the realm of being, " to distinct orders of reality and even to the being of God Himself ", a principle which might be well enough valid in the realm of thought and of " human attitudes or partial apprehensions ".[17]

These examples are sufficient to indicate the grounds, both of faith and to a lesser extent of philosophy, on which Mackintosh contested the fundamental principles of Hegelianism. But it is also important to notice that, completely irrespective of their validity, the conception of God and the religious teaching to which they lead are, at least, totally different from those of the Christian faith. And for one to whom Christianity must be supreme that amounts to saying that the God reached on this basis is not God at all. Thus he can conclude his criticism of Hegel with the words, " The Hegelian interpretation of the Christian religion leaves us with a deeper conviction than ever of the impotence of man to force his way through to the presence of God by the power of speculative reason . . . . If we are to approach, He must stretch forth His hand and draw us near. If we are to know Him, with the knowledge which is life eternal, He must speak His free and gracious Word and we must hear in faith ".[18]

Here we have the heart of the whole matter, on which all else can be only commentary. For a philosophy which seeks God in man as the "Reason within his reason" and a faith which recognises that, whatever the truth of the Divine immanence, God is first and foremost the Eternal and Transcendent One who can be known only as He reveals Himself, are clearly at variance from the start ; and the point of comparisons such as are made in the above examples can only be to illustrate further the width of the gulf between the two. In this way, Mackintosh's conflict with Hegelianism, which is undoubtedly the most imposing speculative system of this kind ever produced, made it clearer to him than it might otherwise have been, how wide the gulf in fact is. And one result of that conflict was certainly to make him exclude from theology, even more emphatically than he might otherwise have done, any use whatsoever of the speculative reason which should make it possible for the theologian to set about his task with any preconceived ideas dictated by that faculty.

But if it was clear that the religious teaching of the speculative philosopher was at variance with that of Christianity on so many vital points, what of the Christian thinker who sought in Hegelianism a justification of his theology, yet without being willing to sacrifice the vital interests of faith? Here the treatment of the question of personality by many Hegelian writers, particularly of the British school, offers a convenient illustration. While Hegel himself seemed, by his insistence on the ultimate identity of finite spirit and Infinite Spirit, at least to imply the denial of the personality of the Absolute, and while his Continental followers, particularly of the left wing, had made this denial explicit, the utterances of the earlier British Hegelians on the subject were remarkably ambiguous. Stirling never made it really clear how far he ascribed real validity to the symbolic truth he found in his religious concepts or how far he regarded them merely as imaginative symbols. Wallace toys with the possible solution of ascribing supra-personality to the Absolute, but without reaching any definite conclusions on the subject. John Caird avoids the question altogether. T. H. Green (who can only in a wider sense be described as a Hegelian, but whose writings are nevertheless at many points closely akin to Hegelianism) seems, for himself, to have believed in the personality of God, or what he called the "Eternal Consciousness", but his references to the subject are ambiguous in the extreme. Edward Caird alone faces the problem explicitly and attempts to save the concept of the personality of God by calling in the principle of evolution —but with questionable success. It is thus not surprising that these writers incurred at least the suspicion that their teaching actually constituted a danger to a religion in which personal relationships between God and man were of primary importance. And that this suspicion was not entirely unfounded, was presently to be shown when Bradley, Bosanquet and McTaggart expressly denied the personality of God and refused to ascribe primary importance to personality even in man.

On this point in itself Mackintosh was perfectly clear: he saw the religion of the New Testament as one in which the reality of personal relationships between God and man is fundamental, and he held that apart from relations on the purely human level in which "self" and "neighbour" meet each other as responsible personal individuals and not merely as "cases" or "instances of humanity", Christian fellowship and Christian love can have little meaning.[19] It was therefore clear to him that, whatever the difficulties of the concept of personality, the question is one on which a scriptural theology cannot tolerate ambiguity, far less denial.[20] But he had also learned from Pringle-Pattison that the Hegelian attitude here was not without objection from the side of philosophy. For as early as 1887 Pringle-Pattison had criticised the identification of the human and Divine consciousness and its twofold result in the denial of God's personality and the disparagement of the human self, by which it was regarded as only a logical, instead of also a real, concrete, responsible and immortal self: this, he had insisted, was a fundamental error of Hegelian thought as also of the related thought of Green, and could only lead in the end to sacrifice of the concrete reality both of God and man and of their relationship.[21] Thus Mackintosh argued consistently for the primary importance of personality both in God and in man, and felt here again that he had good grounds, both theological and philosophical, for doing so.

But it seems as if the treatment accorded to personality by such writers must have appeared to him as symptomatic of something deeper and more far-reaching. For the ambiguity of Stirling or Wallace or Green, the somewhat suspicious silence of John Caird, and the rather unsatisfactory evolutionary argument of his brother, could at least be explained as attempts at compromise between their religious convictions, aware of the importance of personality, and their philosophical arguments which pressed for its denial. And even Bradley and Bosanquet (the latter being specially eager to effect a reconciliation between his philosophy and Christianity) maintain that a distinction between God and His worshipper such that they can stand over against each other in a personal relation must remain to the end in religion, although they cannot allow its validity in metaphysics. Mackintosh can scarcely have failed to notice this in the writings of his countrymen, and to have seen it as a dualism produced by the conflicting claims of philosophy and faith. For he points to precisely this dualism in the case of Biedermann, who considers himself justified as a believer (for example, in moments of prayer) in conceiving God as personal, but as thinker regards the conception as a pure illusion, so that " in his pages the Divine sonship which it was Christ's function to reveal hovers ambiguously between the idea of personal and ethical communion with the Father and a purely ontological relation of finite to Infinite Spirit ".[22]

Nor is the dualism confined in Biedermann's case to personality but it appears again and again—for example when, as philosopher, he insists on making an absolute distinction *in abstracto* between the principle of redemption and the Person of Jesus, yet must as believer allow their indissolubility in concrete fact:

" The principle of redemption, we are told, means the idea of God-manhood, which in the sphere of human life takes reality in the form of Divine sonship. But if Christianity is to remain the absolute religion this principle must not be identified with Jesus. For the Person of Christ we must learn to put the Christological dogma with its literally unbounded speculative value. Yet as a believer, who somehow had found God in Jesus, Biedermann could not merely stop at this point. In spite of all, the principle and the Person come later to be bound up together. We must not suppose, he tells us, that ' the principle would *eo ipso,* prior to and apart from the fact (*i.e.* the historical appearance of Jesus), have realised itself in the development of man '. Thus for all time Jesus Christ remains the Person in whom the principle took flesh ; nay more, it is specifically through Him that the principle has touched and changed human life. Far from being merely the first to exemplify Divine sonship, Jesus, it is laid down before the end, is One who by the efficacy of the redeeming principle in Himself guarantees its triumph in all who are united to Him."[23]

Thus Mackintosh can sum up his criticism of Biedermann by saying that he " meant to be as Hegelian as possible, but always found Christianity breaking in ".[24]

But now, even the personal Idealism of Pringle-Pattison, who was by no means a Hegelian, he found to be not entirely free from objection in this connection. For in his review of the Gifford Lectures, *The Idea of God in the Light of Recent Philosophy,* he writes:

" Christian thinkers who are much surer of their faith than they ever can be of its philosophical vindication are,

I feel, justified in putting these two questions. In the first place, how far is Professor Pringle-Pattison's view of God and the Absolute capable of being combined with belief in the Divine Fatherhood? In the second, can his statements as to the relations of Reality and the time-process be harmonised with faith in the Divine Revelation? We shall find that in both cases his thought exhibits two distinct and even disparate strains, one of which can, whereas the other I am bound to think cannot, be reconciled with what we may broadly call the faith of the New Testament."[25]

And he goes on to quote a series of passages in which God, the Absolute and the All are equated with each other, alongside one in which the familiar Christian distinction between God and the world is at least implied ; and a further series in which " events within the time-series have a substantial value as a significant index of Ultimate Reality " over against another in which " Reality proper is timeless, unchanging, eternally complete, and on that account possesses at best only a negative connection with the incidents of human life ".[26]

Thus Mackintosh not only saw that the Hegelian philosopher could attain only to a religion which ultimately had little in common with Christianity. He saw also that the Christian thinker who sought in Hegelianism a justification of his theology but yet refused to surrender completely to this philosophy the demands of his faith, must be content with contradictions which even the Hegelian dialectic apparently could not reconcile, and that a similar dualism appeared not only in the thought of the Hegelian theologian, but also in that of so highly respected a Christian philosopher as his friend and teacher Pringle-Pattison. The former insight left him, as we have seen, with a deeper conviction than ever of the impossibility of reaching God through the speculative reason, and a stronger determination than ever to exclude from theology any presuppositions to which it might lead. And it is difficult to believe that the latter insight had no effect in convincing him of the futility of attempting to combine philosophy and theology at all in such a way as to provide any sort of justification or basis for the latter in the former.

This at any rate became one of his leading convictions from the beginning. He was himself perhaps too much of a philosopher to wish to deny all value to philosophical argument, but he was prepared, at most, to allow it a value in the purely secondary and optional task of countering philosophical difficulties. It was to meet doubts which might be roused by the Hegelian philosophy that he was concerned to show that the system which caused them might not itself be philosophically sound; and, on the other hand, he granted that in this respect Hegelianism in particular had provided valuable weapons for the refutation of materialism.[27] But that such apologetic undertakings are fundamental, or that theology is subject in any sense to the jurisdiction of philosophy, he steadfastly refused to allow:

" It is well ", he writes, " to buttress the theological edifice with the best available scientific and philosophic argument; it is still better defensively to meet philosophy with philosophy and thus to show those who may be kept from faith by philosophical objections that a deeper and more adequate philosophy will rob these objections of their force. These things are good, but they are not vital to the fundamental things of religion. Were they vital, men could have no right to their faith in God until they had found for it a metaphysical vindication."[28]

This conviction was to receive positive support from another quarter as we shall see. But if it was in any sense, as it seems it must have been, an insight induced at least in part by his opposition to Hegelianism, then this must be reckoned among the most important influences on him of this type of thought.

It seems, indeed, as if what further influences can be traced are all of the same negative kind as the two we have now mentioned, in the sense that, just as his rebellion against Hegelianism seems chiefly accountable for the firmness with which he barred from theology all *a priori* speculative concepts, and at least partly responsible for his complete abandonment of the attempt to provide any ultimate philosophical vindication of faith, so also it was in opposition to Hegelianism that he was led at many important points to define his own position more clearly than he might otherwise have done.

The nearest approach to a positive influence is to be seen in the important place he gives to the thought of a kinship between God and man. Yet it is more than doubtful if he owes much to Hegel in a positive way even here: it is true that Hegel had called renewed attention to this concept and that Mackintosh regards this as one of the services of Hegelianism, but his own treatment of it is different from that of Hegel. His point of departure is certainly not anything he learnt from the Hegelians, but the scriptural thought of the *imago dei;* and it is only in so far as it reflects this thought that he can here find any value in Hegelianism at all. In so far as the place the concept occupies in his Christology owes something to his predecessors, he is more indebted to Dorner than to Hegel ; and while he himself regards Dorner as unduly influenced by Hegel at many points, he holds that it was precisely in his Christology that he most completely and decisively broke with Absolute Idealism.[29] But if it is thus impossible to find here a positive relation which is more than superficial, the importance of the negative influence is yet not to be overlooked: for he saw in Hegelianism a system in which the affinity between God and man was made central, to the virtual exclusion of all else, and in revolt against this he made it very plain that, whatever the place in his own system he might wish to give the concept, he had no delusions as to the fact that it must never be allowed to encroach upon the vital thought of the Divine "otherness".

One is again reminded of Hegelianism when he speaks, as he so often does, of the essentially symbolic character of religious thought—as, for example, when he writes that the thoughts and pictures we form of God " are in no sense precise copies of the Divine fact . . . . We have added to them subjective elements ; the broken mirror of imagination has defaced the higher object." [30] Yet here again it is precisely the apparently all-too-imminent proximity of Hegelianism which made him define his position in such a way as to show that he was, in fact, on a very different track from the Hegelians. For he insists that the symbols are not, as for them, mere imaginative pictures of great rational truths, which can and must be discarded if we will only rise above the lower sensual realm of imagination with which religion has primarily to do, to that of the speculative reason and the purely abstract notion. In the first place, he urges, they cannot be discarded: sense experience necessarily colours *all* our thought from end to end, and when for example Biedermann replaces the " consciousness " of the Absolute by *Insichsein,* he has only substituted for one pictorial expression another one—and that a lower one, for " consciousness " has at least mental and spiritual associations, whereas " *Insichsein,* or ' being-in-self ' . . . is really no more than a spatial term once the suggestions of ' consciousness ' have been set aside ".[31] Indeed, to demand the exclusion of such symbols is only to enter upon " the path which . . . if followed out to its logical termination, is the path of pure negativity which at last plunges down into a blank featureless Absolute devoid of all positive or recognisable attributes and therefore not really capable of description at all ; and this we are blindly to call God "—so reaching " a point which non-Christian mysticism had reached of itself, as the furthest limit of human apprehension ".[32] And in the second place, the symbols are not mere representations of the imagination but rather result from the effort of human thought to describe the God who has revealed Himself to it.

and who in His very richness must ever contain " an element which breaks through language and escapes ".[33] Thus they not only cannot, but must not, be discarded. For they have a real meaning and value: " In religious symbols there is nothing to be ashamed of, and if only the symbols used are the worthiest human experience can furnish, it is precisely by means of them, with all their inadequacy from the intellectual point of view, that we receive true and saving impressions of God ".[34]

The same is true of what Mackintosh refers to variously as antinomy, paradox, contradiction, " double polarity " in Christian thought, which he holds must meet us at " every point where we touch the relations of eternity and time ",[35] and, indeed, all along the line: " Take any true religious conception ", he writes in his clearest utterance on the subject, " and think it out to its logical issue, and you will at last find it confronted by a religious conception not less true because answering just as much to a genuine interest in the believing mind ".[36] But here, too, the similarity to Hegelianism is only formal—if not, indeed, merely superficial. For the contradictions are not in any sense due to a dialectical movement of reality, but to the fact that the human mind is incapable of grasping all at once the infinite richness of Divine truth. Moreover, it is here not even a case of the application of Hegelian dialectic in the realm of thought, the validity of which Mackintosh was, as we have seen, prepared to allow. For in this particular connection it is expressly laid down that the third stage of synthesis is never reached: " Our thinking . . . is obliged ever to swing between two absolute points of view, each of which insists on being recognised as valid, yet both of which we never quite succeed in envisaging as merged in a thorough-going unity ".[37] Faith alone knows that the unity exists and can see each aspect in its counterpart, but it is never allowed to grasp both at the same time.[38] This tension is a vital one for the life of faith, which cannot simply be calmly held but must fight for its existence and be ever won anew. And the duality which it imposes on theological thought is "in no sense a weakness; it is a strength rather, a richness, a fidelity to the living strain and stress of devout experience".[39] It is clear that this dialectic stands much nearer to that of Kierkegaard and of Barth than to the Hegelian: it is born, not of any abstract speculation, but of his own struggle to express his faith in terms which he constantly found inadequate and in need of correction from the other side.

We may notice, lastly, an interest which Mackintosh shared with the Hegelians, yet with a very different result in his case and in theirs. We have seen that Hegelianism gave a new meaning and direction to the interest in history; and for Mackintosh the question of historical revelation and of the relation of the events of time to eternity was, and remained to the end, one of the chief problems of modern theology. But in actual fact the historical *interest* was all he had in common with the Hegelians: their whole approach to, and interpretation of history was completely different from his. He admits that it may seem as if, "by taking history as the *locus* of Divine self-manifestation, and refusing to interpret the Eternal in purely conceptual and *a priori* modes", they "point to concrete events as the medium wherein the traces of Divine Spirit may be read".[40] Yet all history is for them one uniform process, any point of which reveals as well as any other the universal pattern of rational being: there is no room in it for any unique, once-for-all event which can completely change or re-shape the future, but it is "merely an earthly representation and picturing of eternal truths—of validities, that is, which hold good irrespectively of all that may *become* in time and space".[41] For Mackintosh, on the other hand, the events of history "must function substantively in the plan of being" as events in which God is actualising supremely valid truth;[42] and history is "the fruitful sphere and nidus of being" in which a unique event not only can, but must and did, occur in the coming of One who "does more than unveil a relation already posited by the very definition of Divinity and Humanity; He once for all develops a new relation, at a great cost ".[43]   He sums up the difference between himself and the Hegelians here as that between the Hebrew and Greek conceptions of history respectively: " Time for the Greek intelligence and for Hegel is circular in movement and, therefore, subject to logical prediction: for prophets and apostles time receives its direction and content ever anew from the living God ".[44]   And he adds that the latter alone gives meaning, not only to the religious interest, but also to the ethical, for which the conception of the reality of progress and of real relationships between time and eternity is essential.[45]

The sum of the matter, then, is this:—Mackintosh completely rejected the Hegelian position, partly on philosophical grounds, but chiefly from the standpoint of Christian faith; and the only value he could find in it was the rather minor one that it had recalled attention to the somewhat neglected thought of a kinship between God and man, and the still more minor one that it had helped to provide weapons for the philosophical polemic against materialism.   Its chief influence on him was, that in the first place, as a philosophical interpretation of religion, it convinced him more deeply than ever of the impossibility of man's reaching God by " digging into himself ", and thus led him to exclude from theology with the utmost rigour anything which savoured of such a process; while in the second place, in the form which it took in the Hegelian theologian, it urged him further along the road which was to end in his making theology completely independent of any kind of philosophy.   Its chief value for the student of his theology is, that its proximity and dominance in British thought laid him under constant necessity of defining his own position over against it, so that it acts as a foil which brings out at many important points the true character of his thought.

4. THE COMING OF RITSCHL AND THE NATURE
OF THE PROBLEM

Although Mackintosh reacted so strongly against Hegelianism, he nevertheless shared, with one notable exception,
the interests of his time to which we have seen it made its
appeal. The exception was the tendency towards Immanentism. This feature of nineteenth-century thought was
largely a reaction against the extreme Transcendentalism of
the preceding century which had exalted God above all
contact with the world ; and it was supported by the thought
of the dignity of man and expectations of human progress
brought by Romanticism, by the new discoveries of science
and anthropology, and by the social movements attendant
upon the Industrial Revolution. But Mackintosh stood far
enough away from the controversy between eighteenth-
century Deism and the Immanentism of the following century to see that it was really between two mistaken emphases
with a common philosophical presupposition rather than
between genuine alternatives presented to Christian faith ;
while he was near enough to the Free Church tradition to
be on his guard against conclusions of the cult of man. He
had no wish to deny the Divine immanence, and particularly
in his earlier writings he was perhaps at some points influenced by current thought on the subject to a greater extent
than he realised. But his conscious concern at any rate was
primarily with the Divine transcendence and his purpose
was to give an interpretation of it which would rule both
pantheism (or panentheism) and deism alike out of court,
thus guarding against the chief error of immanentism while
at the same time preserving the truth for which, as against
its adversary, and with a certain narrowness of outlook,
it seemed to have been contending—the truth, namely,
that the transcendent God is universally and most intimately
present to, and to that extent in, the created world. In this
sense it could be held that he shared what was the chief

underlying interest and insight of Immanentist thought ; but
however that may be, it is at least certain that he could
neither share its preoccupation with what is at best but a
single aspect of the Divine Being, nor abide its identification
of the world (or any part of it) with God.

As regards the other three interests or needs, however, he
seems to have been, in the best sense, a true child of his age.
For in the first place, if it was from the standpoint of
faith that his chief objections to Hegelianism came, that was
certainly not the faith of late orthodoxy, the reaction against
which had made Hegel's thought so welcome in nineteenth-
century Britain. For he, too, rebelled strongly against its
arbitrary distinction between sacred and secular, and its
basis in a conception of faith as the acceptance of prescribed
or traditional dogmatic formulae as so-called revealed truths.
Only, he felt that Hegelianism provided no true answer to
his needs in this direction : its principle of pantheistic
monism or logical evolutionism violated the vital interests
of the faith of apostolic Christianity as much as did the
rigid distinctions it wished to supplant, nor did the substitu-
tion of rational for revealed truths lead to a better conception
of that faith, which he held did not consist in mere acceptance of truths at all.* Again, he too, like his contemporaries,
was concerned to find a meaning in history and he sought
above all a key which would unlock the mystery of the
historical self-revelation of God and the personal presence of
the Eternal in time. But he found that while Hegelianism
might appear at first sight to answer this need, in the end it
elaborately missed the point and left him seeking as before.
And in the third place, a glance at almost any page of his
earlier works reveals at once the important place given to
moral values, while there are features of his doctrine of sin

* " Pure " orthodoxy and rationalism, he observes in one place, have
this error in common : both imagine " that religion lies in submitting
one's intelligence to a creed—longer for orthodoxy, shorter for rationalism " (*Aspects of Christian Belief*, pp. 202 f.).

and of the Church which reflect the current sense of the importance of community and society. It was, indeed, not from lack of sympathy with the ethical and social interests of his time that he quarrelled with Hegelianism here: on the contrary, it was, as we have seen, precisely because he felt that, in spite of the place it gave on the surface to moral and social values, it at bottom denied their reality, both by its view of history as a uniform logical process, which excluded the possibility of real or significant change in the events of the time-series, and by its fundamental pantheistic tendencies and consequent disparagement of personality.

Thus he was compelled to seek elsewhere the satisfaction of these interests. He found it, at least to a very considerable extent, in a type of theological thought which was beginning to be known in Britain towards the turn of the century—that of Albrecht Ritschl.

It seems as if the British interest in Ritschl was aroused first through his followers, for the chief early works of Herrmann, Kaftan and Harnack were known in translation several years before his own. Mackintosh, too, probably made his first serious acquaintance with him through his studies under Reischle and Herrmann ; and he was rather more favourably disposed towards " the Ritschlian theology " than towards " the theology of Ritschl " which he is concerned to distinguish from it in the sense that Ritschl himself was a pioneer and the faults which almost inevitably attend the work of the pioneer were to some extent made good by his followers Herrmann, Haering and Kaftan.[46] Nevertheless, the fact remains that it was Ritschl who was the pioneer, and that the modifications made by the others, though often considerable, were still made on essentially the same principles. Hence he soon found Ritschl's own work to be of such importance that he made himself jointly responsible for the translation of *Justification and Reconciliation* which appeared as early as 1900.

Of Ritschl's reception in Britain, Mackintosh himself writes with something of native humour: "In our own country his system, or more correctly his leading principles, have encountered that ordeal of rapidly modified criticism which is so peculiarly English when Englishmen are confronted with a new fact. In a situation so difficult they first say, 'We never heard anything like this before'—which is meant to be final. After a second look, 'It is contrary to the Bible'. Then at last, 'We knew it all the time'."[47] To some extent this appears also to have been his own reaction. For his first published essay, "The Philosophical Presuppositions of Ritschlianism", is extremely critical of Ritschl;[48] but when he republished it later in *Some Aspects of Christian Belief* it was with the explanatory note that what he was really attacking was "not the Ritschlian theology, which has taught this generation so much . . . but the Kantian or Lotzian theory of knowledge with which Ritschl buttressed it" and which "was really for him an afterthought: he was apt to work out this methodology, not always felicitously, after putting his methods into operation".[49] At any rate, whatever his first reactions and whatever his objections to Ritschl's methodology, he soon found in Ritschl's thought the answer, or a very large part of the answer, to his own needs both for satisfaction of the interests we have noticed and for positive support of the convictions to which his conflict with Hegelianism had disposed him.

But now, what were the leading features of this type of thought? We may notice six:

(1) It sets out from an intensely practical conception of religion as essentially the answer to man's moral needs—the one solution to the difficulties in which he finds himself in his struggle to meet the moral demands made upon him, and a solution, moreover, which can be attained solely through this struggle and not in any other way. Whatever the implications of this essential and inseparable conjunction of morality and religion may be, it at least gave real validity

and a central place to moral values: indeed, it is so characteristic of Ritschl's thought, and colours it from end to end to
such an extent, that Mackintosh felt justified in discussing
it in his *Types of Modern Theology* under the head " The
Theology of Moral Values ".

(2) It undertakes to bind theology securely and exclusively
to its basis in the historical revelation of God in the Person
of Jesus Christ, and thereby to give the events of history
their proper relation to the Eternal.

(3) It substitutes for the rigid distinction between sacred
and secular a view of the spiritual world as the (essentially
moral) Kingdom of God being realised in and through the
events of the world of every-day experience, and discernible
simply through the (essentially moral) act of entering it;
while it holds that faith is not in any sense the acceptance of
traditional dogma, but rather free, personal surrender of the
will in obedience to a living Person.

(4) As a result of the emphasis laid on the revelation of
God in Christ as the sole source of Christian doctrine, it
completely rejects all natural theology.

(5) On the basis of its practical view of religion and of
faith, it teaches that the religious convictions which it is the
business of theology to formulate are the product not of
reflection but of experience—or in Kantian terms, not of the
pure, but of the practical reason. Thus it seeks to exclude
metaphysics from theology, rejects speculative theism, and
makes theology completely independent of all theoretical
knowledge, *i.e* of all philosophy.

(6) It is the convinced and unrelenting antagonist of all
religious mysticism as representing a metaphysical type
of piety.

It is not difficult to see how great the appeal of such
a theology to Mackintosh must have been. True, the
Ritschlian opposition to mysticism scarcely seems to have
awakened an immediate echo with him; but he was willing
enough to grant its validity, at least up to a point. And at

any rate, the first five of the features we have noticed clearly answer directly to his ethical and to his historical interests, to the difficulties he felt over against later orthodoxy, to his conviction of the futility of seeking a natural knowledge of God, and to his desire to free theology from the patronage of philosophy. It is therefore not surprising that anyone familiar with Ritschl's thought can find extremely significant traces of its influence on him, particularly in his earlier writings.

Yet he was not by any means a blind follower of Ritschl, but was often extremely critical of him: indeed, the extent of his indebtedness is, for the most part, left for the reader to ascertain for himself, and when he expressly refers to Ritschl it is almost invariably in terms of criticism, or at least of correction. Many of these criticisms and corrections were taken over from the younger Ritschlians and could so far be regarded as modifications within the school itself, which had room for considerably wide differences of opinion on many points. But there were also others—some expressed from the first, many only implicit and not attaining their full weight until later—which came from other quarters and whose chief ground doubtless lay in his Calvinist upbringing and in an understanding of Pauline theology such as none of the Ritschlians had ever possessed. These criticisms were the most important, and it was these which, whatever the early attractions of Ritschlianism, were to lead him in the end in a very different direction.

At the beginning, then, he took over so much from Ritschl and his followers that we might be tempted to call him a Ritschlian, though it is clear from the first that we could not do so in anything but a modified sense. But at the end he had reached a position which was clearly and definitely non-Ritschlian. Our task will be to seek to bring to light the nature of this change and the way it came about; and although the Ritschlians are by no means the only factor in the case, yet the comparison with them offers a convenient method of doing so.

The matter may perhaps be put briefly as follows : Mackintosh's debts both to contemporary and to earlier theology were many and varied ; for he had a vast know-ledge of the theological literature of almost every period, and kept his mind extraordinarily open to influences both positive and negative from almost every side. Under these influences his early thought swung constantly to and fro : rebelling against later orthodoxy, not least as represented in certain elements of the Free Church tradition, and just as much against the Hegelianism which sought to replace it—finding in Ritschl the corrective of both which he sought —reacting against the Ritschlians in turn—finding in other writers, and above all in the things his Free Church up-bringing had taught him, the arguments by means of which he sought to correct them. Yet the movement was not that of a cork bobbing aimlessly on the waves : it was rather that of a ship which, if storm-tossed, is still under control. He listened to most and he learned from many, but he was not, in the apostle's phrase, " carried about with every wind of doctrine " : he listened with the Bible in his hand—witness the constant recurrence of such phrases as, " He has the New Testament on his side in this ", or " That is not Scripture's view of the matter "—and his thought, swing as it might, was firmly anchored here.

But that is not all : there is still another thing which im-measurably enhances both the interest and the value of his theology. In the last years of his life, helped chiefly by Barth, he broke through the maze of nineteenth-century thought and found himself on the way to a position which was undoubtedly nearer to the Confession and Catechisms of his Church than to Ritschl, but nearer to the apostolic Christianity he had all along sought to express than to either. Here he stood closer to Barth than he had ever done to Ritschl, so that he would seem to represent the remarkable—

and indeed unique—spectacle of one who, starting as at least in some sense a Ritschlian, finally completely changed his direction and found himself in close proximity to Barth.

It is only—or at least most clearly—on reading his works backwards (so to speak) that one discovers that this seemingly completely new outlook was not the result of a sudden revolutionary change in his thought, but was to a large extent implied and fore-shadowed in elements which were all along present—in thoughts which for a time were obscured by others or lay only on the outer margin, in points which were overlooked or unemphasised in the general trend of the argument, in traces of inconclusiveness and dissatisfaction due to a sense of the inadequacy of the terms which he was using and which, when read in the light of later utterances, are often patient of a very different meaning from that which they might at first seem to bear. What he owed to Barth was not so much a completely new set of ideas as a fresh insight into old problems, not so much a sudden transportation on to a new path, as a clearer sense of the direction of the path he was already on. Yet that there was in the end a new outlook cannot be denied. It represented a change of emphasis or perspective rather than a fundamental alteration, yet it must have entailed a revision, not indeed of his principles, but certainly of much of his former argument. And although he did in fact begin this revision, he died before he was able to do very much more than indicate his new position and express his profound sympathy with Barth.

Thus if his work were to be classified amongst the various "Types of Modern Theology" which he discussed in his last book, it might fittingly be described as the Theology of Transition. If we may put it so, he took over the theological ship in the midst of all the warring currents of nineteenth-century thought, and with Scripture for his chart he set a course for her home port. He picked up many pilots to help him at particular danger-points on the way; but he himself remained master of the ship, and if he found that the pilot was forsaking the chart he would first remonstrate with him and then, if he paid no attention, had no hesitation in dropping him overboard. The last pilot he took on board was Barth; and though at first he found his methods of navigation somewhat unusual he soon discovered in him a master mariner, in whose company he came well within sight of the land he sought. He himself was not to bring the ship to harbour, but the last entry in his log expresses the hope that the pilot may be enabled to do so—the chapter on Barth which concludes the posthumously published *Types of Modern Theology* closes with the words:

" At the moment he stands in the midst of his theological work, which cannot but take years to complete. Nothing more enriching for the whole Church could be thought of than that the time for completion should be given him, if God will, and that more and more of his living influence should pass from land to land."

CHAPTER II

THE FUNDAMENTAL PRINCIPLES OF DOGMATIC

1. *THE SUBJECT-MATTER AND FUNCTION OF DOGMATIC*

IN the opening lecture of his college course, Mackintosh lays down that dogmatic exists to serve the Church—particularly the preaching of the Church—and offers two definitions of it. In one paragraph it is the theological discipline which " sets forth Christianity as it becomes the inner conviction of men through believing reception of the revelation of God in Christ " ; and in the next it is defined alternatively as the " elucidation of the full content of Revelation, of the Word of God as contained in Scripture ".[1] Both definitions, it is clear, are saying essentially the same thing with a slight difference of emphasis, the former on the subjective or human side, the latter on the objective or Divine ; and in both cases it can be summarily regarded as " the full presentation of Christian truth as a coherent system ".[2] But in neither case may the one side be emphasised to the exclusion of the other, for dogmatic is neither a mere psychology of the human mind nor a collection of abstract ideas of the Divine: it is a systematic presentation of truths made known and recognised in the concrete relation between God and man in Jesus Christ, in whom " God takes the initiative " in revealing Himself to us while we are " called to rejoice in the knowledge thus made ours ".[3]

According to whichever side of this relationship claims Mackintosh's more immediate attention at a given moment, he can speak of the function of dogmatic either as interpretative or as normative. And in either case its execution is clearly not a matter of choice, but of necessity. It is not a casual interest which may be pursued or not according to personal inclination, nor is it a utilitarian service which the Church can avail herself of or do without as she pleases; on the contrary, it is a vital concern alike of the individual believer and of the community. For it is part of all Christian obedience to seek the fullest possible understanding of the truth made known to faith;[4] while if the Church is truly to rejoice in *this* knowledge and no other, and is faithfully to proclaim the Gospel of her Lord, then she requires good theology as an "antiseptic" against the "poisonous influences" of bad[5], and cannot dispense with the constant and systematic testing of the truth of what she is saying. It is important, however, to notice that the task of interpretation and that of critical examination, if properly understood, are so inseparably bound up together that the one cannot be carried out independently of the other. Nor can their execution ever produce a system which will include *all* that is to be known, or can claim to be infallible.

On the one hand, then, dogmatic is an interpretative study rather than a creative one. It is not called upon to introduce the Christian mind to truths of which it was hitherto totally ignorant, but "to make explicit the truth which faith contains implicitly . . . , to lead faith to a clearer consciousness of its own nature and meaning",[6] "to fix in lucid conceptual forms the whole rich truth of which faith is sure".[7] In other words, there must be nothing in it which is "a bare external addition to our incipient believing view", but every element must be simply a more complete statement of some point "given, though latently, in the initial confession, 'Jesus is Lord'".[8] The new emphasis on this vital connection between dogmatic and Christian experience which came with Schleiermacher represents a gain which theology should be slow to lose; for it is surely one of our best defences against Traditionalism—whether it be that of the Roman Church, which regards dogmatic as the co-ordination and systematisation of ecclesiastically imposed beliefs, or that of later Protestant Orthodoxy, which lapsed into something very similar, thanks to its doctrine of the verbal inspiration of Scripture.

There is no need here to throw up our hands in horror, as is so often done, and protest that this is to replace the "theocentric" thought of the Reformation, which moves from God to man, by an "anthropocentric" method, which moves from man to God.* For "these adjectives need imply no serious difference of opinion as to ultimate conclusions: 'anthropocentric' must not be confused with 'humanitarian'".[9] There can be no fundamental difference between a theology which starts from a revelation which is apprehended by faith and one which starts from a faith created by revelation; nor should we forget that it was precisely in reaction against the rationalistic and humanitarian attempts of the Enlightenment to dispense with Christ that Schleiermacher set about his task. If we cannot but demur to many of his results, that is not simply because he set out from the human side, but because in doing so he failed to take the other seriously enough—the revelation in Christ. And if we would ourselves avoid similar errors, then we must only remember that what we are seeking to interpret is not the convictions of men—not even of Christian men—but such convictions as are involved in believing response to the revelation of God in Christ. It is a simple fact that the truth of God " is not clear to everybody without exception or to anybody at all times ",[10] but "there are degrees in the appreciation of redemption" much as, for example, there are degrees in the appreciation of art.[11] And the aim of dogmatic is not simply to present " the lowest form of belief compatible with a profession of Christianity " or to establish some sort of working average, but " to formulate,

* In his attitude to Schleiermacher as expressed in this and the next three sentences, Mackintosh is at one with Barth, cf. esp. *Die Geschichte der prot. Theologie*, pp. 409 ff., 415.

if that be possible, *all* that Christ is to the fully surrendered mind ".[12] In so far as it succeeds in attaining this end, it presents to the believer the full range and meaning, not only of what he does believe but also of what he ought to believe if fully Christian and free from misunderstandings or the contamination of falsehood or heresy. Hence interpretation automatically passes over into criticism, and dogmatic as an interpretative study is at the same time also normative.

This may now be put from the other side, by placing the emphasis not on faith, but on revelation ; and then the argument is not so much directed against Traditionalism as primarily against the various forms of Liberalism derived from Schleiermacher. Dogmatic may not, after the manner of Schleiermacher and many later thinkers, reach its conclusions merely by analysis and interpretation of the Christian consciousness, leaving to be understood, or bringing in as a kind of afterthought, the revelation which makes it a specifically *Christian* consciousness. It has to elucidate the revelation of God in Christ, in which He summons men to serve and to rejoice in Him, and is to that extent a normative discipline. As it is most emphatically put:

" What dogmatic is called to do is not to describe or elucidate the existing state of the Christian mind ; its proper task, rather, is to bring out and expound with all possible completeness the *norm* to which Christian piety must conform ; for in revelation God makes insistent *claims* on man. There is such a thing as the obedience of faith ; and theology is summoned to set forth the revealed truth, apprehension of which is thus incumbent on the believing mind. In that sense theology has a definitely authoritative character."[13]

But if we would avoid pernicious errors also on this side, then we must remember that it would be meaningless to speak of revelation apart from any apprehension of it: there is a real sense in which " revelation is no revelation until it takes the shape of human thought ".[14] That is not to say that faith is a normative source of doctrine, for it is only its medium. But it does mean that dogmatic as a normative discipline is at the same time also a human act of inter-pretation: it cannot itself provide a final norm or claim absolute authority for its formulations, but can only seek to expound in human terms the revelation which alone is final, and it is only in so far as it truly corresponds to that revelation that it has any authority at all.

Whichever way we look at it, the dogmatician's task is to present the whole range of Christian truth in a coherent system which shows the vital connection of every true doc-trine with every other. But whichever way we look at it, the system can never lay claim either to completeness or to permanency. On the one hand, it is an exposition of truths of which the human mind becomes convinced—certainly, the human mind as, by Divine grace, it is enabled to respond to revelation, but still the human mind and therefore by no means omniscient. On the other hand, it is an elucidation of God's revelation of Himself in Christ—but a revelation apprehended by human faith, in creating which God does not surrender His own sovereignty or cease to be unfathomable.

It is a complete denial of the teaching of Scripture to suggest either that " from the intrinsic make of our faculties we cannot form ideas about Divine things except as we falsify them in the very act " or that " God, as self-revealed to men, is not God as He is in Himself ";[15] but the fact remains that, although Christian faith has in every sense a *true* knowledge of God, and although He certainly reveals Himself *as He is,* yet we are not thereby enabled to " find out the Almighty unto perfection " (Job 11 : 7) or to do any more than " know the love of Christ—which passeth knowledge " (Eph. 3 : 19). And when it comes to the task of giving systematised ex-pression to the things thus known, then the Spirit and the grace of God are our assurance that the conclusions of the theologian who seeks to do so in faith will be no mere empty words ; yet they remain attempts of a man, who is neither omniscient nor infallible, to formulate the truth of God in human terms, which can only serve but never master it. They may—and surely will—present for the moment vital aspects of it in a coherent form, and so far have a certain completeness and a certain authority. But the most perfect and comprehensive system attainable can neither enshrine the *whole* truth of the unfathomable riches of God's being and ways nor claim to be finally valid. Rather, each new conception we form, no matter what care and devotion may have gone to produce it, soon becomes inadequate and obsolete. Christological theory alone " is in truth like the great cathedral: ' it is ever beautiful for worship, great for service, sublime as a retreat from the tumult of the world, and it is for ever unfinished ' ".[16] So, too, with the whole theological system of which Christology is the heart: " In systematic thought there is no final form. Theologies from the first have perished ; they wax old as doth a garment ; as a vesture time folds them up and lays them by. Nothing save the Gospel is abiding, and its years shall not fail."[17]

Hence it is not only Christian piety which is in need of constant criticism, but also the doctrinal teaching alike of past centuries and of our own day: dogmatic has not only to present to men what as Christians they ought to believe, but also to examine the truth of the doctrines resulting from its own and previous attempts to do so. Since it is often only in their relation to the past that present-day problems can be properly understood, it is through critical examination and reconstruction of the conclusions of former days that the theologian will best be enabled to speak to his own. Thus it is of first importance (as Schleiermacher insisted) that dogmatic questions should be studied historically. But (and this Schleiermacher failed to make plain) in doing so the aim is not simply to give a historical account and explanation of past doctrines: it is to examine their truth and to detach what is of lasting value in them from what is only temporary vesture.

Many of the symbols which these doctrines must inevitably

employ[18] may have conveyed the truth to a particular
age and generation, yet be of doubtful value now: for
example, the Chalcedonian doctrine of the two Natures
of Christ, which served a former day, calls for revision in
one in which " Nature " means " Substance " and the highest
category is moral and spiritual personality, while we shall
now do well to discard the military, legal and commercial
theories of the Atonement in favour of symbols drawn from
" social and family life at their highest ".[19]   Other figures,
again, may have done good service in the context of a
particular set of problems, but must now be abandoned, or at
least corrected with extreme rigour: thus those of Hegelian
theology recalled attention to the neglected fact of the kinship of God and man, while those of Immanentism preserved
an important truth over against eighteenth-century Deism,
both thereby answering a particular problem of the time,
yet both in a way which it is now clear involved errors of a
most pernicious kind.   And still others—like that of the
Divine Fatherhood—are completely indispensable, yet require
to be controlled by a concrete relation to the experience of
Christ and thereby protected against being made the basis
of " inferences far too human to be true ".[20]   " To a large
extent ", we are told, " the progress of theology has consisted,
and so far as can be seen will always consist, in the severest
but also discerning criticism of the symbols familiar to past
centuries ".[21]   Nor is it only the traditional doctrines of the
Church, or the conclusions of past thinkers, that the
theologian must thus submit to criticism: it is also his
own previous findings and formulations, which are likewise
inadequate and equally in need of constant testing and re-
testing.   In one early passage this part of his task is summed
up as follows:

" In this matter, theology is called to be a conscience to
the Church.   Its work is not to purge religious thought of
symbol—this must always fail—but to awaken men to the
fact that their ideas about God *are* really symbolic and hence

perpetually in need of being tested afresh by experience and reflection ; and, in addition, to re-examine current figures in the light of Jesus' revelation of God."[22]

Or as it is later expressed, in a manner not a little reminiscent of Barth, "As a normative discipline it brings a certain standard of truth to bear upon the preaching or the confessions of the Church, and, in the light of this standard—the Word of God—it puts past and present alike on trial".[23]

Thus far the nature and function of dogmatic has been little more than formally outlined—and that in a manner which would no doubt command the assent of a large number of theologians of various schools. A very great deal depends on what is meant on the one hand by the "inner conviction" which comes from "believing reception of revelation", on the other by "revelation" which is "the Word of God as contained in Scripture"; and it is, in fact, the further treatment of these topics, preceded by a discussion of Christianity as a religion, which completes Mackintosh's dogmatic Prolegomena. Thus his precise position only becomes clear in the ensuing discussion, in which the formal concepts of religion, faith and revelation are given a definite content. But before we go on to examine these things, it will be convenient to note three characteristic features of his thought which are already apparent at this point, and with which we shall repeatedly have to do.

One is the habit of putting the emphasis, now on the subjective, now on the objective side of the matter, in view of the vital inter-relation of the human and the Divine—in this case, faith and revelation. But in doing so he did not mean to imply that this is a relation of mutual inter-dependence between two equals. On the contrary, he made it clear (as we have seen) that in revelation God takes and maintains the initiative, while in faith man is summoned to respond with obedience—as it is put elsewhere : "Revelation is God speaking ; our part is to hear and trustfully obey. The Word of God, His revealing utterance, is not to be argued with, but something we have to listen to on our knees ".[24] It was, indeed, explicitly for this reason that he chose the term "faith" rather than "Christian consciousness", "feeling" or "experience" to designate the subjective aspect.* For he felt that it unambiguously includes the transcendent reference and "expresses better the receptive attitude proper to the believer": [25] it is essentially both a fully human act and the work of the Holy Spirit, an act of submission, obedience, loyalty, and the gift of God.[26] For the same reason he could not regard the interpretative and normative functions of dogmatic as simply on a par with each other: the former receives the emphasis—and then never an exclusive emphasis—only in polemic against false conceptions which would ascribe authority of an absolute or external kind to dogmatic formulae, and it is clear that, just as it is not with faith but with revelation that the supremacy lies, similarly also it is not the interpretative but the normative function of dogmatic which is the primary one.

It is worth noting here that his treatment of the function of dogmatic in this respect is but one application of the view of the Divine-human relationship around which all his thinking revolves. We shall meet further examples in different contexts and different forms ; and if we would avoid misunderstandings then it will be well to be clear from the start that (taught no doubt by his Calvinist upbringing) he invariably regarded the relationship as one in which the supremacy and initiative is, and remains throughout, with God. That is not to say that God is and does everything, man nothing: it means,

---

* He had no fundamental objection to the other terms, but he disliked their ambiguity. They too, he recognised, can denote "a mode of objective apprehension" and need not exclude the view of God "as confronting the soul in His real and infinite causality" ; but he found that "consciousness" and "feeling" as Schleiermacher uses them slip over all too easily into the terms of pure psychological subjectivism, while "experience" in later theologies too often "has the air of setting the religious experient free from all dependence on Divine revelation" (*Types of Modern Theol.* pp. 47 f.).

rather, that it is only because God is everything that man is anything, and "only because God does everything that man can do something, not as price but in gratitude ".[27] Thus the vital relation, as Mackintosh conceived it, is clearly not between equals, but between the Creator and His creation, the Lord and His servant, the Father and His child. And it would therefore be a mistake—if sometimes it lies near at hand—to liken the thought which revolves round it to an ellipse with two foci: it is not, and if at times it may have a somewhat elliptical appearance, it is really much more a circle whose true centre is God—God in Christ, Immanuel.

A second characteristic feature is the two-edged polemic, directed on the one hand against certain tendencies of later orthodoxy, on the other against Liberalism of the more extreme type represented by the left wing. And here a most significant development can be traced: the polemic against orthodoxy recedes into the background, while the front against Liberalism becomes the chief one and broadens out towards the right.

It would seem to be largely the reaction against late orthodoxy which gave the initial impetus to Mackintosh's early thought. And in our present context this means that the scattered references to the topic found in his earlier writings so emphasise the interpretative function of dogmatic that even a not-too-superficial reader might gain the impression that it is the chief one: revelation is relative to faith, and therefore dogmatic is not so much a creative as an interpretative study—though we must not go to the other extreme of disregarding or subordinating revelation and holding that the theologian is called to do no more than to report and interpret. Presently, however, he found it necessary to distance himself not only from orthodoxy and from the Liberalism which ignores or subordinates revelation, but more particularly from that which regards it as *merely* the correlate of faith. Thus we find him writing against Stephan, "Revelation is more than relative to faith ; it is sovereignly evocative of faith and throughout its stimulating and controlling 'authority'".[28] Or against Wobbermin:

"My lack of faith does not make the promise void. . . . It will not do even to *seem* to invest faith with a quasi-creative power, when, in point of fact, it is but a response to the initial self-unveiling act of God. Any ambiguity on this point—and in theology we are inevitably judged by our words rather than our intentions—immediately forms a full justification for Barth's insistence on the sovereign priority of God in everything that concerns salvation." [29]

It was doubtless to remove any possible shadow of ambiguity that he now changed the title of his College lecture on "Revelation as the Correlate of Faith" to "Revelation as the evoking Cause and Object of Faith". And thus, too, the references in his last book to the theologian's task place the emphasis unmistakably on the normative, not excluding the interpretative but never explicitly mentioning it at all. This is nothing fundamentally new: he had often enough insisted that revelation is creative of faith, while as early as 1904, in the inaugural lecture to his Chair,[30] he had made it reasonably clear that it is the normative task of dogmatic which is primary. But here, as so often elsewhere, the change of front has brought to the fore what had been lurking in the not-too-distant background all along, and resulted in clearer expression of what, at bottom, had been his position from the first.

Finally, we may notice that already there are signs of a certain proximity to Ritschlian thought. Mackintosh felt himself to be one with Ritschl in regarding dogmatic as primarily a normative discipline whose sole standard of reference is the revelation in Jesus Christ—indeed, he found that to have brought out this fact afresh and made that revelation the avowed basis of his whole theology was the most fruitful feature of Ritschl's thought and the one which most clearly distinguishes his method from that of his immediate predecessors both of the Liberal and of the Mediating

schools.[31] Moreover, the introduction to his Prolegomena
(above all in the Lecture Synopses) has some striking parallels
with that of Ritschl's disciple Kaftan.[32] In particular, Kaftan
likewise insists that the vital interrelation of faith and
revelation is the one safeguard against false conceptions of
dogmatic (whether as a collection of mere psychological
reports or as a system of abstractly conceived dogmas imposed by external authority); while he, too, contends that
faith here is only the medium of knowledge, not its normative
source, and that (as essentially obedience) it at once includes
the objective reference. Not only so, but the whole plan of
Mackintosh's Prolegomena also seems to owe something to
Kaftan. For he, too, follows up his introduction by discussing successively religion, believing knowledge, revelation and
Scripture as the Word of God.[33]

At the same time, however, Mackintosh felt himself compelled to qualify his favourable judgment of Ritschl's method
by adding at once that " whether his actual performance was
equal to his intention is quite another story ". And although
he follows Kaftan both in the order of topics and occasionally
also in detail, yet his treatment is rather different on the
whole, and ultimately gives a decidedly different content to
the concepts concerned. Thus we already have indications
of an outward identity of purpose with a difference of performance, a similarity of form with a difference of content.
And this is worth noting chiefly for two reasons. In the first
place, it gives us from the start a pointer to the fact that
Mackintosh can often make statements which appear to be
Ritschlian, but are only formally so and really have a very
different meaning. Secondly, it was here that he found the
link between Ritschl and Barth: —

"That Barth is definitely a more Christian thinker than
Ritschl," he writes, " no one, I should suppose, can doubt who
takes revelation seriously. But in declared intention and
programme the two theologians are much nearer to each
other than has often been supposed. The difference may,

perhaps, be shortly put thus: that Ritschl undertakes to
furnish a theology inspired throughout by Scripture, but too
often fails to keep his promise, whereas Barth is set upon
thinking out something that will deserve to be called a
'Theology of the Word of God', and has so far proceeded
with a consistency and power which is engaging the attention
of the whole Christian Church. It is in performance, not
in chosen aim, that the two men stand so far apart." [34]

2. THE NATURE OF RELIGION

The simple fact that while we speak naturally of " the
Christian religion ", we can also speak of " religions " in the
plural and find that there is no people which does not profess
one or other of them, impels us to ask what this phenomenon
is which we call religion. And the further fact that we
believe the Christian religion to be the true one and feel ourselves called to convert the adherents of others to it, immediately thrusts upon us the question of its relation to them.
For these reasons Mackintosh follows the tradition of the
nineteenth century in general and the Ritschlians in particular by setting in the forefront of his Prolegomena a
discussion of the nature of religion.

He begins with a characteristic protest against the practice
of the older dogmatic down to Schleiermacher in restricting
the idea of real religion to Christianity and its Old Testament
preparation. This view provides a simple method of circum-
venting the problem, and there is certainly truth in it. But
he feels that it must largely have been lack of missionary
enterprise which made such a circumvention possible. While
he finds that it preserves only one aspect of the truth to the
complete exclusion of another: " Such a view no doubt
gives expression, however unsympathetically, to the certainty
that Christianity rests upon a perfect revelation, and in that
sense is in a class by itself. But it takes no account of the
fact that a certain psychological similarity, as well as a
certain identity of aim, characterise all known forms of

religion."[35] The former aspect of the truth is not, of course, to be denied, but here the purpose is to seek an understanding of the latter, and this for two specific reasons: such an understanding is not only necessary if Christianity itself is to be fully intelligible, but still more it is essential for the work of evangelism among the adherents of other faiths.

What, then, is religion? Etymology is of little help here. And it is also clearly impossible to proceed by logical deduction from what is known of God and man, for " we cannot make up a definition of religion out of our heads or by adding ideas together ". [36] The answer must therefore be sought in the concrete facts of history by examining the great religions of the past. Yet in doing so it would be useless, as Ritschl also held,[37] to seek the " greatest common factor " of all religions and call that the essence of religion: such a procedure is too baldly arithmetical, and the answer, even if it could be reached, would be hopelessly and unworkably vague. What is wanted is thus not " an abstract statement of all the common characteristics belonging to every known worship, whether existing or imagined as yet to be ", but " a dynamic conception of the living tendency which, with more or less fullness or definiteness, is operative in all religions ".[38] For religion is for Mackintosh, as for Ritschl,[39] not stationary and immutable, but something which grows and develops in a multitude of different forms ; and what he seeks is not a strict definition in terms which do not imply the special qualities of religion itself, but a description which may fairly claim universal recognition. That being so, he again follows Ritschl,[40] in insisting that the presence of Christian convictions which cannot be even temporarily suspended is no disqualification since the question is one of facts and not of evaluation—the present enquiry is not as to the truth or value of any particular religion, but simply as to what religion is.

With that by way of preface, he embarks upon a study of religion according to its essential content, its relation to

4

science and art, its psychological character, and its origin.*

In *intrinsic essence*, we are told, it may be broadly described as " dependent faith in spiritual beings or powers, or in a spiritual being or power, superior over man and the world, together with the felt need to have personal fellowship therewith ".[41]　　And the following four points are then emphasised : —

" First, there is an awareness of a ' Supreme ' or ' Holy ', apprehended as somehow disclosing its nature through the world and the course of human life, though not necessarily conceived as will and individual personality. . . . Secondly, in religion, man is conscious of certain grave difficulties which surround and trouble his life, of a kind which neither he nor his fellows unaided can remove. Thirdly, the thought is present of a blessing by which these difficulties can be overcome. And fourthly, some idea prevails, however rudimentary, of a way or method by which this life-giving value or blessing can be secured." [42]

So far, it is clear, we have a concept of religion which is little more than formal and could be applied without serious difficulty to almost any particular faith. One might be disposed to query the remark about the self-disclosure of the Supreme, if it meant that every religion claims to be revealed. Yet it must surely be meant in a more general sense, for (unlike Ritschl) Mackintosh himself insists elsewhere that there are religions which have never heard of Divine revelation and for whose adherents " the one source of religious knowledge is tradition—what they learn from the old men of the tribe, not from God ".[43]

But however that may be, in the ensuing exposition a remarkable thing happens, which we do well to note at once and to which we shall presently have to return : the formal concept receives such a content as makes plain that his

* This framework seems to have been taken over from the younger Ritschlian Haering (*Der christl. Glaube*, pp. 27 ff.). The treatment is also parallel to Haering's at many points, with the exception that the discussion of origin is completely different.

Christian convictions do not only affect the question of value, but have had an important influence also upon his view of the facts. For it soon becomes evident that, whether or not a particular religion claims to be revealed, he wished to assert as emphatically as Ritschl [44] that *all* religions are a response to Divine revelation. So, too, if the Supreme need not be conceived as will, it is laid down in the very next paragraph that it "is conceived as possessing what we can only call 'will'"—and this "of at least partially moral character, as being interested in the lot of man, and as bearing towards worshippers such a relationship that they are not only dependent on the Supreme but responsible to it". Likewise, if Deity need not be conceived as individual personality, it presently transpires that we—again this "we", so unemphatic and yet so significant*—can only properly speak of "religion" when gods with some sort of personal character are believed in: the animistic belief in spirits or demons "though probably from its rise allied with religion is not necessarily in itself religious at all", and was in any case almost certainly preceded by a truly religious belief in *mana,* which is conceived as "less or more personal".[45] And although the last three points suggest a view of religion as simply the solution of man's difficulties, Mackintosh at once makes it clear that he is well aware that God is to be sought for His own sake, irrespective of benefits ; and he claims that "we" can find some recognition of this in all religion.

A comparison between religion and science reveals that they resemble each other in the impulse to seek behind appearances an understanding of the course of things, but differ radically in two respects: the believer's passionate interest in his faith forbids the attitude of cool scientific detachment, and (still more important) he does not seek so much a *causal* explanation of the processes observed in the world of outer and inner experience, but is concerned to relate them to a

* *Cf.* pp. 56, 64 *infra.*

Divine *purpose*. Again, like art, religion addresses itself " to the soul rather than to the disinterested intelligence ",[46] stimulating the inner life of contemplation and revealing amid the tensions of the world an ideal realm of harmony and blessedness ; but again there is a radical difference in that art has no concern for the objective truth of its creations and, in appealing only to the aesthetic sense instead of the whole personality, makes no claim to control conduct.

These two comparisons, by bringing out the facts that religion is interested not so much in causes as in purposes, and that it is all-embracing in its appeal and ethical in its claims, suggest that it is rightly described as a " practical concern " and is bound up with needs which are at least in part moral. And now it is expressly laid down that " the basic impulses behind religion are more practical than theoretic, and the needs which religion comes to satisfy are not those of the analytic intellect but those of man as a living whole ".[47]

In *psychological character* it involves in a living unity all three ultimate modes of being conscious—knowing, feeling, willing. The curious suggestion has been made that religion can exist without any particular ideas of the Divine. But while the possibility should not be hastily dismissed, it is clear that no such phenomenon as a " godless " religion has ever existed. Even primitive Buddhism is not an example, as some have contended, for " it is more than doubtful whether Buddhism would have survived as anything more than a high type of morality, or a philosophy, unless it had gradually made room for belief in God and immortality by deifying Guatama and transforming Nirvana into something more positive than a mere absence of desire ".[48] Likewise Confucianism only *became* a religion with the deification of Confucius. Nor does extreme mysticism, which professes to abandon all claim to knowledge, really succeed in doing so, for the " feeling " by which knowledge is supposedly replaced is not mere feeling but at least *involves* knowledge —" not merely an emotion moving purely within the mind itself, and unrelated to any confronting object ; but rather an emotional type of knowledge ".[49]

Thus Mackintosh considers himself justified in holding that all religions—at least all known forms of religion—include some idea of God. He likewise urges that such feelings as awe and reverence, fear, trust and love are vital to religion, arguing that the emphasis on fear as the dominant emotion is a misleading half-truth, for " in religion reverence is fundamental, and reverence includes fear and love together ".[50] And he declares that religion cannot exist without willed activity, whether in sacrifice and prayer or, more generally, in the striving after ethical ends which springs from the sense of obligation to the Deity and the impulse to serve. He also emphasises the inseparable unity of the three elements: " All three are fused in one vital moment. They are not successive but simultaneous and inter-dependent." [51] And much as Ritschl argues that, while no greater importance can be assigned to any one than to any other, yet it is permissible to give the preference to one,[52] so Mackintosh tends elsewhere to show a greater interest in moral will, but warns most strongly against stressing any one in such a way as to try to secure a monopoly for it or even partially neglect any other: " Religion without an element of knowledge would sink to the level of magic ; without feeling, it would be heartless formalism ; without will, it would justly incur the charge of exerting an anti-moral and even anti-social influence ".[53]

The *origin* of religion is obscure, and discussion of it has been spoiled by a certain prejudice in favour of the primitive. Yet its origin back in the mists of time cannot be different from its origin in men to-day, and the cause of its rise in the past cannot be other than the source of its present power. It is thus permissible to say that it has its source in human need, whether for explanation, aid or fellowship, or for all three. Permissible, but not sufficient. For " to point to felt human need could not in itself be an ultimate explanation of religion ",[54] and we must go on to ask why the need is felt.

To that the Christian can give but one answer: man needs God because God has created him for Himself and because " the impact and challenge of this great Presence lies upon him from the first ".[55] It is in virtue of this unanalysable and ineradicable kinship, given and maintained by God Himself, that man is susceptible of religion. And it is likewise God Himself who makes the susceptibility active—by revealing Himself in Nature and history, presenting to man in these two realms of experience the " objective facts which go alike to stimulate and to satisfy his longing for perfect life, and to convey the assurance that there exists a Superhuman Power (whether conceived as plural or singular), capable of bestowing the boon thus longed for ".[56] Thus for Christian thought the origin of religion is not in man, but in God. The full and final revelation in Jesus Christ, confirming as it does " all that is true and prophetic in lesser forms of faith, however rudimentary ", is " proof that in religion, right on from its lowest stages, man has not been stretching out his hands into a universe empty, blind and deaf. Rather at every point he has been responding to the touch of a God who creates the higher longing and in anticipating love stirs our prayer." [57]

It is obvious that the student of Ritschlianism will find himself here on somewhat familiar ground. For a great many of the variations from Ritschl himself would seem to be either modifications due to the influence of the younger Ritschlians or else mere variations of detail. Nevertheless, in spite of all obvious similarities, we can see at once that there is a difference of starting-point and that this has no inconsiderable effect upon the treatment as a whole.

Ritschl starts by assuming that Christianity is *a* religion, of one kind with others, and his chief concern is " to seek a solution of the question how Christianity, as a religion, is related to general philosophical knowledge ".[58] This has two important consequences. In the first place, because his primary concern is with the question of knowledge, he never troubles with an exhaustive or detailed comparison of religions: he simply asserts that they can be arranged in ascending stages, formulates the general conception of religion which he holds can be abstracted from such a comparison and which he employs at once in the service of his theory of religious knowledge, and for the rest allows to other religions only "passing glances" designed to "point out the modifications for the worse which they exhibit when compared with Christianity ".[59] In the second place, because it is a fundamental presupposition of his whole argument that Christianity is of one kind with other religions, the only distinction he can make between them is one of degree: Christianity differs from the rest simply as the highest of them all, the one which brings the most perfect realisation of that (moral) freedom from the (sensual) world which the others secure only in part. And the only purpose there can be in comparing them at all is "to promote among Christians mutual understanding" of this fact.[60]

Mackintosh, however, sets out from the fact that in virtue of its relation to the revelation in Christ, Christianity is "in a class by itself", but as a human activity has also "a certain similarity " with other religions ; and the question which he seeks to answer is, What is the nature of this similarity, and what does it mean for the work of evangelism? Thus on the one hand, because his chief interest is in the missionary task, the topic of religious knowledge in general is no more than touched upon, while the comparison of Christianity with other religions is important enough to require a special treatise to itself. And on the other hand, since he begins by laying down that Christianity is in a class by itself, he is clearly aware that, whatever is to be said of its relation to the others, it differs from them not only in degree but in kind.

This can often be detected with a little care even where the emphasis is on similarity: for example, if Christianity, with its conception of a self-revealing, personal God who demands moral obedience and who is not sought for His blessings but for His own sake, imparts to the formal description of religion a content which in the other cases it simply does not have and which only " we "—Christians—can somehow read into them, then surely the whole concept " religion " is here fundamentally altered and by a " certain " similarity can only be meant a formal one. But the qualitative difference here implied can also be set in the forefront elsewhere—as when we are told on the first page of the special study that its concern is with the elements of the Gospel message which " are new, and not merely new but so intensely charged with native truth and power as to entitle Christianity to displace its rivals ", so completely different from all else as to make it not just superior to the rest, but *the* religion, " destined for, and deserving of, permanent sway over the best human life ".[61] It can scarcely be said that all this forces itself on our attention: on the contrary, it is apt to be somewhat obscured amid all the ins and outs of the argument and often requires some care to detect. But if for that reason it should have escaped our notice, it is most forcibly recalled when it finally becomes the basis of one of the chief criticisms of Ritschl: that for all his protests against rationalism, he has himself fallen a victim to it by applying his general idea of religion to Christianity as simply its highest manifestation, and thus obliterating " the absolute distinction between a universal religion without a Mediator and a definite revelation *with* a Mediator ".[62]

The immediate result of the difference of starting-point is thus to leave Mackintosh's argument open to the recognition of a qualitative distinction between Christianity and other religions which is automatically excluded from Ritschl's. This, however, imposes upon his treatment as a whole what appears to be a curious dualism—as if he did not wish simply to contradict Ritschl, but to have it both ways.

The relation of Christianity to other faiths, it is plain, is conditioned by the fact that it rests on the revelation given by the Mediator, Jesus Christ. But now, *all* religion apparently is based upon revelation: " Outside Christianity there is more to be observed than a fruitless search on the part of unaided man for the Divine reality: there has been a positive self-disclosure of God. We cannot but relate *all* the phenomena of man's religious history to a vast redeeming Divine plan ".[63] And it is suggested more than once that the revelation in Christ, which is the basis of Christianity, sums up and completes that in Nature, history and conscience which underlies other worships. If these things are so, then it would seem that the difference is only in the degree of perfection or completeness of the revelation concerned and Christianity no more than the perfect crown of man's religious development.

And yet, if he can insist that all religion is a response to Divine revelation, he can urge just as emphatically—in one case on the same page—that there has in fact been no response. " Neither Nature nor history ", he writes on this occasion,[64] " has made on man a sufficiently deep impression. Even conscience has proved unavailing ; for as the apostle declares, uncontrolled sensuality renders men at last incapable of recognising the imperatives of God within the soul." And thus, he goes on, this revelation actually results only in " vain attempts of idolatrous heathenism to make a religion for itself ". Likewise, the passages which suggest that the revelation in Christ is distinct only in degree of comparative purity must be off-set by others which imply a qualitative difference. If, for example, the " primary revelation " in the general course of things can be read only by Christian eyes (if at all), then the " remedial revelation " which makes it so must surely be not merely higher and purer, but of a different kind—a blind man will not see a landscape any better for going higher up the hill, and if one cannot read the Hebrew Old Testament the remedy is not a purer text, but either a tutor or a translator. Or again, the passages in which we hear of the creative and transforming effect of the Christian revelation surely also imply that it is absolutely new in comparison with all else, not just relatively so. This indeed is made particularly clear when he urges that it creates in the believer a conception of the love of God which is not only lacking to the rest of mankind but flatly denied by them, and goes on:—

"It is only a relic of old-fashioned rationalism, so often naively indifferent to history, when men persist in talking as if *this* were part of the normal furniture of human understanding, instead of being what it obviously is—an insight, a conviction, that rose like a new planet over the world's horizon at a definite point in history. . . . To speak strictly, in apostolic thought the Cross is not just one illustration of love chosen from a number of possibles. It is rather a creative revelation—that is to say, a revelation which entails a revision and transformation of every former thought, and raises the mind which has taken in something of its wonder to an absolute point of view." [65]

In a word, this revelation " taken seriously means a revolution in religion " [66]—which is surely a different thing from bringing the final stage of its evolution towards perfection.

Thus from the beginning it seems as if on the one hand there is a revelation of God in Nature, history and conscience, consummated in Jesus Christ, and a corresponding development of the human religious faculty quickened thereby, which culminates in Christianity. While on the other hand the one true revelation is utterly unprecedented and Christianity absolutely different from all other faiths.

This, one might be disposed to say, is really not Ritschl but Schleiermacher. There would indeed be some justification for saying so, for the fact is that a score of parallels could here be quoted. And yet here, too, a difference is noticeable at once. For Schleiermacher succeeded in maintaining both sides of the antithesis ; but while the Divine self-manifestation in the general course of things and the ascent from lower worships to Christian faith was, so to speak, the child of his heart, the necessity of Christ and the uniqueness of Christianity was a sore trial and maintained only by dint of severe dialectical discipline. Whereas with Mackintosh the contrary seems to have been the case: it was the former that was his problem child—so much so that far from being maintained it had eventually to be disowned. One often feels, indeed, that when he is speaking in generalities, the argument for general revelation and religious evolution wears well enough; whereas when he comes to particulars, he is never able either to point to anything which man has actually learned from the former or to find anything in the latter beyond the provision of concepts and forms of expression to which the Christian revelation gives a totally new meaning. But however that may be, this much is certain: if at first he may have wished to assert both points and emphasise whichever suited his particular context, by the end the second had forced its way to the centre, pushing the first so far out to the periphery that there is now no revelation apart from Christ, and Christianity means the complete reversal of everything for which religion in general stands. Thus he finally urges, in express agreement with Barth:—

"Revelation is far too great a name for the faint and ambiguous suggestions of God which are all the sinner can detect in creation. Objectively, no doubt, they are present: the heavens declare the glory of God. But for one thing they are audible solely to faith, which is evoked only by true revelation in Christ; and secondly, they are definitely not such as lead men into reconciliation with the true God. . . . There is no real revelation which is not a Divine unveiling of *grace to us,* to me, the sinful. This, once we recognise it, strips us bare of that pride which would lightheartedly and self-confidently cast around for revelations in other quarters." [67]

And of religion in general he writes (against Troeltsch and the religious-historical school):—

"As has recently been contended with great force, the

movement of human religion in general is regarded in Scripture as a movement from man to God, whereas the Christian Gospel testifies rather of the movement of God to man. It is, by its very nature, such a judgment on all human religion as is, in ultimate meaning, the judgment of grace." [68]

So far, then, we have found in Mackintosh, as distinct from Ritschl, an apparent dualism in the form of an antithesis somewhat reminiscent of Schleiermacher, yet differing also from him at least in so far as it seems to be finally resolved by the simple denial of one side. But this last comparison is worth pressing a little further. For the underlying principles of Schleiermacher's argument are so essentially similar to those of almost the whole nineteenth century that by far the greater part of its thought in this connection (including that of Ritschl) can be brought with greater or less completeness under the title " variations on a theme by Schleiermacher ". And a comparison with him will bring out the fact that the immediate differences we have noticed are but symptoms of a deeper and more significant one, which not only separates Mackintosh fundamentally both from Schleiermacher and thereby also from Ritschl, but also provides a clue to the real nature of the dualism and of the change which took place in connection with it.

Schleiermacher, who succeeded in combining to a truly remarkable degree the best qualities of modern man with those of a Christian theologian, felt the advance of modern culture to be identical with the realisation of the Kingdom of God. And the problem to which he here* addressed himself was that of presenting Christianity to the " cultured despisers of religion " among his contemporaries as the crown of civilised man's spiritual development, in order that they might be induced to become active Christians and take the

* Especially in the *Reden*—a book, incidentally, which reads less like a scientific treatise than a great poem.

full share in the advancement of human life and culture which that means.

His method was first to maintain on general philosophic grounds that man as such is essentially a religious being, with a religious faculty alongside his moral, aesthetic and other faculties ; so that the existence of religious fellowships is not an " aberration ", but rather " a necessary element in the development of the human spirit ".[69] And then he assumed the rôle of the " religious virtuoso "—the expert in the philosophy of religion, as much the complete master of his subject as the virtuoso in, say, art or music or politics is master of his—in order to demonstrate that of all the specific forms of religion produced by the progressive development of this faculty, Christianity is the most perfect because it corresponds most closely to the speculative ideal.[70] This being so—and one has only to understand the facts properly to recognise that it is so—it is obvious that a civilisation without religion in general, and Christianity in particular, is an imperfect one, and the modern man who is not actively religious, and in particular actively Christian, is neglecting an essential part of his make-up.

Schleiermacher, however, was not only a typical representative of his " enlightened " age, well qualified to address his cultured contemporaries on an equal footing: he was also—yet without any sense of contradiction—a Christian theologian, who had a somewhat different story to tell. For both, Christianity is, according to his celebrated definition, " a monotheistic faith, belonging to the teleological type of religion, and is essentially distinguished from other such faiths by the fact that in it everything has relation to the redemption accomplished by Jesus of Nazareth ".[71] But if the religious historian can regard it as a stage in the orderly development of a particular group of religions (monotheistic faiths), the theologian has no option but to treat it as a new and unprecedented revolutionary movement with a separate significance of its own.[72] If for the philosophy of religion it is the highest yet known but might one day be surpassed, for the Christian it is final, perfect, absolute. If the modern man sees in the Redeemer and His Work the highest point in the normal (if mysterious) evolution of spiritual powers inherent in human nature from the first,[73] for the Christian believer He is distinct from all others in virtue of the unique indwelling of the full power of God in Him,[74] and brings a new creative principle into human life.[75]

Thus it was vital to him in his two-fold capacity (as representative of modern culture and as Christian theologian) to maintain that the Christian faith both crowns the series and also transcends it—because the redemption in Christ which is its distinguishing mark is both the natural culmination of the historical advance towards the triumph of Spirit over Nature and also a sudden new departure in the course of things, a unique and revolutionary Divine event. This antithesis he had to reconcile without denying either side, and he did so from the standpoint that it is not absolute, but rather a fluid antithesis between one unavoidable over-emphasis and another: it is due to the inadequacy of intellectual forms to express the movement of life, and the truth lies in an inexpressible dialectical middle-point between the two.*

* There were few things more calculated to rouse his ire than the assertion of absolute or even sharp contrasts. And although his thought abounds in antitheses, he is never tired of reiterating that they are only relative : always—with the sole exception of the primary antithesis between the Infinite, in which being and knowledge are identical, and the Finite as a whole, in which they are divided—the opposition is only between " more " and " less ", one element predominating over the other, but never excluding it. The result may not always appear entirely convincing, and in particular one may doubt whether it does justice to the Christian revelation, the uniqueness of Christianity and the Divinity of Christ. Yet one cannot but wonder at the vastness of conception and the dexterity of the argument. It is easy to throw stones, as has repeatedly been done—all too often, perhaps, by the tenants of glass houses. But understanding criticism is a very different matter : he was far too many-sided to be so easily dealt with as is often imagined.

Not so Mackintosh. His fundamental interest in the missionary task gives his argument a very different cast for all the many verbal reminiscences.* For it means that at bottom he is less concerned with the advancement of culture than with the proclamation of the Gospel to a sinful world. Thus he has no apparent desire to identify civilisation with the Kingdom of God, but rather to separate them: " the forward movement of humanity is itself sinful, lying under the judgment of God " [76]—it belongs to what the New Testament calls the " world ", and has meaning only because already the transcendent " ' powers of the age to come ' project themselves in manifold ways into the present age, diffusing harmony and order throughout what is otherwise a chaos, and preparing ultimately to supersede the laws of the present dispensation ".[77] For the same reason there is an obvious absence of the interest in apologetics which played so great a rôle with Schleiermacher: he has no need to justify

* Schleiermacher was not actively opposed to missionary enterprise —indeed, in a note later attached to the first of the *Reden* (p. 27) he found it to be possibly (but only possibly !) a redeeming feature of the British national character, of which he had earlier (p. 11) painted such a delightfully black picture. But he rather suspected it of being bound up with interests which were commercial rather than religious. And in any case he was inclined to deprecate it on the ground that every religion has its right and proper place at a particular level of culture and it is mistaken to attempt to force a specific form of faith upon peoples who are not ready for it (pp. 183 ff.)—although on the other hand he was later prepared to allow a certain justification to missionary endeavour which was no more than a sympathetic attempt to accelerate the natural process of development (pp. 220 f.). The fact is, however, that far from being deeply interested in the work of foreign missions he seldom mentions it at all, and it could not have anything like the formative influence on his thought which it had on Mackintosh's. The difference is understandable enough. For on the continent this matter was—and still is—left to special independent societies formed for the purpose, and thus it was by no means unusual for a German theological professor to be indifferent or even sceptical towards it. Whereas in Scotland missionary concern first arose within the Church itself, and since then has always been an integral part of its work ; so that it could not but be a living issue for one of its professors.

Christianity to "the world" by arguments from a general anthropology and the philosophy of religion, but can adopt throughout the standpoint of the Christian believer and the "age to come". Indeed, he not only can do so, but does— as can be seen at both stages of Schleiermacher's argument.

In attempting to define the essence of religion Mackintosh does not construct a speculative conception of it by a process of philosophical deduction: rather, he explicitly rejects such a method, seeking instead a general description of the basic tendency more or less discernible in all the religions of history. And it is clearly the standpoint of the Christian that he adopts in doing so. For he finds in other religions things of which their own adherents and the philosophical observer would no doubt often be surprised to hear; but he evidently means that it is *Christians* who must see as it were an unconscious shadow of these elements (the idea of a God who reveals Himself, is personal, makes ethical claims upon His worshippers, is sought solely for His own sake) invariably present to some extent in ethnic conceptions of the Supreme, although in actual fact it may not be so conceived. When, indeed, he comes to examine other religions in themselves, it is to call attention repeatedly to the absence of most or all of these elements.

So, too, with man's religious faculty. If he can say that man is "susceptible to religion", this is the voice not of the philosopher but of the Christian, speaking of man not simply as man but as he stands before the living God: he has this susceptibility because he has been created for God and cannot alter his constitution for all his sinning.* When, on the other hand, man in himself and as such does become the subject of discussion, then it is rather of a sinner that we hear, blind and deaf to the things of God, heading for chaos and death. And thus if concern with religion in general will bring home to the Christian afresh "how incurably religious a being is man",[78] the conclusion is not that

* *Cf.* p. 54 *supra.*

man as such has a true capacity for God. Rather, because it is a feeling of dissatisfaction and restlessness which makes him religious and because Christian thought can only explain this feeling as a " symptom " that God never ceases to claim him for Himself,[79] it means that the Christian has here (as the sentence at once goes on) a fresh indication " how constant has been the pressure of God's seeking love upon His blinded and dying children ".

At the second stage of Schleiermacher's argument it is the same. Mackintosh is no " religious virtuoso ", adopting the standpoint of an impartial observer " above Christianity in the logical sense of the word " [80] with an expert's mastery of facts to be measured against a speculative ideal. Rather, he takes his stand within Christianity, as a Christian believer who, however inexpert he may be, can endeavour to make the revelation of God in Jesus Christ the light of all his seeing. Thus if he can describe man's religious history as a progressive " response to the touch of God ", that is not because in themselves the various religions lead gradually up to Christianity as ever more perfect approximations to the ideal, for in themselves " religious phenomena in the non-Christian world display no steady or consistent advance " and are preparations for Christianity only in the negative sense that " the alternatives to Jesus Christ are as it were tried in advance and found wanting ".[81] It is because the Christian can see in them an ever more determined attempt to satisfy a feeling of need whose origin is in God, and thus a continued acknowledgment of the fact that He has never abandoned those who would abandon Him. And when it comes to the question of truth and value, then the standard he applies is again not a philosophical ideal, but God's revelation of Himself and His ways in Jesus Christ; with the result that non-Christian teachings are not found to be growing approximations to the truth, but only scattered verbal parallels—some perhaps nearer, others more distant, and to that extent describable provisionally as more or less true, but one and all with such a totally different meaning and content that ultimately they can only be described as false.

Such differences may appear to be subtle. Perhaps in the result they often are. For it cannot be denied that at first the influence of Schleiermacher and later thinkers on the form of Mackintosh's argument was such as to produce considerable ambiguity at many points ; so that the reader of his earlier works is often in some doubt as to whether this is nineteenth-century theology with a subtle difference, or something of a very different kind obscured by nineteenth-century influences every here and there. But in view of the evidence of his last work there can surely be little doubt that the latter is the case. And however subtle or obscure the difference may often appear, it is one of extraordinary importance. For it provides the key both to the real nature of that contradiction which is at first sight so strange, and also to the development of Mackintosh's thought in this connection.

First the contradiction itself. At one moment we are told there is a general revelation in Nature and history, the next there is none ; on one page we hear of a progressive religious education of mankind and a response to the touch of God in every religion, on another progress is haphazard and there is no response. But from here we can see that this is neither a mere inconsistency on Mackintosh's part, nor an attempt to compromise between modern thought and Christian faith with the aid of a dialectic based on the relations between the Infinite and the Finite: rather, it is imposed on him by the fact that he sets out from the relation of Divine grace to human sin revealed in Jesus Christ. The antitheses are neither arbitrary, nor due to the limitations of finite thought and the consequent necessity of regarding each of the several phenomena of life, now as an element of a greater whole, now as an individual entity with a peculiar significance of its own: they are due rather to the fact that the creature has sought to sever the relation with its Creator but is nevertheless maintained by Him, so that it must be seen alternately in view of Divine grace and of human sin.

Because God is the Creator who sustains and rules the world in grace, He is fully present and knowable in a multitude of forms throughout creation, and there is a Divine self-disclosure in Nature and history as well as in Christ. But because man is a sinner who rebels against his Creator and insists on interpreting creation in his own way, he can only be blind to the indications of God there, and must be totally ignorant of Him until grace overcomes sin in redemption; so that Nature and history in fact reveal nothing, and the Redeemer alone brings a revelation worthy of the name— which must then mean not only deliverance from the self-confident search for revelations elsewhere but judgment upon it. Again, because God in His grace never ceases to make His claims on man at every point of his life, the religious activity which this calls forth is a response to the touch of God, and that of Christianity one among others. But because man in his rebellion has repudiated the God whose claims are the true source of his need and who alone can satisfy it, his religious activity can only issue in the sporadic appearance of " varied plausible but fruitless attempts at self-redemption ";[82] so that there is in fact no true response, and the faith which lives not by human effort but solely by the grace of Christ is the only true religion, absolutely distinct from the rest—a religion whose message must then be one of judgment on the endeavours whose place it takes.

These contrasts are indeed absolute and mutually exclusive, not fluid antitheses between a relative preponderance of one element and a relative preponderance of the other; for there can be no mere relative opposition between the grace of God and the sin of man. And the missionary cannot disregard either side; for he is called to proclaim a message of Divine grace to sinners, in the knowledge that " only those know

the grace of God who have trembled at His judgment ".
If God is not One who has all along disclosed Himself to
man and at every point " furnished all the conditions for the
rise and progress of true religion " [83]—One, that is, of whom
he has always had knowledge and to whose claims his
religious activity has been a response—then the hearer cannot acknowledge that he has ever had to do with Him before.
And if man has not persisted in completely ignoring God
and making his very religion an out-and-out act of rebellion,
so that in fact he has no knowledge of Him whatsoever and
has not responded in the least, then the hearer can neither
see himself and his religion unreservedly under His judgment
nor know His grace and embrace the true faith.   Yet
ultimately there is here no pure, irresolvable paradox, for the
unity does exist—not in an indefinable point of identity
postulated by thought beyond, or midway between, the
opposing elements, but as a certainty of faith in the God
with whom there is forgiveness of sins and whose judgment
is ultimately the judgment of grace.

   This dialectic, grounded as it is in the Christian revelation
and worked out for the sake of its bearing on the missionary
task, surely reproduces faithfully the teaching of the apostle
which Mackintosh called upon in its support.[84] For Paul,
likewise, is speaking of non-believers in closest connection
with Christ and the proclamation of His Gospel, not
abstractly in themselves.   And in these concrete circumstances he urges that God " has not left Himself without
witness " but has made Himself known in His gracious care
of men (Acts 14:17) and His sovereign control of nations
(Acts 17:26), that " His eternal power and Godhead are conceived and perceived on the strength of His works " (Rom.
1:20), that all that can be known of Him " gives clear evidence of itself among men " and is manifested to them by God
Himself (v.19) ; so that (as they must now admit when the
Gospel message comes home to them) " they knew God "
(v. 21) and can be taxed with that knowledge.   And yet they

did not in fact know Him or give Him the slightest recognition: "they suppressed the truth in unrighteousness" (v. 18), they "became vain in their thoughts and their foolish heart was darkened" (v. 21), "they changed the truth of God into a lie" (v. 25) and "refused to maintain the true knowledge of Him" (v. 28)—and thus He must now be "declared" to those to whom He is in fact "Unknown" (Acts 17:23).

So, too, with religion in general. Paul's hearers are indeed "very religious" (Acts 17:22), and it is owing to God they are so: it is because He has created men for Himself and guides the whole history of mankind that they can "seek after Him, if haply they might find Him" (vv. 26 f.). And yet they have not responded in the least, but have indulged instead in an "ignorant worship" (v. 23). Although He has made Himself known as Creator and Ruler of all things, they have fondly imagined that "He is to be ministered to by human hands as though He needed something" which their efforts could provide (vv. 24 f.); although He has disclosed Himself in all the nearness of a Father (as their own poet has unknowingly borne witness), they have gone off seeking Him on their own and turned Him into "a product of man's artifice and reflection" (vv. 28 f.); "although they had come to knowledge of God, they glorified Him not as God, neither were thankful" but "changed the glory of the uncorruptible God into an image resembling corruptible man, and birds and beasts and reptiles" (Rom. 1:21, 23).

There is no suggestion here that man as such has a true (if dim) knowledge of God and practices a true (if largely erroneous) religion, or that the preacher can link his message to these things and bring them to perfection. On the contrary, it is the revelation in Christ which now for the first time (Acts 17:30 f., Rom. 1:18) makes plain to the hearer that he could have known and worshipped God. And thus he must now recognise himself as "without excuse" (Rom. 1:20), seeing his imagined knowledge and the best things in his very religion as "vanities" from which he must now turn aside (Acts 14:15), wilful ignorance of which he must now repent (Acts 17:30), "ungodliness and unrighteousness" which can only be the object of Divine wrath (Rom. 1:18).

Here, then, we have surely the same insight as Mackintosh was seeking to express—at first, perhaps, with here and there some momentary departures in the direction of nineteenth-century thought, but latterly with perfect consistency and clarity. Or if we would seek a parallel in a theologian nearer his own day, then it will not be Schleiermacher or any of those who, like him, were concerned first of all with modern man and the advancement of his culture, but— Calvin, with his primary interest in God and the proclamation of His Word.

In this context Calvin, too, maintains that apart from the "redemptive" revelation of God in Jesus Christ there is also a "primary" revelation in creation and providence, in which He is manifest as our Maker and the sole "Fount of all good"[85]—in other words, there is "a certain knowledge of His Divinity given to all men" and "continually brought to mind afresh" by God Himself,[86] "a consciousness of His Godhead indelibly engraved upon every human heart".[87] This knowledge, moreover, "is an adequate teacher of the piety from which religion springs":[88]* thanks to it, indeed, "a certain seed of religion" abides perpetually in all men,[89] so that religion is no mere accidental invention "contrived by a few men's subtlety and cunning"[90] but a necessary human activity called forth by God Himself. But he goes on at once to say that men in fact totally disregard the general revelation, and that the seed of religion, far from

* Piety is here defined as "the combination of reverence and love of God produced by the knowledge of His benefits", and in the next paragraph the "pure and genuine religion" springing from it is "faith united with the earnest fear of God, inasmuch as fear both includes spontaneous reverence and brings the proper worship as prescribed by the Law"—a general definition not so very different from Mackintosh's, although the biblical standpoint is more immediately obvious.

bearing fruit, never even ripens at all: [91] " they do not apprehend Him as He reveals Himself but imagine Him according
to the picture they have constructed in their own temerity " [92]
—and hence all their religious strivings are inevitably only
" the worship of their own heart's dream ",[93]—their religion
becomes " a vain and deceitful shadow of religion, scarcely
worthy to be called even a shadow ",[94] and the " seed ",
though it remains " ineradicable ", is " so corrupted that it
produces only the vilest fruit ".[95]

Thus in Calvin we again find the same thing. There is a
difference between the two writers in that Calvin, following
the scholastic tradition, concerns himself more with the
general knowledge of God than with religion, whereas
Mackintosh, in the wake of the nineteenth century, concen-
trates more on religion than on knowledge. But since Calvin
also insists that knowledge which did not issue in worship
would be mere idle speculation,[96] whereas Mackintosh urges
that religion without knowledge would be no more than
magic, the difference is only one of perspective and not of
principle. Both adopt the same standpoint—the revelation
in Jesus Christ. For both, there is then a universal self-
disclosure of God, yet the sinner remains in culpable ignorance of Him. For both, religion is no chance phenomenon
but an inevitable result of God's claims on man, yet it is an
act of open rebellion against Him. And just as Mackintosh,
in his special concern with other religions, can find vague
glimmerings of truth in them all, only to conclude that in
fact they are mere vain attempts at self-redemption whose
true Source and real sinfulness are both made plain for the
first time in Christ; so Calvin, in examining the natural
man's knowledge of God, finds [97] that he is a good Christian—
indeed, a good Calvinist Christian—only to add at once [98] that
actually he is nothing of the sort, but an inexcusably ignorant sinner who cannot know either God or his own guilt
except through the revelation of His Word.

From the vantage point now obtained we can also see that

there was really no sudden or radical change in Mackintosh's thought here, but rather an orderly development. It seems, indeed, that from first to last his fundamental concern was to maintain the New Testament teaching on the subject in all its fullness, and that the difference in his final position is due partly to greater clarity, partly to a change of front.

At the beginning his thought was largely conditioned by opposition to late orthodox discussions both of the " natural knowledge " of God and of religion in general.

In the former case he felt that the very term " natural " was apt to suggest a knowledge which " had grown up of itself, in untended and unenriched soil ",[99] and could be studied abstractly on its own ; and he found that later orthodoxy, by making the topic an almost independent interest and giving it a thoroughly rationalistic treatment, had rendered this interpretation practically inevitable. This, however, ran clean counter to two elements of New Testament thought: first, that if there is in any sense a knowledge of God anywhere, or any possibility of it, then that is not due to man but solely to God's disclosure of Himself, second, that its nature is not a matter of rational observation but is known for the first time in Christ. And it was in order to counteract these errors that he insisted so firmly both that there is a general revelation and that it is only readable to Christian eyes.

In the case of religion he rebelled against what he calls " the simple but unhappy method " of dismissing non-Christian religions out of hand as due to " human error or wickedness ".[100] It is unhappy, he felt, not because they are true, but because it is in danger of so asserting their falsehood as to forget the power of God and suggest that " man has been stretching out his hands to a universe empty, blind and deaf ".[101] Whereas faith knows that " while we in our sin are infinitely distant from God, you do not state the whole truth, or even its more important side, by laying down that He is infinitely distant from us. He is near as well as far." [102]

Recognised or ignored, served or rebelled against, He is there, and since it is only because of this that man can be religious at all, his religion *could* be true although in fact it is false. But the method is unhappy also for another reason: it tends to obscure the fact that Christianity rests upon the revelation of God's grace *to men* and that, whatever else it is, it is certainly a response *of men,* so similar to others in psychological character and apparent aim that its absolute difference from them is not a matter of simple assertion or observation but is known only in faith. What he writes in one place of its finality applies also to its uniqueness:—

"Christianity is absolute only if it dares to be so. The persuasion of its supremacy is not something that can be obtained once for all either by the Church or the individual Christian, entered correctly in a creed or private notebook, and left thenceforward to maintain itself in life and power. No: we lose the truth except as we continually regain it, fighting the good fight of faith with decisive and fearless trust. The great certitude that Christ is final belongs not to the sensible men, but to the martyrs—to all who are willing to spend and be spent to the utmost in a cause greater than life itself." [103]

He had no desire to dispute the fact that Christianity is unique and other religions sinful. But he considered it a fatal mistake simply to ignore the other side of New Testament teaching: that in virtue of its origin in God all religion could be true, and that Christianity as a fully human activity has certain similarities with the others for all its difference. He found that later orthodoxy, by losing sight of this, had left the real sinfulness of man's religion and the true nature of Christianity's uniqueness open to question after all, grounding them on a mere naive human assumption instead of on the revelation of God. For false religion is not sinful because we say so, but because we see in the light of Christ that God has provided the conditions for true religion; while the uniqueness of Christianity does not lie in its being observably different from the rest, but in the fact that here God in Christ enables man thankfully to accept and live from the profferred grace which the rest try to earn for themselves. Thus here again it was with an eye on the shortcomings of later orthodoxy over against the New Testament Gospel that he conducted his argument: it was in an effort to remedy them that he felt bound to maintain so emphatically that all religions are a response to the touch of God and to point to similarities between Christianity and the rest.

But in thus seeking to avoid the dangers which he found in orthodoxy, he left himself open to dangers of another kind. For he came under the influence of nineteenth-century writers who were also insisting upon general revelation and the similarity of Christianity to other religions.

At first, perhaps not fully aware of the fundamental difference between their standpoint and his, he was sometimes led astray by their argument into temporary lapses from his own. Hence the occasional suggestions that the general revelation has actually been recognised, at least to some extent. Hence, too, the passages which seem to imply that the outstretched hand of man's religion does in fact grasp something of the truth, that his ineradicable longing for God does find true (if only partial) satisfaction, that Christianity surpasses and crowns all other religions in virtue of its new ethical purity and the unrivalled moral inspiration which it brings. Yet it is clear that such suggestions never occur in their own right: rather, like certain traces of scholastic thought which one may find in Calvin's discussion of the natural knowledge of God, they seem to have insinuated themselves under extraneous influences into an argument which would not be adversely affected by their excision, but rather the clearer for it. Their intrusion was no doubt facilitated by the natural tendency of all reaction to indulge in hyperbole. But they were never anything in the nature of an independent interest, nor was there ever a lack of statements at least equally emphatic which contradicted them ; and in the course of time they become noticeably fewer while those on the other side become more numerous and more clear.* Thus we are told emphatically enough that the primary revelation has *not* been recognised. While there are increasingly plain indications that the stretching-out of the hand is *vain* (not because God is not there but because He is not to be found that way) ; that God shows His love precisely in creating at every point an *unsatisfied* longing and thus frustrating every attempt to find satisfaction in anything less than Himself ; that in so far as an ethical standard can be applied to the evaluation of religions it is not a general one (as with Ritschl) but exists only as it is called into existence by the revelation of Christ.

Whatever ambiguity such contradictory statements may at first have caused, we can see at least that from the beginning his interest lay first and foremost in the uniqueness of Christ and of Christianity, and only then and for that reason in their relation to primary revelation and religion in general. And thus it required only the exaltation of the latter by Troeltsch into the sole concern of theology, together with a certain stimulus from the writings of Barth on the other side, to make him state his position in a manner which left no room for doubt. For then he came to see as his chief enemy no longer late orthodoxy with its rationalistic tendencies, but first and foremost the thorough-going rationalism of the "Theology of Religious History" and then also that of Schleiermacher and Ritschl from whom it had come.

Against this he felt himself bound to assert in no uncertain terms that in fact there is no general revelation and all religions are wholly false. But there is here no denial of the contentions formerly upheld with such tenacity: that there are indications of God in Nature and history, and that all religion has its origin in the ceaseless impact of God's

* One can compare in this respect *The Originality of the Christian Message* (1920) with *The Christian Apprehension of God* (1929).

love upon man which provides all the conditions for its proper rise and development. The point is, rather, that because the indications are never apprehended by man and in fact mean nothing to him, although the Christian knows that objectively they *are* there, they should not be called " revelation " as if they were of one kind with the only real and effectual revelation in Jesus Christ ; and because the conditions of true religion, although the Christian knows that they are continually provided by God at every stage of man's development, are in fact used only to rebel against Him, it is better not to speak of their provision as a " religious education of mankind " as though men were thereby being led gradually to the point where they could quietly step over into Christianity. Thus both sides of the antithesis are still maintained ; but the emphasis now falls on the side on which Paul and Calvin placed it—on the side indeed, on which from Mackintosh's own starting-point it was inevitable that it should be placed.

One might perhaps briefly describe the progress of his thought by saying that he was sure enough of his general direction, as pointed out for him by Apostle and Reformer, to be able to trim his sails to suit the wind. When it blew a late orthodox gale, he shortened sail and made all possible speed away from the danger-point in the direction of general revelation and religious development. But when he found he had gone far enough, and that the wind was now religious-historical and threatening to carry him on to the rocks of Liberalism, he immediately swung round and set off on a different tack which brought him to his goal in the end. If he had not been able to approach this goal directly, he had never forgotten where it was ; and although circumstances had made veering necessary, he was too skilful a mariner ever to have got very far out of the direct course.

3. *THE SPECIFIC NATURE OF BELIEVING KNOWLEDGE*

We have seen that a definite knowledge of God and His relation to man is an essential element in true religion. It is not the only element, since then religion would be hardly distinguishable from science or philosophy, but it is an important one: —

"The people who in the past have counted for most in religious progress have been the thinkers—not the mystics who lose themselves in ecstasies of feeling, nor the practical men, whose one aim is to get things done; but the prophets and thinkers. The men who best understood religion and revealed in it new power to conquer the world, have been figures like Origen, Augustine and Luther." [104]

The nature of this knowledge has now to be determined. And Mackintosh's chief purpose in doing so appears to be (like that of the Ritschlians) to establish the relation between faith and science, theology and philosophy: just as religion and science were seen to resemble each other and yet at the same time to differ radically, so also with scientific and believing knowledge. It is worth noting, however, that although he can call it "religious knowledge", it is not with religious knowledge in general that he is concerned.* He does begin by referring to this question, and adds: "It is a topic on which long and interesting debate was held throughout the nineteenth century; it cannot indeed fail in any age to fascinate those who care deeply for religion".[105] But he goes on at once to take his own starting-point in the fact that "for Christian minds religious knowledge means first

* The terms "religion" and "religious" when used alone seem to be practically synonymous with "Christianity" (the only true religion) and "believing". When they are meant in a wider sense they are always qualified by some such addition as "all", "in general" or "as such".

and foremost that knowledge of spiritual reality, and supremely of God, which we have through *faith* ".[106] Therewith the question of religious knowledge in general is quietly laid on one side, and the knowledge of the Christian believer becomes the sole topic of discussion.*

On the one hand, we are now told, faith and science resemble each other. For religion is based upon Divine revelation ; and that means that, like science, " faith is apprehending facts, not inventing them ".[107] Or, to put it otherwise, in objective quality the two kinds of knowledge are similar: the self-revelation of God "is as definitely presented to, but not created by, the knowing mind, as the natural world is presented to the scientific intelligence ".[108] Nor does the essentially symbolic character of believing thought† destroy this objectivity any more than is the case with science, for it is simply the nature of *all* human thought that it must use images derived from sense-experience: the thought of an electron, for example, owes as much to the imagination as that of Divine Fatherhood, and if science can verify and correct its symbols by further research, so also faith can, and does equally well test *its* symbols against the revelation which called it into being.

But there is also another side to the matter. For religion is no mere exercise of the intelligence, but a practical concern of the human soul, *i.e.* of " the complete nature in its most personal aspect ".[109] And this means that believing knowledge is not purely theoretic but is so closely interlaced with feeling and volition that, however much its objective conditions may resemble those of science, its subjective conditions

* It is in keeping with this that the word " religious ", which so long stood in the title of his College lecture on the subject, was finally altered to " believing ".

† Here Mackintosh comments, " the intellect goes hand in hand with imagination and clothes ideas in symbolic vestures " (*Apprehension of God*, p. 31 n.)—which is clearly an almost verbal quotation from Haering (*Der christl. Glaube*, p. 30).

are decidedly different.[110] Scientific knowledge is cool and detached theory ; that of faith is heartfelt conviction. Science proceeds by reasoned hypothesis to be tested by trial and error ; the prophets do not reach their knowledge of the truth by scientific or philosophical argumentation, but " perceive it intuitively by spiritual insight or inference, however much they may seek to defend it by inductive reasoning should it be attacked ".[111] In the one case truth has the assurance of logical certainty and cannot be doubted once the argument is understood ; in the other it is held by " moral or spiritual " certitude and often clung to in spite of " what seem the hard facts of the world ",[112] though not with any less assurance. The knowledge of science is strictly departmental in character, for it is the result of " intellectual operations which leave conscience untouched and do not open the door into a new kind of moral experience ",[113] so that it appeals only to the intellect and neither to the whole man nor to all men ; the knowledge of faith, bound up as it is with the whole range of man's physical and spiritual life, is completely universal in its appeal. The one kind of knowledge need not imply the recognition of independent moral values, the other must inevitably do so.

These differences, Mackintosh holds, are best covered by saying that " science operates with theoretic judgments, faith with value-judgments ",[114] the former being simple statements of fact, the latter adding the value or worth which the object has for the speaker as a personal being. To quote his favourite illustration of the distinction :—

" ' Christ lived and died in Palestine 1900 years ago ' is a historical statement which might be made by a Mohammedan or a Buddhist. But ' God was in Christ reconciling the world to Himself ' is a statement into which the believer has put that which Christ means to him personally. It brings out the worth and preciousness of Christ for faith. It expresses what the fact of Christ involves for sinful men. That fact has mastered and subdued us, it has made us the forgiven children of God, it has become as it were a part of our life of which we could not bear to be deprived. Hence we proclaim its reality in a judgment which is more than a judgment of cold fact, because it is in addition a glowing and heartfelt judgment of value. In a word, a religious value-judgment is a *personal conviction,* on which we stake all, and which we hold because the influence of Christ upon us leaves us no option." [115]

Such personal convictions—" judgments of trust, of conviction, of personal and kindling response to absolute values " [116] —do not call for any great intellectual powers : they are truths to which any Christian can witness, and knowledge of which can be attained by the simplest peasant capable of moral and personal relations. For the way to them is not intellectual perception, but simply the sympathetic and trustful insight, the desire to recognise goodness and worth, and the will to submit to the deserved influence of another will, which are the indispensable preconditions of all true knowledge of persons and essential even to the personal relations of human friendship.[117] And likewise the proof appropriate to such truths is not that of logical compulsion, but of appeal to the whole moral and spiritual being : the evangelist instinctively does not seek to overwhelm his hearers by irrefutable argument, but to subject them to an irresistible impression, generally made specifically upon the conscience, by whose " inward witness the authority of the heard message is recognised and owned ".[118]

Thus Mackintosh subscribes to the theory of religious value-judgments which, deriving from Kant, Schleiermacher and Lotze, was first given real prominence by Ritschl and his followers. He also joins the Ritschlians in the attitude towards philosophy they grounded upon it. For the knowledge of faith thus given in the form of personal convictions is the very stuff of which theology is built. And since it is so different from theoretic knowledge both in its nature and in the manner of its attainment and verification, the dogmatic which is its full elucidation and systematised presentation must be wholly independent of the theoretic disciplines of science and philosophy.

Thus he found in the Ritschlian conception of the nature of religious knowledge the positive support for the conviction of the need to separate theology and philosophy which we saw arising in his struggle with Hegelianism. And on this same ground he objects not only to the practice of Hegel in making theology definitely subordinate to philosophy, but also, like Ritschl,[119] to that of orthodoxy in attempting to combine the two on a more or less equal footing—by setting a universal natural knowledge of God alongside the revelation in Christ, and uniting the Christian conceptions of God, of Christ and of Redemption with purely speculative ideas derived largely from Aristotle and scholastic philosophy. The so-called universal natural knowledge of God, he urges, neither exists (witness the very fact of polytheism) nor can exist (since the purely speculative use of the theoretic reason simply cannot in fact attain to any true knowledge of God); and the convictions of faith have so little in common with the logical abstractions of philosophy that such an attempt to combine them can only lead to inconsistency and confusion. A proper dogmatic therefore cannot find a place for such things. Nor does it require to do so. For all that can be known of the things of God is fully and completely revealed in Jesus Christ and needs neither supplement nor substantiation from the side of speculative metaphysic: the full content of the concepts in which Christian doctrine is expressed is, either immediately or by implication, contained without remainder in the convictions of faith resting solely on that revelation.

He finds it necessary, however, to add three comments in defence and explanation of the theory.

First, it is no new invention of Ritschl's: in actual fact it goes back to the New Testament itself. For when Christ says, " Everyone that is of the truth hears My voice " (John 18:37), or, " If any man wills to do the will of My Father, he

6

shall know of the doctrine " (John 7 : 17), or when Paul writes,
" The natural man receiveth not the things of the Spirit, for
they are foolishness to him ; neither can he know them, for
they are spiritually discerned " (I Cor. 2 : 14), the meaning is
simply that spiritual knowledge is morally conditioned. The
man who does not care for goodness is inevitably blind to
the truths of the Gospel, and they can only be a mystery
to him : —

" He cannot see what Christ is for. He cannot believe that
Christ is of any use to him. It does not dawn on him that in
this Man the Father Himself is stooping down to bless and
save us. Why? Because to the eye dulled with sloth or
pride or lust these things are invisible. Such a mind, as long
as it remains so, sees no more than a dog in a picture gallery.
But the man in earnest about living right makes the discovery. It comes home to him, instantly or by degrees, that
here in Jesus the love, the gracious friendship of God is
seeking him out and soliciting his trust, to help him inwardly
to love and to do that Will which he has been endeavouring
to obey, but with constant shame and failure." [120]

According to the New Testament, then, " there is no true
knowledge of God which does not come through faith, and
faith, while a Divine gift, is also a morally qualified human
attitude ".[121] Or, more shortly, " Obedience is the organ of
spiritual knowledge ".[122] The meaning and power of Christ
—and likewise also the whole range of God's providential
government of the world and the whole meaning of life—can
only be perceived by those whose hearts are set upon
obedience to God's will. And Mackintosh urges that all the
theory of religious value-judgments does is to give technical
elaboration to this view.

Secondly, he is at pains to defend the theory against the
charge that it means that religious knowledge is purely subjective so that in religion " fancies are as good as facts " or
" people may believe what they like, if only they like it very
much ".[123] Some of Ritschl's earlier statements may, he

admits, have lent colour to this charge ; * yet it is quite unfounded, for in living experience fact and value are inseparable and a judgment of value is *ipso facto* a judgment of fact. If, for example, we affirm the infinite worth of Christ, we at once affirm also the fact of Christ, and if there is a subjective quality in the sense of value, the fact is none the less objective. Moreover, "the believing affirmation refers not to the inward experiences of the person making it —though it may and does spring out of such experiences—but to something real and objective, in this case the Personality of Jesus. That reality is *there,* confronting us whether or not we attend to it, possessing its worth for men whether or not we feel it." [124] Thus religious value-judgments are not mere postulates, clung to because of their indispensable value to our inner life and affirmed solely on the strength of that value: rather they express a response to objective revelation.[125] We do not argue from our desires to the reality of the desired object, but rather we rest our convictions upon the self-revelation of God in Christ: "it is because God has shown us that in character He is such and such that we are sure of this and that ".[126]

Finally, he urges that, although scientific and believing knowledge are thus so different, issue from and appeal to different mental interests, and are reached and verified in different (though equally valid) ways, this cannot mean the existence of an ultimate and irreconcilable dualism in knowledge. He rather suspected the Ritschlians of at least a tendency in this direction ; for in an early essay he finds that Ritschl, in his various editions, wavers considerably as to the possibility of uniting the two, while for Herrmann any

* In his early essay on the Philosophical Presuppositions of Ritschlianism (1899) Mackintosh had himself made almost precisely this same criticism of Ritschl (*Aspects of Christian Belief*, pp. 139 ff.). But in republishing it twenty-five years later he adds the note that the more vulnerable points of the argument were strengthened, and the objective reality of spiritual values clearly exhibited, by later members of the school, chiefly Reischle in his *Werthurtheile und Glaubensurtheile.*

attempt to do so is simply treachery to religion and sacrilege.[127] And although he later recognised that such suspicions may have been unfounded,[128] for his own part at least he could allow no uncertainty on the point : " faith that every truth when scanned from the ultimate point of view, is in harmony with all the rest of truth is part of faith in God Himself, who will not put us intellectually to confusion ".[129] The world investigated by science is the same world in which the believer lives ; and without some understanding of the course of things, *i.e.* without science, we could not offer to God the life of service in the world which He demands of us. Thus the two kinds of knowledge, far from being mutually exclusive, or even hostile to each other, are really complementary, and are both required for " even an approximately satisfying view of the universe as a whole ".[130]

This does not mean that the unity is easily attained. There is, and probably always will be, an acute tension between science and faith ; for it seems to belong to faith that it must fight for its existence as much in the realm of thought as in that of action.[131] But what is here being maintained is, that no specious methods of getting rid of the tension may be adopted—whether by attempting the impossible task of setting up two completely water-tight, hermetically-sealed compartments in the mind, or by seeking to apply purely scientific methods to religious problems. Rather, whatever the difficulties may be, " the true task of reflective faith is to search for spiritual law in the natural world. . . . Or to put it more comprehensively, what we are summoned to do is so to interpret the realities of history and of Nature by selective insight as to catch the message they bring us from the self-revealing God." [132]   And now it should be noted that this relation between faith and natural science has its parallel also in that between theological and philosophical thought. There will be tension between the convictions of the believer and the conclusions of the scientist, but no final contradiction provided the believer remains free from superstitions or false traditions and the scientist restricts his methods to the sphere in which they are valid. And similarly there will be tension between the theologian who presents faith's convictions in a coherent system and the speculative thinker who seeks to give scientific conclusions their place in a harmonious view of the universe, yet there can be no ultimate dualism if the former gives speculative thought its proper place and the latter recognises that human reasoning alone can never provide a satisfactory account of existence or of life.

The Ritschlian tone of all this is even more unmistakable than in the earlier discussion of religion. Indeed, there is so little obvious trace of any thorough-going difference that it would not be difficult to make out a case for designating the whole argument as pure Ritschlianism. And yet it is precisely at this point, at which Mackintosh appears to be nearer to Ritschl than anywhere else, that appearances are most deceptive. The root of the deceptiveness is simply this, that while the two writers appear to be saying much the same thing, Ritschl claims to be speaking of religious knowledge simply as such whereas Mackintosh is concerned solely with *believing* knowledge.

This difference is by no means so insignificant as one might think. For believing knowledge is knowledge given and created by the revelation of God in Jesus Christ; and this means that Mackintosh's whole argument is conducted against the background of that revelation. The result is that although he can appropriate so much of Ritschl's argument to his own purposes, he is aware that he is here discussing only one side of the matter—the knowledge of God as apprehended by man—and that there is also another and more important side—the sovereign supremacy of the God who makes Himself known. It would be hard to over-estimate the significance of the fact that he never lost sight of this side of the matter and always regarded it as the more important of the two; for it is this which gives rise to some of his most telling criticisms of Ritschl and most important differences from him—criticisms and differences which separate him fundamentally both in his conception of the standard and medium of faith's value-judgments and in the relation he wishes to assert between theology and speculative thought.

We take first the standard of value and the medium of believing knowledge. For Ritschl religion, and supremely Christianity, seeks by Divine help " a solution of the contradiction in which man finds himself, as both a part of the world of nature and a spiritual personality claiming to dominate nature " [133]—earlier he had described it even more bluntly as " the spiritual instrument which man possesses to free himself from the natural conditions of his life ".[134] Such moral freedom from the natural or sensual world is man's highest end, and the Power which has the highest value for him as a means to it is known through his moral sense to be Divine: " God is the power which man worships because it maintains his sense of spiritual selfhood over against the restrictions of nature ".[135] That is to say, man possesses a standard of ethical perfection and is conscious of a desire to attain it, but also of limitations imposed by the sensual world upon his ability to do so ; and when he finds in Christ the perfect means of overcoming these limitations and attaining his ideal, his conscience recognises that here he has to do with a Divine Power and expresses this conviction in the judgment that Christ has for his moral and spiritual life the value of God. Thus for Ritschl the standard of value is a purely ethical one, possessed by man simply as man, and the moral conscience is the one medium of all religious knowledge, including that of the Christian faith.

Mackintosh, on the other hand, felt that the only thing to do with most of this was to deny it outright. From as early as 1899 he consistently and vigorously protests that Ritschl's theory is utilitarian and intra-mundane, based on a purely rationalistic examination of non-Christian religions ; whereas the fact is that true religion does not seek union with God as a solution to human difficulties but for its own sake, and we do not recognise Him as God because He maintains our spiritual self-respect but because the impact of Christ upon us leaves no option. To speak as Ritschl did, he urges, ultimately implies that man is and remains the centre of religion and that the idea of God, or of union with Him, is merely something supplementary—" a mere necessity of his present unfortunate situation " which would no longer be required " in the limiting case of a perfect harmony between the spirit of man and its natural environment ".[136] He acknowledges that these conclusions were not actually drawn until the next generation (notoriously by Bender), and finds that Ritschl has here done much less than justice to his real opinions as reflected in other parts of his work. Yet if he could speak even for a moment as if the function of God were to secure the realisation of man's purposes, the damage was already done. His theory is at bottom thoroughly rational-istic, and the fact that the purposes are those of the moral conscience does not make it any less so: it merely makes it a moralistic rationalism.

For his own part, accordingly, Mackintosh could not insist strongly enough that, as he puts it in one passage, " The first thing declared in Scripture concerning God is that He is the Creator. . . . The God of Christian faith is in no sense a means to our ends: He is the Lord, whom we and all things serve." [137] Man certainly has needs (and moral needs among the rest) ; but the Christian knows that his one need is for the God who created him for Himself. And when He reveals Himself in Christ we truly recognise Him as the One who alone can satisfy this need and with it all others besides ; but it is maintained often enough that this revelation is an act of Divine pardoning grace which " makes all things new ", which " revolutionises our natural thoughts of God ", which has a creative and transforming effect upon our whole sense of values, as indeed upon our whole thought and being.[138]

These things surely imply that man as such has neither any means of recognising his needs nor any true standard by which to estimate the value of the object which satisfies them, but the capacity to recognise even need and value must come to him from without, by the gift of God.

That this was in fact Mackintosh's meaning, may be seen from the attitude which, like Barth, he later adopts towards Troeltsch's theory of the religious *a priori*. He grants it may reflect the truth that in revelation man receives the capacity to know God in a way " empirical sense-perception could never do " ; but he finds that in view of its Kantian ancestry it " is better put aside as misleading "—for among other things it suggests that this is a normal human capacity similar to those which underlie our ordinary intellectual, moral and aesthetic knowledge, and obscures its essential relation to " the transcendent fact of God who cannot be likened to, or included within, that material of experience which elsewhere it is the function of the *a priori* factor to shape and organise ".[139]   No doubt all this was rather relegated to the background at the time his own theory of value-judgments was constructed ; but it is clear that it finally pushed its way to the fore in this context also.   For when he comes to discuss the topic in his last work it is on this side that the accent falls.   The God who meets us in Christ, he declares, does not " accredit Himself to our moral canons " but " breaks creatively into our life " in a manner we can only call miraculous ; hence it must never be forgotten that " while Christ does appeal to our sense of right and wrong— and thus is acknowledged and appraised in what may suitably be called a judgment of value—yet His effect is to transform from end to end our very capacity to judge what is good ".[140] And elsewhere he urges that the whole truth of the theory of value-judgments depends upon the recognition of this :—

" The vital issue is whether the standard we apply in thus affirming our recognition of God in Christ is merely moral, or also transcendent ; or, to put it otherwise, whether in confronting Christ and forming the judgment of faith upon Him and His work we bring with us, as it were ready-made, the standards by which He is to be estimated, or have them new created in us through specific revelation, by the Spirit of God. In the one case, revelation comes through One of whom all we can say is that He is morally indistinguishable from God —One whom man by himself can recognise as such ; in the other, the sovereign, unanticipated God is revealed through a Person in whom He gives Himself in utterly free grace, declaring His will sovereignly and creating thereby the very faith by which he can be apprehended." [141]

If, however, the standard by which God is recognised is thus not one possessed by man as such, is it possessed by the believing man as such? Is it a standard given as it were into his hand, a sort of extra capacity for God which he did not have before and which distinguishes him at once from other men as a specifically Christian man? This is a question which in Ritschl's case, of course, could not arise, since for him the ability to recognise God is the common possession of believer and unbeliever alike. But it is worth raising here, since it not seldom happens that theologians who repudiate any suggestion that man in himself has a capacity for God subtly return in the end to a similar position by ascribing one to the Christian in himself. With Mackintosh, however, it is reasonably clear that the answer must be as definitely negative as Barth's: [142] even the Christian believer possesses no such capacity of his own, but has it only as he receives it in the continual act of responding in the Spirit to the claims of God in Christ.

This is surely implied in the repeated statement that the sovereign initiative and absolute supremacy is, *and remains throughout* with God. It is even made explicit in at least one passage where he insists that the first step in conversion is with God who takes the initiative in calling us to Himself, and then goes on: —

" In responding by faith to His call we act indeed, but it is the activity of taking. It is not otherwise in later Christian

life. There we are still the receivers, He is the Doer of all.
A communion has arisen between God and sinful hearts
whose permanent quality is identical with that of its incep-
tion ; to the end it is a communion resting not on any self-
produced activities of pardoned men but perpetually and exclusively on their response to the movement of God's creative
love." [143]

It is this, too, which underlies the importance he attached
to the Christ-mysticism of the New Testament,[144] to which
we must not be blinded, as Ritschl was, by a justified
antipathy to mysticism in general. According to the New
Testament the vital mainspring of all Christian life and
thought is the union between Christ and His people, a union
so deep and intimate, so much more than merely moral,
so utterly dependent throughout upon our Lord's truly
miraculous and mysterious communication of His life to us,
that we can only call it mystical.[145] And here, he declares,[146]
" is the *punctum stans* of all Christian theology ". For it is
only in virtue of our union with Christ, in which (to speak
with Luther) our sins and death become His while His
righteousness, victory and life are ours, that we can be reconciled with the Father and can know and love him. With
Christ believers have died to sin, with Him they live as sons
of God, but the moment they are abstracted from this vital
relation to Him they can only be seen as sinners who can
neither know nor serve God and for whom no atonement can
avail.

There is also a third point at which the same insight
emerges : the question of assurance. In maintaining that the
certainties of faith are held with no less assurance than those
of scientific knowledge, he was accustomed to raise in his
lectures the question, " In what sense then is faith a ' venture '?".[147] And the answer is : it is a venture because there
is no means of proving it and nothing in man or the world
on which it can be grounded, but it must abandon every
imaginable support and rest solely upon God. It is, indeed,

precisely for this reason that faith is held with such an assurance as nothing else can be: "what is of man takes and must take the chances of time, and may be lost in shipwreck; what is of God moves on in triumph to the end "—hence the note struck by the angel message "He shall have His people from their sins" rings through every page of the Bible and is unfailingly echoed "in every form of Christianity worthy of the name", with the calm and unshakable certainty that "it is all as sure as if it had already happened ".[148] But what interests us most at the moment is, that the "venturous" character of faith's assurance is explicitly said to remain throughout the whole Christian life: there is nothing even in the believer which can produce certainty, and Christians who base their hopes on anything in themselves—be it the memory of some great experience, or the apparent presence of a new capacity for higher life—"are building their house upon the sand ".[149] No doubt in our daily life of prayer and service we shall be granted experiences which will "confirm and nourish the assurance", but nothing in us can be its ground: "the foundation-stone of the faith that can be lived by is, always and unconditionally, the love of God in Jesus Christ our Lord ".[150]

For Mackintosh, then, the standard by which God can be recognised is not at the disposal either of man or of believing man, but is given only in God's self-revelation and maintained only by His power. What, now, of the medium of believing knowledge? There is no doubt whatever that, especially in his earlier works, he was inclined to put the emphasis here on the moral conscience. Yet it is also clear that he did not mean this in any exclusive sense, but took much more seriously than Ritschl the contention that faith is concerned with the whole man. For one thing, he urged repeatedly that the believing life has as much to do with thought and feeling as with will—indeed, it can even be held to involve also the recently canvassed " subliminal consciousness ", provided we recognise that, whatever else that may be,

"it is the permanent deposit of conscious processes", not
just a happy "tumbling ground for whimsies ".[151] And just as
the life of faith involves every single element in the human
make-up, so also its origin cannot be confined to any one :—

"Why should we believe that God's presence invades the
soul at some one ascertainable spot? . . . . It is surely more
worthy to conceive the Divine indwelling as relative to the
human spirit as a whole, not entering at some isolated orifice,
but taking possession of, because directly appealing to
conscience, thought, feeling. The Divine does in the end per-
vade the whole man ; why should it not do so directly? . . . .
It has been said that unanswerable questions in philosophy
are many of them questions which ought never to have been
asked. And the wish to fix some fitting point in soul-life,
where, and nowhere else, God enters, must, I am afraid, be
repelled on the plain ground that the problem has been
stated in an unintelligible form." [152]

For another thing, he took strong exception to the
Ritschlian disparagement of the reason. It is not simply that
the believer requires science as well as faith in order to serve
God in the life of the world—to this every Ritschlian could
agree—but still more important, faith itself *includes* an
element of intellectual cognition and is not only trustful submission of heart and will. This is clearly brought out in one
early criticism of Ritschl :—

"The older theologians used to divide faith into *notitia,
assensus, fiducia,* and it is in the disposition of the heart and
will that *fiducia* consists. But the Ritschlian position comes
finally to this, that *fiducia* is made to do the work of *notitia*
as well as its own ; while in reality it denotes the trustful
apprehension of an object recognised in *notitia* as real. Into
faith then enters, not only faith as surrender of the heart,
but also the *faith of cognition. . . . Notitia* may exist without *fiducia,* for a man may defy God ; but *fiducia* without
notitia is blind." [153]

It would seem that at first Mackintosh's main desire here
was to stress that faith is not just given to us lightly or from

above, as he felt some forms of orthodoxy (both Roman and Protestant) tended to suggest, but is a fully human act of response to the claims of God upon our whole being, intellectual, emotional and sensual, moral, even (though the term is suspicious) " subconscious ". And in doing so he was inclined to put the emphasis (though by no means an exclusive one) on its relation to the moral conscience, for two main reasons. On the one hand he found it a convenient means of upholding the personal and spiritual character of believing knowledge against materialistic and naturalistic thought ; while on the other hand the relating of faith to conscience, defined as " the sense of unconditional and infallible obligation ",[154] served to bring out its practical character as obedience over against the theoretic and unbridled use of the reason in speculative Idealism.

But later, faced not with a false Supernaturalism but with a humanitarian psychology of religion run riot, he shifted the accent from the faith called forth by revelation on to the revelation which creates it ; and then, since the creative nature of this revelation at once ruled Naturalism and Idealism out of court along with all other forms of rationalism, there was no need to emphasise any particular element involved in faith's response. Hence in his last work the terms " conscience ", " moral ", " ethical ", earlier found on almost every other page, are no more conspicuous than those which relate to feeling or intellect. One might be tempted to find a lingering trace of the old predominating interest in the ethical when he maintains that Christ does appeal to conscience yet also completely transforms it. Only, it is obvious that the first half of the " paradox " is determined by the context—Ritschl's theory of value-judgments—and that the emphasis is not on it but on the second : in other contexts, surely, he could equally well have said, Christ does appeal to our intellect, our feeling, our hidden instinct, yet His effect is to transform our thoughts, emotions and instincts from end to end.

The second great difference we have mentioned affects the relation of faith and science, or rather, theology and speculative thought. On the surface of the argument, the difference is not at once apparent. For Ritschl was as definite as Mackintosh that conflict between faith and science can arise "only when laws which are valid for narrower realms of nature or spirit are erected into world-laws and used as a key to open up a view of the whole", and that "it must be possible to harmonise the scientific study of nature and the Christian view of the world in the same mind ";[155] while if he was less certain about philosophy, he at least refrained from pressing the distinction to the very limits, and even went so far as to suggest in the end that the philosopher's only hope of achieving his purpose rests on his taking over the Christian conception of God.[156] So also with Herrmann: Mackintosh's suspicion that he wished to make an absolute distinction had been roused by an early statement to the effect that a man could well be a materialist in philosophy and a Christian in religious faith,[157] but it was presently removed by the discovery that Herrmann later repudiated this [158] and was clearly as sure of the ultimate unity of knowledge as any one else. There is, indeed, nothing to which any Ritschlian could object in three of the conditions which Mackintosh laid down for the attainment of this unity: that faith must remain free from superstitious traditions, that science must restrict itself to its own sphere, that philosophy must recognise the limitations of human reason. But he made one more condition: theology must give speculative thought its proper place. And it is this which separates him at once from the Ritschlians by a wide remove.

Whatever possibilities they might be prepared to allow to a philosophy which cared to take over the Christian conception of God, their demands upon theology were uncompromising: Christian faith is a thoroughly practical affair which has nothing to do with the purely theoretic reason, and theology must therefore exclude as "speculative rationalism " all doctrines of which, by their very nature, we can have no experiential knowledge—those, for example, which deal with the Trinity, with the pre-existence and exalted life of Christ, with the question of His two Natures, or with the complex of problems connected with the character of the future life. But for Mackintosh this was too much like throwing good money after bad. It is one thing, he tells us, to reject speculative rationalism of the kind of which Hegelianism is the classic example, and quite another to exclude all " speculation " as such : it is one thing to refuse to allow reason in the form of purely rational principles to dictate to faith what its experiences must be, and quite another to forbid reason to work within concrete believing experience with a view to bringing out not only its immediate utterances but also its remoter implicates. In the former case Ritschl was fully justified, and indeed performed his greatest service to theology ; but in the latter he completely ignored the fact that " we are all speculative rationalists in one sense, in so far as we endeavour to think out and think through the implications of belief ".[159] Men do not leave their reason behind on becoming Christians, but will insist on asking questions which go beyond the bounds of what is immediately verifiable in experience.[160] And once the questions are asked the theologian must do his best to answer them or—no less important—to show clearly why no answer is possible.[161]

The truth is, that such questionings are neither optional nor arbitrary but derive from faith itself: saving faith in Christ is compatible with very different degrees of knowledge,[162] yet, although not attainable by reason, it is not irrational, but is bound to seek the fullest possible understanding of what it believes. And in attempting to answer them the dogmatician is only bringing to full and clear expression what is implicit in faith from the first, if not immediately and consciously realised. For, to recur to the problems just mentioned, faith cannot know that there *is* an eternal life without thereby implying at least some idea as to its nature,[163] and since the knowledge of opposites is one, some conception of the fate of those who reject redemption is implicit in what we know of the redeemed.[164] Or again, since God is eternal and is one, faith's immediate conviction of the Divinity of Christ implies at least some conception of His pre-existence and of His relation to the Father within the Godhead ; while since Godhead is not manhood some theory of the relation between the Divine and the human in the life of Jesus underlies the assurance that He is not only God but also Man. It is indeed true that these things " are *only* implicit, not actual ingredients in that of which faith is directly conscious ", so that opinions on the precise formulation of the teaching to be given on such points is bound to differ and on occasion it may be well to separate the discussion of them from that of faith's immediate utterances on which Christians are unanimous. Nevertheless they *are* implicit and therefore form a true element in doctrine.[165]

In some ways this last distinction recalls similar ones made by the Ritschlians. Herrmann, for example, distinguishes between the " ground of faith " (*Glaubensgrund*) in the " inner life of Jesus " and " convictions generated by faith " (*Glaubensgedanken*) such as the Divine origin of Christ, His resurrection, His exaltation to universal sovereign power.[166] The ground is the same for all men, and to describe how faith arises from it is the primary task of dogmatic proper as a normative discipline ; but the presentation of the resulting convictions is a purely secondary task in which it cannot claim universal or normative character, for " different people see different things and, because they must be truthful, must also express them differently ".[167] More especially are we reminded of the distinction which Haering, in precisely the same terms as Mackintosh, makes in his Christology between " the immediate utterances of faith " and its " presuppositions and implicates ". The continual improvement of the argument for the former and the " ever more exact " formulation of them "remains the highest Christological task"; whereas if the latter—the pre-existence of Christ, His relation as Son to the Father, the unity of Divine and human in the Incarnate Word—must also be asserted because of their "religious value", yet they can be so asserted only as conceptions lying just across the border-line of our knowledge (*Grenzgedanken*), which may be discussed "in complete inner freedom, since they do not affect the inmost sanctuary of our faith", and whose discussion must always be judged and controlled by the standard of faith's immediate utterances.[168]

Such parallels, however, serve only to bring out more clearly the difference between Mackintosh and the Ritschlians here. For the convictions in question are not, as with Herrmann, those of particular individuals, framed in doctrines which may be true for one believer but false for another: * they are implied in *all* authentic Christian faith, and the doctrines which express them are no less universally valid and no less authoritative than any others. Nor is it enough to recognise, as Haering does, the universality of the things thus implied, and then simply to assert their truth as religiously indispensable facts, assigning every attempt at further elucidation to a relatively subordinate place as something which does not affect the kernel of faith and which passes beyond the scope of our knowledge. For their assertion is demanded not by their religious value, but by the obedience of faith in the revelation of Jesus Christ as Lord. And still more important, that the Son came "from the bosom of the Father" and lived as very Man for our salvation *is* the kernel of New Testament faith ; while if it

* Barth has pointed out that in the last form of his Lecture Synopsis Herrmann suddenly speaks at one point as if here, too, we have to do with convictions "in which religion expresses itself in every case" (Herrmann, *Dogmatik*, § 23) ; but as he goes on to remark, if this is meant seriously, then it can be no mere marginal correction but involves a *fundamental* change in Herrmann's whole position. *Cf.* Barth, *Die Theologie und die Kirche*, p. 245, note 16.

7

is true that pre-existence, incarnation and Trinity are really symbols for realities which " lie on the farther side of terrestial knowledge ", it is also true that such an " immediate utterance " as the present sovereignty of Christ is equally symbolic, and that the symbols have a real meaning whose unfathomableness does not exonerate us from seeking to express it as best we can in a fully articulated doctrine.[169]

If Mackintosh chose to put the " speculative " doctrines second in point of order, that was partly to emphasise that the speculation is not guided by general philosophic principles but conducted *within* the realm of *faith*, and partly in view of the extreme difficulty he felt in formulating them. But he had no intention of implying thereby that they are answers to merely individual questions, or subsidiary intellectual exercises. For the questions must be raised by every believer who recognises that God claims the love of the whole mind as well as of the whole heart ; while the attempt to answer them, however much the answer may defy adequate formulation, is not dictated by mere intellectual ambition but by the service of Christ.[170] Hence he found it a grave fault of the Ritschlians that they were content with the question: Is this doctrine speculative? For its exclusion or subordination simply on the ground of its speculative character can be demanded only by a positivist philosophy and is therefore not to free theology from subjection to philosophy, but only to exchange one master for another and equally objectionable one: Ritschl " had discarded Hegel: but Kant remained, and at times Kant and the New Testament disagree ".[171] The fact is, the use of the speculative reason to construct a doctrine in itself determines nothing: what really matters is whether reason is being used in obedience to principles of its own or to the revelation in Christ. And thus the question Mackintosh put here was a different one: " Will it preach? "[172] *i.e.* will it serve the proclamation of the Word?

All this means, in more technical language, that he refuses

to follow Ritschl in excluding metaphysic from theology. There is a kind of metaphysic which, like that of Hegel, operates with general ideas and seeks to force faith into harmony with its principles ; and in objecting to this, Ritschl was certainly right. But in calling for the exclusion of metaphysic simply as such, he was asking for more than can be granted. For metaphysic in itself is concerned simply with objective ultimate Reality and its meaning for our experience as a whole. But the Reality known to faith is both objective, since it exists entirely independent of our perception or appreciation of it, and ultimate, since there is no more final Reality to be known ; [173] while, as Ritschl himself suggested, it is precisely this Reality as known to faith (the Christian conception of God) which alone can make our experience truly luminous and lead to a unified view of things if that can be attained at all. And even if it be asserted that the knowledge of ultimate Reality is here given chiefly " through the medium of conscience ", in " the moral certainties of redeemed men ", and is to that extent ethical, it is not therefore any less metaphysical than if it is attained by the purely theoretic reason working with *a priori* principles: " the ethical, when taken as ultimately true, *is* the metaphysical ".[174] For these reasons, there must always be metaphysic in theology—but " the implicit metaphysic of faith ".[175]

It is clear that the two theologians are working with different conceptions of what metaphysic is. For Ritschl regarded it as essentially indifferent to the distinction in value between nature and spirit.[176] But Mackintosh urges that this interpretation is much too narrow and rests on an erroneous identification of metaphysic with epistemology: the latter science indeed makes no such distinction, but the former, concerned as it is with the *whole* of experience, " is bound to include all the distinctions on which that experience rests and among them the distinction of value or worth—otherwise we should be forced to adopt the strange conclusion that the ultimate philosophy must remain entirely silent on the subject of our moral and aesthetic beliefs ".[177] If this be so, then ideas which have metaphysical significance cannot be excluded from theology simply as such, and one must agree with Barth that whether or not they are permissible depends entirely on their context.[178] This, however, is an understanding of metaphysic which Ritschl explicitly refused to accept ;* so that to a large extent the difference is perhaps more one of the word than of anything else. And Mackintosh, recognising this, issues an explicit warning against making too much of Ritschl's attitude here—adding that as Ritschl himself allows it what he calls a " regulative " rôle in defining such concepts as cause or final end, his real intention was apparently " not so much to expel metaphysic as to keep it firmly in its right place ".[179]

The difference might indeed have remained little more than one of the interpretation of terms had not Ritschl gone on to label as " metaphysical " the doctrines we have mentioned, and consequently failed to give due consideration to them. Against this Mackintosh urges that while the orthodox forms of these doctrines certainly contain much against which Ritschl's criticism was justified, yet a more adequate conception of the nature of metaphysic might have enabled him to distinguish what is to be rejected as purely speculative metaphysic from what, if metaphysical, is the permissible kind of metaphysic and not pure ontological theory. But the real point at issue is not so much whether, or in what sense these elements are metaphysical, but whether or not they are to form a part of Christian doctrine. And while Ritschl was resolved to omit them, Mackintosh was convinced, as we have seen, that they must be included in any

* " If others ", he writes, " understand by metaphysics : not that elementary knowledge of things in general which ignores their division into nature and spirit, but such a universal theory as shall be at once elementary and the final and exhaustive science of all particular ordered existence, they do so at their own risk " (*Rechtfertigung und Versöhnung*[4], iii, 16).

system which seeks in the obedience of faith to give a comprehensive account of what it believes.

Looking back from here we can see what a wide gulf actually separated Mackintosh's theory of value-judgments from Ritschl's. He took over much of Ritschl's argument—at some points, perhaps, rather more than he would later have done. But he took it over for his own purposes and in full awareness of the fact that it deals primarily with the human and subordinate side of the relation between God and man.

Over against all suggestions that faith is given by some irrational means (extreme orthodoxy) or instilled by a somewhat mechanical infusion of Divine grace (Romanism) it served to emphasise that faith is a fully conscious human act of judgment—he would later have said of *choice* or *decision* —which involves man's whole rational, emotional and personal being. But this is a judgment of *response,* a decision to *accept.* It does not imply that man in himself has, or ever will have, at his own disposal either the means to judge or the God for whom he decides ; for he has the capacity to judge only as he receives it in the act of response, and his decision is to accept and submit to Christ as from first to last his sovereign Lord.

The theory also served at the same time to provide a convenient and (at least on the surface) fairly convincing argument for making theology independent of philosophy, and in particular for the rejection of Hegelianism, Naturalism and certain rationalist elements in orthodox theology. But it neither means any subordination of the reason nor does it involve the simple discarding of the doctrines which contain rationalistic elements. For revelation makes its claims every bit as much on reason as on conscience ; while to dismiss doctrines without more ado simply because they are constructed by the theoretic rather than by the practical reason, instead of trying to correct their false elements by a *proper* use of speculative thought, is to base theology upon philosophy all over again—a philosophy which is no less rationalistic for the fact that this time it is a moralistic and positivistic rationalism, and which forgets that in revelation the practical reason is as much transformed as the theoretic.

For such purposes, it can hardly be said that the Ritschlian theory was indispensable. Irrational or mechanical views of faith were well enough guarded against in any case. And even the independence of theology, in support of which Mackintosh chiefly used it, clearly does not stand or fall with the validity of this particular argument. For his real reason for making the separation is not that theology employs chiefly the practical reason, philosophy chiefly the theoretic: it is that theology employs both in the service of the Gospel and in obedience to the demands made by God in Christ upon the whole being and powers of man, whereas philosophy, irrespective of whether a particular form of it may prefer the speculative reason or the practical, knows no criterion but the principles of reason itself. Moreover, the different background of the argument, and the corrections thereby introduced at such vital points, so transformed the whole theory that at bottom it has little in common with the Ritschlians at all. In view of all this it is clear that, whatever the appearances, Mackintosh actually stood much less near to Ritschl than to Barth.

4. THE REVELATION IN JESUS CHRIST

Christianity as a human religious activity is the true religion in so far as it rests upon revelation. The convictions of Christian faith as a human act of judgment or decision are true convictions in so far as they arise in a true decision made in obedient response to revelation. The dogmatic system in which the theologian attempts to expound and co-ordinate these convictions is true and authoritative in so far as it corresponds to revelation. And the primary task of dogmatic is to test and re-test the preaching, the beliefs and the doctrine of the Church against the standard of revelation. We have now to consider what is meant by the revelation which is thus the criterion of religion, of faith and of doctrine, and the standard by reference to which the theologian has to test their truth.

Much has already been anticipated in the foregoing discussion. We have seen that the only real revelation is the one given in Jesus Christ; for although the Christian knows there is also a universal presence of God throughout creation and history, it is one which in fact is never recognised and therefore not a revelation in the proper sense. We have also seen that this is a revelation of God as He is in Himself, not one which is meant merely to regulate human life while God Himself remains unknown and unknowable in the transcendent background. And we have seen that in revealing Himself God takes and maintains the sovereign initiative, creating and sustaining the faith by which alone His revelation can be recognised. He does not accredit Himself to any existing human canons, whether they be speculative as with Hegel, moral as with Kant and the Ritschlians, or aesthetic as in mysticism: He transforms all existing canons from end to end. Nor does He give an absolute criterion into the possession of men to be administered by them either in the form of a Christian consciousness, as with Schleiermacher and his followers, or in that of the infallible tradition of an infallible Roman Church: He remains throughout the sovereign Lord, and the place of believers (whether individual or corporate) is to recognise and to obey. But there are still three further points of very great importance for Mackintosh's conception of the revelation in Jesus Christ which is thus the sole, complete and finally authoritative norm or criterion of dogmatic as of faith.

The first thing to be noticed is, that it is identical with the Word of God as contained in Scripture. That, however, is not to say with later orthodoxy that it is a supernatural communication of Divine truths in the form of the verbally inspired teachings of Holy Scripture. For then the Bible becomes once more, much as in medieval orthodoxy, " a book full of Divine information or infallible truths about doctrine and morals ", and saving faith is " assent to correct propositions, found in the Bible, about God, the universe and the soul of man ".[180]

Such a view makes nonsense of human freedom and sacrifices all over again one of the great principles for which the Reformers stood: if revelation is simply the disclosure of facts, then our beliefs are dictated to us by some external authority and to be accepted upon that authority—and it makes little difference whether the authority is an infallible Church or an infallible Book. But the truth is, that in revelation God does not overwhelm us by display or compel our submission to any external authority: He demands our free and willing self-surrender in a personal encounter. What He gives us in Christ is *Himself*, not just facts *about* Himself ; and true faith is not mere intellectual assent to propositions but free submission, in willing obedience and trust, to a Person who calls it forth by His very nature and not just by command. That for one thing. But for another, no human propositions—not even those of Scripture itself—could ever express the whole truth of the living God: " The greatest truths can never be all enshrined in words ; they must wait for a life in which they are incarnate ".[181] And however true the propositions which man is enabled to make in response to revelation, they cannot properly be called revealed truths: strictly, they are only attempts, which must always be inadequate, to express *the* revealed truth become flesh in Christ. What is revealed, then, is a Person, not a doctrinal code. There are certainly facts to which faith will assent, and doctrines in which they will be truly formulated. Yet our assurance of them is not attained by mere submission of the intellect, but is freely and spontaneously generated by the new personal relationship into which God brings us in

Christ. And in themselves they cannot rank as infallible truths, but it is only in concrete relation to Christ that they are true at all.

Yet all this does not in the least deny the unique position of Scripture as the Word of God: it means rather a much more vital and dynamic conception of it. It is true that the legal and mechanical theory of verbal inspiration must go ; so that the theologian cannot regard the Bible as a doctrinal code-book of material lying ready to be lifted, but must proceed selectively—as indeed all in fact do.[182] But for all that, it is no less true that Scripture is and remains the Word of God, in the sense that it is the medium through which God speaks to us His sovereign Word.

As the record of God's self-revelation and the witness to it, the Bible mediates to all later times the livingly fresh impression of that revelation. It does so because it is not only narrative, but also testimony. For what reveals God to us is not just the account of His mighty acts, culminating in the career of Jesus: it is these acts evoking the faith of men and inspiring them to a unique believing witness brought home to us by the Holy Spirit.[183] It is indeed of the utmost importance that Scripture should be studied historically, for as the record of God's dealings with His people *in history* it conveys to faith the assurance that in these events He is speaking to us and that the same mercy and judgment with which He treated them are being shown also to us. But that, as the Reformers saw, is only one half of the truth: " The other half, of still greater importance, is that nothing but the Spirit of God in the heart of the believer enables him to realise that in very truth it is God, and none else, who is seen in the history ; none else than He who speaks in the Word, coming near to unveil Himself and declare His saving purpose ".[184] And if we would make a distinction, as the Reformers did, between the Word of God as spoken by holy men moved by the Spirit, infallibly and authoritatively true, and the Bible in which their message was thereafter put in

writing, whose teachings cannot in themselves be unconditionally binding, then we must also follow them in never
losing sight of the vital and inseparable bond between
the two :—

   " It is only in and through the Bible that God's Word of
judgment and mercy reaches us. Where, except in Scripture,
is Christ offered to sinners? Thus the tie between the Word
of God and the Bible is an absolutely vital tie ; His Word is
recorded and conveyed in the Bible and the Bible alone." [185]

For Mackintosh, then, the revelation in Jesus Christ means
the personal revelation in which God Himself uses the
Scriptures to confront us in Christ and to speak to us His
sovereign Word in Him ; and it is only through the biblical
record and witness, as illumined by the Holy Spirit, that
the revelation can be recognised and obeyed. Hence the
theologian, in seeking to present in a coherent system the
truth thus made known and recognised, must invariably set
out from that record and witness, and let his thought be
controlled throughout by it. It is not necessary that every
detail of his system should have verbal prophetic or apostolic
sanction but it *is* necessary that his construction as a whole
should truly reflect the biblical picture as a whole. To that
end it is best that we " let the portrait of the historic Christ,
contained in primitive testimony, be brought to bear directly
upon our mind, saturating it through and through ; and
thereupon let us proceed to give free systematised expression
to the thoughts which arise within us. This is, as a fact,
what has happened whenever theologians have spoken
worthily of Jesus Christ, and it is clearly the procedure which
harmonises with the native freedom of the Gospel." [186] And
if this is to free theology from the fetters of a narrow and
mechanical legalism, it certainly does not alter in the very
least the fact that apart from Scripture as, through the influence of the Holy Spirit, it becomes the living Word of God
there can be neither true faith nor a true system of doctrine.

The second important point is, that the Person thus revealed through Scripture is not the " Christ-idea " of Hegelianism, but the *historic* Christ. Yet in saying this we are not making faith and doctrine subject all over again, as in the " Life of Jesus " theology, to the findings of historical criticism. For on the one hand, even if purely historical research could succeed in providing a complete picture of Jesus as He was, it " can no more give us a Saviour Christ than science can give us the living God ".[187] While on the other hand, there is really no such thing as a *mere* historian ; for with the best—or worst—will in the world, no man can escape the claims of God. Thus, however detachedly and impartially he may seek to examine the record which is the chosen medium of God's Word, he cannot " be guaranteed against finding himself in the presence of One who deals with us in ways which we know to be God's ways. . . . And if this should happen, he will know, with a certainty which no history can give or take away, that in this Jesus he has touched and met with God." [188] Historical criticism may point to uncertainties, gaps and discrepancies in the Gospel narrative ; it may and does demand a revision of the traditional methods of Scripture proof ; but it cannot touch the apostolic witness to Jesus Christ. It may even succeed at some points in casting more light on Jesus as He lived ; but it cannot affect the fact that this Jesus is in very truth the Christ of God. And it is not simply with Jesus of Nazareth that theology is concerned, but with the historic *Christ* as He gives Himself to faith.

This last point has been brought out with peculiar power by Kähler, who urges against the " Life of Jesus " theology that it is impossible to reach a scientifically reconstructed picture of Jesus of Nazareth and that we must therefore content ourselves with the apostles' witness to Him. Yet Kähler's argument, although for the most part it is manifestly sound and contains much that must be gratefully accepted, is unsatisfactory in one respect : it leaves untouched the question whether the Gospel can rest for us merely on the testimony of others. Clearly, however, we can have no real knowledge of God or faith in Him until the apostles' experience becomes *our* experience and Christ is revealed *to us*. The truth surely is that " the apostles' faith is for us a mirror reflecting the actual Jesus, and enabling us to know Him for ourselves ".[189] Christ is indeed mediated to us by their testimony, yet in such a way that at the same time He is made known to us directly.* And it is only as the historic Christ, in history yet not of it, known in a personal relationship thus mediated yet direct, that He is the norm of dogmatic and of faith.

The third thing which must be emphasised is, that our direct knowledge of the historic Christ is the work of none other than Christ Himself. At this point the argument turns against the limitation imposed by Ritschl and Herrmann upon the conception of the " historic Christ ". Ritschl confines revelation to the historical work of Christ in founding the Kingdom of God, Herrmann to the " inner life " of Jesus ; and both thus limit our understanding of the historic Christ to the events of our Lord's earthly life between Bethlehem and Calvary, as reflected in the consciousness of the early believers. But that is to leave out the crucial element of the resurrection. This cannot be, as Herrmann holds, merely a conviction generated by faith as distinct

---

* To this, Kähler too must surely have agreed. For if it is perhaps not brought out so clearly in the work to which Mackintosh refers (*Der sog. historische Jesus und der geschichtliche, biblische Christus*), that is surely because the primary question there is not whether the relation is direct as well as mediated, but whether the medium is a historical biography of Jesus of Nazareth or a testimony to Jesus Christ. Elsewhere the directness is emphasised often enough. Thus, for example, he speaks of our communion with Christ as mediated by the preaching and sacraments of the Church and the testimony of the apostles, and goes on, " But it would still be no communion if He only worked upon us as One who is hidden from us, inaccessible to us, merely an object which we thankfully picture to ourselves because of what we have heard of Him " : it is a communion which " is mediated in various ways, and yet in the confidence of faith and the practice of devotion is immediate " (*Angewandte Dogmen*, pp. 163, 173 f.).

from an element in the ground of faith—as though revelation
were given simply in Jesus' " inner life " and the faith evoked
by it went on to form the (optional) conviction that He was
too great to be bound by death. Rather, " the resurrection is
itself part of the revelation ", an integral element of the
Gospel and one " which enters vitally into the creative ground
of faith ".[190] Indeed, it is difficult to see how there could be
any authentic Christian faith without it. For it was only
after the resurrection that the veil, which except for a few
fleeting moments had lain upon a hidden life, was lifted and
the disciples given to see it as the life of God:[191] it was the
Risen Lord who called forth their faith, in an act which the
apostle (II Cor. 4:6) " can compare with nothing but that first
creative hour when God said: ' Let there be light ' ".[192] At
any rate, a Christ who certainly rose from the dead and
appeared as the Living One, and a Christ who may or may
not have done so, are very different indeed and must evoke
very different kinds of faith. But He who is held forth in
the Gospel is One who is revealed not only in His life and
death but also in His rising from the dead.

Nor is this all. For if by the " historic Christ " we thus
mean, or ought to mean, the earthly Jesus and the Risen
Lord as two aspects of one and the same Person, then " the
historic Christ is identical also with the Lord present in
experience now and always ".[193] It is only as such that Jesus
Christ is the revelation of God—as One who not only was,
but is and is to come, and to whom all power in heaven and
earth is given. It is thus that He is presented in the testimony of Scripture. And it is He who speaks through that
testimony as the true and living Word of God, thereby
making Himself known to us directly as One who suffered
and died on earth for *our* redemption, and who rose and lives
that *we* might live with Him: " the transcendent Christ,
active ' all days unto the end ', guarantees the Jesus of Palestine, for ever anew He grants to men the very experiences
undergone by the primitive group of believers ".[194] It is, of

course, through the Holy Spirit that He does so. Yet the Spirit neither comes as a mere " compensation or substitute for the absent Christ " nor overshadows Him " by opening a new and loftier stage of revelation "; He is the Spirit of Christ, or Christ as the Spirit, and if the two are distinct in their intra-trinitarian relationship, they are indistinguishable in their working in the heart.[195] Thus the direct knowledge of the living Lord who is the revelation of the Father may be regarded either as the work of Christ Himself in fulfilment of the promise, " I will not leave you comfortless ; I will come unto you " (John 14 : 18), or as that of the Spirit, the Comforter, whom He promised to send (John 15 : 26).

Here, where the revelation which was the background of the discussion in the last two sections has now become the foreground, it is no longer the similarities with Ritschlian thought that are most striking, but the differences. Ritschl too, and above all Herrmann, protested vigorously against the conception of revelation as something which can be formulated in doctrines to whose truth faith must assent. Yet the root of this protest lies not so much in a recognition of the transcendence of Christian truth (though something of that may perhaps be detected in the background), but rather in an anti-intellectual insistence on the moral autonomy of the individual and his freedom to believe only what he finds true for his own particular case. Whereas if there are still traces of something similar in Mackintosh's earlier works, it is clear enough that from the beginning he placed the emphasis rather on the sovereign freedom of God over against all human attempts to fix the truth of His revelation in words.

Again, all agree in making Scripture the one source of doctrine. But for Ritschl it is a Scripture read and expounded in the light of his own particular moral view of the world ; and for Herrmann it must be controlled by a picture of the moral and personal life of Jesus which *we* form.[196] Whereas for Mackintosh the one and only interpretative principle is the illumination of the Holy Spirit. And if at first he could speak of a normative " Gospel picture of Christ ", in language sometimes dangerously near to Herrmann's, yet even then it was a picture given by the Spirit through the Gospel testimony that he meant—indeed, the central place held by the Spirit in his thought is in marked contrast with the meagre treatment afforded Him by Ritschl and Herrmann.*

Most significant of all, perhaps, is the attitude to the historical character of revelation. For this, too, is a point on which both Ritschl and Herrmann were peculiarly emphatic ; yet here, too, the difference is obvious at once. Ritschl appears simply to identify revelation with the historical life of Jesus. Herrmann, feeling that this is to make revelation subject to historical criticism, seeks to avoid the danger by maintaining that it is not given in the external events of Jesus' career, but in His inner personal life.[197] Yet he insists that this " inner life " is knowable in precisely the same way as all other personal lives which " bring us to moral reflection " by compelling our " respect and trust ", that it can be a revelation " only if at first we do not believe in Jesus but are willing simply to look at Him ", that it is " a fact which thrusts itself upon man as real, which he therefore does not first need to ' believe ' but simply contemplates as real " [198]—in other words, it is historical in another, but equally secular sense.

Mackintosh's attitude, on the other hand, is very different indeed. Once more, it is true, there are some early passages which seem so close to Ritschl and Herrmann that we have to be wide awake to detect the difference. For he can often speak of the life of Christ as revealing God to His followers

---

* For Mackintosh " the Holy Spirit is no one casual factor by the side of others, but that to which everything else converges, and apart from which nothing else—not even the revelation of Jesus—could take effect " (*Person of Jesus Christ*, p. 508). Ritschl, on the other hand, has not much to say on the subject at all, and though he complains at one point (*Rechtfert. u. Versöhn.* [4], iii, 501) of its neglect by traditional theology, he does remarkably little himself to remedy matters.

and calling forth their faith. Yet he knew equally well that as a historical fact it did not end in faith and witness, but in denial and desertion ; and it is clear that when he speaks of it as revealing God and evoking faith he is not regarding it in itself as a piece of history, but is adopting with the apostles the standpoint of faith in the Risen Lord and looking back (so to speak) upon His earthly life as that of God incarnate. Hence it is really little more than an explicit clarification of his earlier position when he later insists that if Christ is indeed *in* history—else He would not reveal God *to men*— yet it is only as One who does not belong to history in any ordinary sense of the term* that He is the Revealer *of God*. The events of His life both outward and inward can reveal God only because they are the history of One who " in a sense upon which everything depends has come ' from the other side of reality ' ", One in whom " God is present *incognito* " ; and therefore to approach them as ordinary historical realities " is inevitably to confuse the issue ".[199] Thus in his final assessment of Ritschl's thought he sets along- side the charge of moralism—of which he regards the insist- ence upon moral autonomy, the cavalier method of dealing with Scripture, and the neglect of the Holy Spirit as but further examples—the second charge of an intolerable historism.

The limitation of revelation to the events of Jesus' earthly life, he points out, involves a disastrous modification in the conception of the exalted Lord as ever-present in sovereign Divine power : —

" The full significance of the words 'All power is given unto Me in heaven and on earth ' must be capable of being found, without remainder, in the Gospel story. In conse-

* He joins Barth in distinguishing " two ordinary and secular " senses : " Historical, first, means that which can be vouched for by scholarly research working on universally accepted scientific rules. And secondly, historical means that which is apprehensible by a neutral observer, devoid of faith." (*Types of Mod. Theol.*, p. 305). If Ritschl's Christ is historical in the former sense, Herrmann's is so in the second.

quence, that transcendent declaration is translated into the merely ethical judgment that Christ is still Lord of circumstance in the same sense (but no other) as when He triumphed over the world by accepting the Cross." [200]

Hence, although Ritschl can maintain that "our faith in Christ is not faith in Him as One who was, but faith in Him as One who continues to work",[201] yet His present action is turned into "a merely posthumous influence" [202] lingering on through the mediation of Scripture and the Church.

But however much we may welcome the emphasis which must then be set upon the truth that Christ is mediated to us through the testimony of Scripture and the preaching and sacraments of the Church, it is a truth gained at the expense of others equally important, if not more so. For mediated though He is, He meets us in a direct relationship, in which He is known not just as One who once companied with men and whose influence still lives on, but as One who Himself is with us still. Not only so. But if His present power were but a survival of that visible in His earthly life, would there be either apostolic testimony or Church preaching to mediate Him, or what could they mediate beyond the knowledge of an ideal moral character which we can emulate? For it was the Risen Lord, appearing to the disciples in a power not previously manifest, who created in them the faith which testifies of Him ; and it is only because, through that testimony, He is ever present in the Spirit in all the unique and incomparable power of Godhead that sermon and sacrament can be veritable means of grace. In other words, a revelation given only in the historical life of Jesus as such would not be merely an imperfect one : it would be no real revelation at all. That life in itself neither could nor did reveal anything. It *could* reveal, not as an ordinary historic life but as the hidden life of God ; it *did* so, not as an object of ordinary observation but when its true nature was manifested by the appearance of the Risen Lord in the power of the Spirit. And so it will always be : —

8

" The Gospel picture of Jesus, the events of His career, are not in themselves an immediate or transparent disclosure of God. To be that they must be illumined from above. For one thing, they must embody the personal presence and act of God, as events in which God is approaching and addressing us ; and for another, the Spirit operating within us must open our eyes to their transcendent meaning. Only as God is in past facts do they reveal ; only as His Spirit brings home their import does the revelation become effectual." [203]

It is clear that all this, though urged directly only against Ritschl himself without any express indication how far his followers are to be included, separated Mackintosh by an equally wide remove also from Herrmann. But in the case of certain other Ritschlians the difference is not quite so immediately obvious. For Kaftan, and above all Haering, attempted to improve matters by including the resurrection in the revealing history, identifying the exalted Lord with the earthly Jesus, and seeking to do more justice to the Holy Spirit in whose power He is ever present to the Church. Yet they do so upon principles which are still fundamentally Ritschlian ; so that ultimately one is forced to ask whether they have after all done much more than improve the face of a watch which really needs a new mainspring. Thus Kaftan's Exalted Lord in the end has all too great a resemblance to a disembodied moral principle—as, indeed, his earthly Christ has to an embodied one—while his Holy Spirit likewise uncomfortably suggests an ideal version of the human spirit at its ethical best. And if these things are less apparent in Haering's case, yet when all is said and done, even his thought is vitiated by the positivism which forbids him to assert more than a suspiciously modal Trinity ; for the failure to recognise a Trinity which is definitely immanent, inevitably makes it impossible to maintain decisively the unique and incomparable transcendence of Christ and of the Spirit.

Such weaknesses, however, ultimately derive from the fundamental method of approach which is common to all the Ritschlians and precisely the opposite of Mackintosh's. Ritschl and Herrmann place Christ as the Revealer of God firmly and, to all intents and purposes, exclusively within the realm of history as we know it ; while the others set out from the fact that, whatever else He may be, He lived within that realm and is still known within it, and then go on to enquire what our knowledge of historical reality will permit us to say of His transcendence. Mackintosh's argument, on the other hand, takes its stand upon the certainty that God is revealed in a Christ who " is not *of* history, and for this very reason His being in history at all is a Divine marvel " ; [204] and from this standpoint he puts the question, What then is to be said of the history in which He is? This problem of revelation and history was one which occupied him from beginning to end, and to which he never found an answer which completely satisfied him. But from the start he was convinced that the answer could be given from this standpoint alone, and vigorously protested against the opposite method which ascribes the certainty to our notions of what history is and puts the question-mark opposite revelation : as early as 1912 we find him urging that to adopt such a method, even with the purpose of giving Christ the highest place history can afford, is the surest way of missing the truth, for " to-day as of old He hides Himself from those who would take Him by violence to make Him King ".[205] Here indeed we have the bedrock of his whole theology. For the problem is one which recurred in a multitude of forms, and always his approach was the same : he took his stand upon the truth of a revelation which puts all else in question, in order to ask what is then to be said, not only of the world's history, but also of its religion, its knowledge, its values, its " experience " and all that it contains.

To sum up, then, the one all-determining factor which is the ground of all theological thought and throughout its guiding and controlling authority, is the revelation of God in

Jesus Christ. And by that revelation is meant "The Person of Jesus in His sovereign redeeming power, as apprehended by the faith which in Him finds God ".[206] It is the *Person* of Jesus, known in the freedom and intimacy of a direct personal relationship, not any impersonal code of facts about God contained in the Bible, through which He is indeed mediated but to which He can never be bound. It is the Person of *Jesus*, the *Incarnate* Son of God, who lived at a definite time in a definite place, not the mere " Christ-principle " of Hegelian philosophy. It is that Person *in His sovereign redeeming power,* Christ our Saviour, the Incarnate *Son of God* beyond the reach of scientific criticism—not simply Liberalism's dim and distant religious Genius, the Carpenter of Nazareth and Hero of humanity. And it is that Person, not just as He once was or as He is reflected in the faith of the apostles, but *as apprehended by the faith which in Him finds God*—that is, as through Scripture, sermon and sacrament He makes Himself known *to us,* creating in us the faith which recognises Him as our ever-present and everlasting sovereign Lord.

Since this revelation calls forth in man a fully human response in the form of activities which we can only call religious and which outwardly resemble those of what is commonly known as religion, the theologian has to examine the relationship between Christianity and other religions. Yet it is not merely for interest's sake or on the ground of a general conception of religion that he does so, but from the standpoint of the one true religion based upon the revelation in Christ, and in the strict context of the missionary task committed to the Church by Him. Similarly, since the faith by which the revelation is apprehended involves a fully human act of cognition, he has to make clear its relation to the intellectual activities of science and philosophy. But in doing so he must not take his stand upon any particular theory of knowledge, whether to exalt the human reason as supreme and all-sufficient or to debase it as something which faith can do without or whose conclusions must inevitably be false: rather, he must start by recognising that God, as revealed in Christ, created all things well (including man and his reason) and demands the service of all creation, and from there he must go on to separate himself from all speculative efforts which in fact do not recognise God's claims and to welcome any which do.

The real subject-matter of dogmatic, however, is neither the religious beliefs and practices of mankind nor any theory of science or philosophy (although a position will have to be taken up towards them): it is the convictions born of believing response to Jesus Christ as the Revealer of God, together with the preaching of the Church which seeks to proclaim Him. And the proper task of the theologian, as a servant of the Church, is in the first instance to test the truth of her beliefs and preaching against the revelation to which they profess to be a response, and then also to protect her against heresy by seeking to bring out the full range and implications of what according to that revelation is to be believed and proclaimed. If thereby dogmatic has to present in a coherent and comprehensive system the truth as it is in Christ, then it is solely by constant and ever-repeated reference to Him that it can do so: everything involved in the obedience of faith in Him (no matter how " speculative ") must find a place, nothing may be included which is inconsistent with what He gives us to know of Himself, and the unity of the whole rests upon the fact that each doctrine only brings to expression some aspect of the truth which is in Him and the several parts have thus a vital interrelation with each other. This system, of course, can never be all-comprehensive or infallible ; nor is there any *legal* guarantee against individual vagaries, or any assurance of unchanging orthodoxy. For Christ remains throughout the sovereign Lord, who neither enables us fully to comprehend the unfathomable riches of His grace, nor provides us with an inflexible standard by which theological correctness can be measured.

But it is the glory of the Gospel that it should be so, and better sureties are given us in Him than we could ever have in ourselves:—

"We have the promise of the Spirit, to lead the Church into all truth; we have the Word of God which liveth and abideth for ever, and to which the Spirit bears witness perpetually in the hearts of men. These are the real—these, when we speak strictly, are the only and the sufficient—guarantee that the mind of the believer, working freely on its data, will reach conclusions that are in line with the great faith of the past." [207]

Such, in briefest outline, are the fundamental principles of Mackintosh's thought as brought to light in the preceding discussion. No doubt they were long overlaid, at first rather heavily, by elements from Ritschl and his followers which make their true nature not always easy to discern. Yet when we scrape away the Ritschlian deposit—as Mackintosh himself had fairly completely done by the end of his life—we find that all along they were of a definitely non-Ritschlian character. At the beginning, it is obvious, he looked a great deal to the Ritschlians for arguments and forms of expression, and took over much from them which for the moment appeared to suit his purpose, but which in fact ill-consorted with his own principles and by the time of his last work must surely have been denied or at least differently expressed. Yet he did not look only to the Ritschlians: he looked still more to the Bible, in which he saw things they had never seen. And if at first their influence somewhat obscured his view, yet it was only a morning haze which later rose to leave the peaks of biblical doctrine clearly outlined against the evening sky.

CHAPTER III

THE CONCEPT OF GOD

1. *THE BEING AND ATTRIBUTES OF GOD* [1]

AS we should expect by this time, Mackintosh cannot find himself in agreement with the orthodox doctrine of God. His objection is, in fact, twofold: he expresses dissatisfaction both with the way in which the conception of God is reached, and with the content of the concept itself.

In the first case the older dogmatic starts with a natural knowledge of the Being and Attributes of God which is the common possession of all men, completed and vouched for by Christianity, but obtainable in the first instance by the ordinary methods of reflection; and alongside of this it sets the specifically Christian knowledge of the Divine Trinity, reached only through the revelation of Scripture. But that, as we have seen, is doubly objectionable, since God cannot be known by the ordinary methods of reflection, and since in any case the simple juxtaposition of two such heterogeneous kinds of knowledge must inevitably produce confusion and dualism: it is only by adopting throughout the one standpoint of the revelation in Christ that we can possibly attain to a unified doctrine of God.

As for the traditional concept itself, it seeks—inevitably on such a method—to combine with the God and Father of our Lord Jesus Christ one or other of the various interpretations of the featureless Absolute of ancient philosophy. Now, there can be no objection to the epithet absolute provided it bears a Christian meaning. But to set alongside the Christian conception of God a speculatively abstract or impersonal idea, whether it takes the form of Substance as in the mystical writings of Pseudo-Dionysius, of arbitrary Will (which is not equivalent to ethical personality) as in Duns Scotus, or of Law as prominently in Protestant Orthodoxy, can only destroy the basis of Christian assurance. For, as Luther so passionately protested, it implies that Christ is no sufficient guide to the Divine nature, but there are still hidden and terrible regions in God which He does not guarantee. The truth is, the two conceptions are incompatible—indeed much of the interest in the historical study of theology consists in watching the conflict between them. And a Christian dogmatic must leave aside all such logical abstractions and relics of paganism, and build solely on the revelation in Christ which, if it does not enable us fully to comprehend the unfathomable being of God, nevertheless gives the assurance that there is nothing in its hidden depths which is not Christlike.

The God who meets us in that revelation may be described as " the absolute Personality in whom Holiness, Love and Power are perfect and are one "—provided that, if we do not here enter into a full discussion of " the baffling problem known as the doctrine of the Trinity ", the term Personality is left open to " the further interpretation which might come from reflection on the Divine life of Christ and on the Holy Spirit " as indicating necessary active distinctions within the one personal Being.[2] But before attempting an exposition of this all too inadequate definition, we must be very clear what we are about. No amount of analysis of the general concept God may be expected to yield a definition in these or similar terms ; nor, on the other hand, can there be any suggestion that God is a combination or perfect unity of what we generally understand by them. Rather, our method must be to attempt an answer to the question: what conception of God corresponds to the faith evoked by Christ? In other words, we can offer no independent proof that God is such and such, but are concerned, here as elsewhere, with what faith already knows. Our task is, first and foremost, simply to bring to full expression what Christian faith means by God and, without adding any new truth, to unfold its definition in a discussion of attributes which are real (not just nominal) distinctions in His one indissoluble being ; and then perhaps also to seek as far as may be to answer objections (particularly to His personality) which serious thinkers have raised.

(*a*) *The Personality of God.* The fundamental conviction of the faith evoked by revelation is, that in Christ we are redeemed into fellowship with God. But that means at once that God is a Person who enters into personal communion with men—a relation which is not any less personal for the fact that it depends, both for its initiation and for its continuance, on the absolute initiative and supremacy of God. This immediate conviction that God is personal is, in fact, the simple presupposition of the whole round of spiritual life ; for apart from it trust and love, penitence and prayer, service and religious obligation would be meaningless. It is also a fundamental assumption of Scripture which, although it does not use the modern category personality, nevertheless freely assumes the truth of what is meant by it—indeed " what *is* the Bible but the personal converse of God and man? " [3] The fact is, that the biblical writers, and every believer of the biblical type, have lived in such fellowship with God that it would have seemed superfluous to raise the question of His personality at all.

In modern times, however, objections to the concept have been raised. And once such difficulties have been expressed the theologian must give some consideration to them—they cannot simply be stifled, for " violence in theology is the offspring of fear ".[4]

The first objection came from the side of Idealistic Pantheism. For such writers as Spinoza, Schelling and

Hegel, God is in one form or another merely an absolute World-principle, devoid of any real self-consciousness and self-determination, and therefore impersonal. But now, it is clear that the argument cannot simply be stopped there: it must, if consistent, go on to depersonalise man also—to assert that he is simply an element in the unfolding of the world-process and not a responsible moral being, thus jeopardising the whole of morality and contradicting one of the most deep-seated convictions of mankind. Moreover, pantheism simply ignores all distinction between the universe and its Creator. And an objection to the Divine personality which rests on an identification of the cosmos with God cannot be taken seriously by Christian thought, which knows that He is neither just the world, nor even the soul of the world and therefore limited by it as soul by body: " God as Christian faith conceives Him is high and lifted up, ineffably transcending earth and heaven ".[5]

Yet traditional theology is not altogether so safe from the objection as might appear. For the Aristotelian conception of God as essentially Intelligence—" thought thinking upon itself "—still lingers on in it. And if it is a simple step from there to Deism, it is still more fatally easy to reach an exclusive emphasis on the Divine immanence which is little better than pantheistic: * if He is merely a Universal Thinker, " all we are then in a position to affirm is God as contemplating the universe, or as sustaining by His dynamic thought the relations of one thing to another ".[6] But if we cut ourselves free from Aristotle and the baneful influence he has all too often been allowed to exercise on theology when it would have been better to follow Scripture, and if we fix our eyes solely on Christ, then we must affirm that there exists alongside of the Divine Mind a centre of enjoyment in which love, blessedness and joy can find a place, and one of will, in virtue of

---

* Cf. Ritschl's still more emphatic assertion that the Platonic and Aristotelian elements in the orthodox doctrine of God must, if taken seriously, inevitably lead to " the different species of Rationalism—Deism and Pantheism " (Rechtfertigung und Versöhnung [4], iii, p. 216).

which He directs all His activity to a freely chosen end. The God who meets us in Christ is our Saviour—One who not only knows but also wills and loves, and who in His conscious purpose, loving activity and free self-impulsion "most absolutely lives a life incommunicably His own ".[7] But such a God must be described as personal if He is to be represented in thought at all.

A second objection rests on the view that personality is essentially finite, exclusive and subject to development, and therefore cannot be predicated of God. This argument was given extreme and classical expression by Strauss when he wrote: "Personality is the selfhood which shuts itself up against everything else so as to exclude it: the Absolute, on the other hand, is the All-comprehending, the Unlimited, which excludes nothing at all except just that exclusiveness which attaches to the idea of personality ".[8] Here we may note in the first instance that it is a simple fact of life that personality, however exclusive it may be, has yet also some power of transcending its own isolation and entering into the lives of others (as for example in speaking and understanding speech, and still more in love), while on the other hand God does not include everything, even our evil desires, as part of Himself; so that the incompatibility of the two ideas as Strauss defines them need not worry us much.

But more than this can be said, for this particular instance affords a good illustration of how philosophical objections can be countered by philosophical argument. As a preliminary point we may notice that although we first reach conscious selfhood through awareness of the impact of others upon us, yet it is only our self-consciousness which is thus called forth, not our selfhood; and if even *our* personality is thus not produced by these external stimuli, there is all the less reason for holding that God must be subject to such foreign contacts, and therefore finite, before He could be personal. But waiving this, we may call upon the argument of Lotze,[9] that although personality in man is limited and is largely conditioned by external influences, such limitations are simply due to the fact that we, as human beings, do not contain within us the conditions of our being and development. They are marks of *human* personality, and indicate that we are persons only in a secondary sense. In other words, they are defects ; and it is logically fallacious to argue from them to personality as such. Just as the prerogative of the Crown was exercised in seventeenth-century Britain in a defective manner which impeded the free expression of the nation's will, and yet was essential to the constitution of a free Britain, so personality can take a defective form in us, depending for its recognition and development on the interaction of the self and the not-self, and yet be essential to the being of God who has no not-self over against Him : He can both be personal and know Himself as such although He is influenced by nothing which is not the product of His own will. Personality is not, in fact, limiting and confining, but essentially the opposite and as such can and ought to be predicated of God : —

" It is no mere negative idea diluting and reducing, as it were, the energy or range of life. On the contrary, it is affirmative and dynamic in a degree elsewhere unknown ; it is intensely and uniquely positive, and so far from confining life is, when complete, a note of the highest level to which being can attain. It is the power of Spirit over itself, and this power may be finite or infinite. In us, of course, it is finite, since we do not create our own nature ; we receive it and never gain more than partial control over it. But in God, who is the ground of His own being, it is infinite, perfect, absolute." [10]

In such ways, then, it can be shown that the metaphysical reasons for preferring personal to impersonal names for God are after all as good as the religious ones. But if the objection is thus not a serious one even for the philosopher, it is nevertheless not without value. For just as the other stands to warn us of the danger which attends the mixing of *a priori* speculative concepts with theology, so also this one is a salutary reminder that in ascribing to God the qualities of intelligence, feeling and will, of self-consciousness and self-determination—in a word, personality—we do not of course mean that these things are precisely the same in Him as in man, but only that in speaking thus we come infinitely nearer the truth than if we use instead terms from the realm of physical nature. There are no higher terms at our disposal (the "supra-personal", so often suggested as a solution of the difficulty, turns out in the end to be only thinkable as the equivalent of "infra-personal"). And in view of Christ we can say no less. Nor is this (as Hegelians urge) merely a limitation of religious thought from which a higher philosophy can release us ; for there is no more ultimate Reality to be known than that which is known in Christ. Thus, since the concept is not one which we can fully think out, visualise or apply, we must hold that God is personal and at the same time recognise the inadequacy of even our best thought of Him, simply acknowledging that His personality has only a dim analogy in ours, not an exact copy, and regarding it as, so to speak, lying at some infinitely higher point on the line occupied by human selfhood at its best (which is but the converse of the Scripture principle that He has made us in His image) : —

"To express the whole truth of which faith is aware, we must strive to balance together these two convictions : first, that personality in Him utterly transcends ours, being inexpressibly higher, richer, more living than its earthly type, and secondly, that none the less to deny Him personality would be infinitely further from the truth than to affirm it in the properly expanded sense. Of our thoughts concerning the spiritual being of God it is supremely true that *omnia exeunt in mysterium*—unfathomableness is the end of all." [11]

So much for objections. Mackintosh's primary concern, however, is with the fact that whatever intellectual difficulties may attend the concept, it is one which, as we saw, is vital and fundamental for faith. And now, as though to mark the discussion of objections expressly as only a digression, he draws a line and returns (as he says, " from these altitudes ") to the teaching of Scripture with which he had left off.

The Bible speaks, not indeed of the *personal*, but repeatedly of the *living* God, which is just the same : " when we speak of the Divine personality, we are thinking of an infinitely rich and mobile form of being that inwardly enjoys its own blessedness and ponders its own vast purpose, and, outwardly, reacts with sensitive awareness on human life in mercy and judgment " [12]—which is precisely what Scripture means by the " living God ". And, according to the Bible, it is through His great redeeming acts that He is known as such : not by the way of the mystic, retreating into the inner mind, nor by that of the *a priori* rationalist, analysing ideas, can the personality of God be known, but simply—and solely—by the Spirit-inspired appropriation of historic facts. It was through the impact of Divine events, made luminous by the Holy Spirit, that the prophetic knowledge of the living—the personal—God was attained ; it was the " mighty works of God " (Acts 2 : 11)—supremely the coming and going of Jesus Christ —that the apostles preached, leaving them to make their own impression as to who or what the Doer of them was ; and it is through these same events, and passionate testimony to them, that the believer in every age learns to know God as a personal Father.

Thus the one conclusive reason for asserting that God is personal is, " that it is in this character that He encounters us in Christ, the great Doer of redeeming things ".[13] Whoever comes by this Way to know the living God, and to live in communion with Him, is soon raised " above the temptation to conceive of Him as ' a magnified non-natural man ' and to ascribe to Him an inner life closely modelled on our own ".[14] He knows indeed that he cannot claim to comprehend God and that his language can never be adequate to describe Him. But he knows also that unless He is personal in a real sense, then no positive meaning can be attached to the purposes, thoughts and feelings He manifests in Christ, to the way He deals with us—loves, and therewith claims, rebukes, pardons and inspires—or to the life of fellowship we have with Him.

We must now go on to describe this personal God further under two main aspects, one represented by the expression " Holy Love ", the other by the word " Power ".

(b) *The Holiness and Love of God.* Discussion of the Divine *Holiness* must not be confined, as was usually done in the early part of the century, to the moral perfection and purity the word usually conveys to our minds. Purity, no doubt, is an element in it, but in the scriptural witness to revelation, and therefore for theology, the Holiness of God is in the first instance virtually His Divinity : —

" The biblical conception of holiness, properly understood, stands for all in God's being that transcends reason in the narrower sense, all that towers up in infinite sublimity over man and the world. The holy is a category—*i.e.* a fundamental conception—by itself. . . . It cannot be derived from any other idea or grown out of it. . . . Holiness, in short, is not (if the Bible is any guide) to be taken in a simply or exclusively ethical sense, but has a nature of its own ; it is not reducible to elements which do not already contain its distinctive quality." [15]

In the Old Testament it signifies first and foremost the awe-inspiring majesty and " wholly other " sublimity of God, " akin to the blinding *glory* of the Lord " of which Isaiah spoke. And if this thought is accompanied invariably and in ever-deepening degree by the other, that as holy in this sense He is also the sole Author of the moral law and demands unconditional obedience in His people, yet the epithet holy in its primary sense is scarcely distinguishable from Divine. In the New Testament, although God's holiness is seldom spoken of directly, the same two lines of thought remain. The ethical element, indeed, has now reached a new depth and prominence ; yet this must not be allowed to obscure the fact that the awe-inspiring element is still not only present but vital. For Paul God dwells " in light unapproachable " (I Tim. 6:16), while to the writer of Hebrews He is " a consuming fire " (12:29) and One to whom even Jesus prays in " fear " (5:7). The Kingdom of the Gospels is specifically Divine, belonging to another realm than ours and coming, not out of the world but into it ; while the heavenly Father whose gift it is, is not less sacred and unfathomable or " high and lifted up " for Jesus than for the prophets, but rather more so. And Jesus Himself is holy in this sense, so that it is with " amazement " and " fear " that His disciples follow Him to Jerusalem (Mark 10:32) and those who seek to arrest Him " go backwards and fall to the ground " (John 18:6). The *new* element in the New Testament—the wonder and glory of the Gospel—is, that this unsearchable and unapproachable God makes Himself known to us and draws near in love, as our Father in Jesus Christ.

The second element mentioned now calls for special attention : God is exalted not only in unapproachable majesty, but also in purity and goodness—which indeed in Him alone have wholly real existence and cease to be simply abstract nouns. He is therefore utterly intolerant of sin, and yet we must never regard His holiness for that reason as merely exclusive and menacing : on the contrary, it must always be set in indissoluble relation to His grace. Ritschl was of a different mind. He had learnt from Diestel that in the Old Testament holiness is primarily not God's moral perfection but His absolute " otherness "; and because the ethical significance of Christianity was everything to him, he rejected the term altogether, urging that in this sense it is inconsistent with the Divine love and in its New Testament meaning " obscure ".[16] Here he has had no followers, but he provoked a debate which has drawn fresh attention to the " self-imparting " quality of the Divine holiness : repelling and awe-inspiring as it indeed is also in this second aspect (for it involves most dire and terrible wrath at sin), it has yet above all a redemptive quality, and " the opposition to sin which is central to its meaning is an opposition exhibited at least as much in forgiveness as in judgment ".[17] For it not only repels the sinner: it also cannot tolerate his continuance in sin, and therefore bends to his redemption.[18]

It is often precisely to the *Holy* One of Israel that the Old Testament believer looks for redemption (*cf.* Ps. 22:3 f., Is. 41:14, 47:4, 48:17, 49:7, 54:5); and for John it is the *Holy* Father who redeems and keeps men (17:11). It is plain, too, that the Gospels present a Jesus who in His attitude to sinners displays a holiness which is essentially both repelling and gracious (*cf.* Matt. 7:11, Luke, 5:8 ff., 7:36 ff., 19:5 ff., John 4:16 ff.). And for the faith which has found God in Him " the partition between love and holiness has broken down and the nature of each of them has diffused through the whole ".[19] What meets us in Him is the holiness of a *loving* God: it first breaks upon us—baffling, stupefying, menacing—in " an experience of God so great . . . that it throws the mind, as it were, off its balance and produces a feeling of sheer inability to grapple with what has been presented "; yet underlying this sense of tension and contrast is " a quite definite and unified conviction—*viz.* that God is encountering us in grace ", in which " His severity is absorbed, yet does not disappear ".[20]

Finally, this God, both sublimely exalted and lovingly near, both holy and gracious, is also righteous and at the same time merciful. The *Righteousness* of God means that He is morally perfect in His government of the world, and that His character and ways are wholly self-consistent and trustworthy, uniformly true to His own nature and worthy of it. Now, one inevitable expression of this righteousness is, that " He will by no means clear the guilty " (Nah. 1:3) but will surely punish evil. There can be no suggestion that such punishment is unworthy of Him, nor can Ritschl be right in holding that it is merely accidental and regarding righteousness as indistinguishable from grace. For only by an exegetical *tour de force* can it be argued that God's righteousness in the Bible, and especially in Romans, does not issue in active condemnation of sin. Moreover, it can surely only be in the righteousness of its Creator that the moral order which makes for retributive justice as part of the constitution of things can have its ground ; and indeed, it is in Him alone that we can find the true basis of our own penal law.* Yet the Western philosophic and juristic tradition in theology is equally wrong in conceiving God on the analogy of an earthly state as "a scrupulously precise Dispenser of prizes to the good and afflictions to the bad"; [21] for it is monstrous to suggest that, even apart from Christianity, any of us is treated "exactly as he deserves". Thus if we cannot follow Ritschl in denying the reality of judgment and simply identifying righteousness with mercy,† we shall do well to let him remind us of the inseparable bond between them.

The Old Testament conceives God as Judge ; and since for it the judge's task consists "not merely in bringing home his responsibility to the sinner, but in lifting up the oppressed and the down-trodden ",[22] it is easy to see how God's mercy to those weakened and oppressed by sin should have His very

---

* "Those who administer law fulfil a holy office, for they act—with whatever inevitable failure perfectly to achieve their end—in God's name. They are engaged in a cause by all odds higher than mere expediency, for it rests on the inviolable distinction of good and evil ". (*Apprehension of God*, pp. 174 f.). This has a striking parallel in Kaftan, *Dogmatik*[6], p. 360 : "That God punishes evil is the foundation of all penal law. Those who administer it act in God's name as His servants, fulfil a holy office at His command. Its ordering is therefore never merely a matter of expediency, but rests on the *inviolable* ideas of good and evil which are grounded in God's holy will."

† The chief passages in Ritschl are : *Rechtfert. u. Versöhnung*[4], i, 163 f., ii, 154 f., iii, 306 f., 446, *Unterricht*, § 16. From these it will be seen that strictly (as Mackintosh was aware) he did not deny the reality of judgment outright, but allowed it in an eschatological sense : God will at last destroy those who oppose Him to the end. This, however, in fact amounts to a complete denial, since "if wrath in God is inconsistent with love now, it can never cease to be inconsistent with it " (*Experience of Forgiveness*, p. 161).

righteousness as its ground. At any rate, supremely in Deutero-Isaiah, it is His righteousness which causes Him to bring in righteousness: the Old Testament never thinks of "a righteous God and *yet* a Saviour", but of "a righteous God and *therefore* a Saviour" (*cf.* Is. 45:21 f.) [23]—once even contrasting righteousness with the judgment which would normally be its technical expression: "Answer me in Thy righteousness, and enter not into judgment with Thy servant" (Ps. 143:1 f.).* And in the New Testament the background of God's righteousness in Romans is the Cross—the medium of salvation—while for John it is as "faithful and righteous" that God forgives the penitent (I John 1:9). Thus there can be no such conflict of attributes in God as has played so great a part in traditional doctrines of the Atonement. These doctrines indeed contain the truth that the sinner as such is compelled to conceive God as a wrathful Judge and can find no hope of mercy in His righteousness—it is simply the penalty of the guilty that it should be so. But the faith evoked by the revelation in Christ, on which theology ought to build, knows that His sternest righteousness expresses itself in mercy and moves in perfect harmony with love:—

"His righteous character is fulfilled and crowned in the Gospel for a world of sin. His method of saving men through Christ, far from being the contradiction or reversal of His righteousness, is its utterly effective expression. . . . For the rightness of mind and heart which He demands from men He now freely bestows; He not merely convinces of evil, but redeems us from it. Here righteousness moves hand in hand with perfect love. Whatever men's thoughts, it has ever been so. There has never been a time when God punished for punishment's sake, but at each stage the manifestation of His righteousness has opened the way by which love might enter, and the apprehension of His love in turn has enabled men, as nothing else could, to rise up and fulfil the challenge of His righteous will." [24]

* Haering cites the same passage with the same purpose, *Der christl. Glaube*, p. 324.

It may perhaps be a helpful approach to the concept of the Divine love, if we consider first the biblical idea of God's *Nearness,* which answers in part to that of His sublime holiness. Here it is notable that, although every religion has some idea of the Divine nearness, the biblical conception has a peculiar quality of its own.

Already in the Old Testament it has a particularly central and vital place: not only does every reference to the Covenant recall how wonderfully near God has drawn to His people, but His nearness also to the individual is a frequent theme especially of the Psalms (*cf.* Ps. 34:18, 85:9, 119:151, 145:18, Is. 51:5, 55:6). And it is noteworthy that the adoring recognition of this nearness rests solely on God's own act in making it known, not on any general conceptions of Divine omnipresence. This is most clearly shown by the agony which results from His withdrawing Himself, or from the fear that He may do so; for only those who have been given to know His nearness agonise over His distance, and the pain of this most terrible of all afflictions can be removed by no rational assurances as to His omnipresence (which is never questioned), but only by a fresh encounter with Himself. In the New Testament the nearness of God is given a new and ineffably more profound meaning—the same New Testament which knows a sublimity never dreamed of before. Thus here again we come at once before the wonder and glory of the Gospel: " the very Person in whom the unapproachable holiness and loftiness of God is once for all made palpable to human feeling, is He in whom God comes closer than breathing, nearer than hands and feet ".[25] Hence the Christian assurance that nothing whatsoever can come between us and Him (Rom. 8:38 f.)—an assurance which is not confined to moments of peculiar ecstasy, otherwise hovering vaguely in the half-forgotten background, but rather lives and abides continually in all authentic Christian faith as one of its unique and most fundamental elements.

From this distinctive thought of the nearness of God we

may pass to the equally distinctive and even more profound conception of His *Love*. Here theology again owes a debt to Ritschl as the first modern theologian to give the topic more than perfunctory treatment. He cannot, it is true, be followed in regarding love as the essence of God and bringing in personality only in a secondary manner to determine its nature. For Pringle-Pattison's argument for the relative independence of human selves [26]—that it takes two to love and to be loved—implicitly proves also that love can be real only as the characteristic of personal spirit ; we cannot hypostatise it in its own right or ascribe abstract reality to it, as though persons could arise out of it or disappear within it, but as essentially self-bestowal it clearly has personality as its presupposition :—

"Unless the self is there in order to self-impartation— there as an actual, meaningful, independent Ego—love could only amount to an endless self-creation out of nothing. Self-communication has self-possession as its antecedent. Despite the Ritschlian argument, then, we must persist in holding that in essence God is Spirit, with love as its leading active quality." [27]

Yet it is only a logical priority that is here demanded, and we must certainly follow Ritschl in placing love at the very foundation of our thought of God—for what is more fundamental in the New Testament than the Divine love to which it witnesses on every page? We must not fail to recognise, too, that the Christian conception of that love, alike in content and in origin, is utterly and distinctively new: it has nothing in common with the benevolence of Plato's God, the vital cosmic force of Graeco-Roman philosophy, or any other human conceptions of love, for the simple reason that it is not derived from human thought of any kind, but solely from the creative revelation of the Cross of Christ. And this of course means at once that we must beware of deriving from our normal experience of human love the meaning of the love we predicate of God, and must take revelation alone as our guide.

In that revelation it breaks upon us as the love of the Father, in which He not only receives the penitent, but actually, at inestimable cost, goes forth in His Son to seek and to redeem—the ungodly! (*cf.* Rom. 5:6 ff., I John 3:16). And this, surely, is a conception of love which reason not only cannot discover for itself, but whose wonder it cannot even comprehend once it is revealed: only in faith in Christ dare we assert that the love of God pours itself out in literally unbounded measure on sinful men—a truth which must strain to breaking point, and beyond, all ordinary human conceptions of what love is or can be. And now, just as the knowledge of God's holiness must lead only to despair were it not the holiness of a loving God, so also here we do well to say not simply " God is Love ", but " God, the Holy One, is Love ".* This must be our guard against all complacent, or shallow, sentimental interpretations: God's is a stringent love, and were it not so, He would not be more loving—He would cease to be God.[28] It may also be our warning that *this* love is not the reflection of human love, but rather its pattern (*cf.* Matt. 5:44 f.), and our reminder that it is not called forth by any worthiness in its object, but flows down from the heights of God's free majesty in order to raise the unworthy and the frail. It is a subduing love this, and one " presented to us not merely as the guarantee of pardon but as the abiding pledge of permanent and unsleeping care: ' He that spared not His own Son but delivered Him up for us all, how shall He not with Him also freely give us all things? ' (Rom. 8:32) ".[29]

But now, God is not only holy love: we must go on to speak also of His righteous *Mercy* and His pure, sovereign *Grace*. Here we may begin by noticing three points. Firstly, love, however it is to be defined, cannot have an impersonal

* The argument here comes remarkably near Haering, *Der christl. Glaube*, pp. 216 ff.

object; and thus, while God's goodness extends to all creatures, only those made in His image are the objects of His love. Again, it is here that we may see the ground of creation: "God, if He is to enjoy from without a true response to His own affection, must call into existence beings possessed of independent personal life ".[30] And finally, since the response, to be true, must be spontaneous, the satisfaction of God's love must then depend on its being freely reciprocated by these His creatures. Such considerations at once exclude certain conceptions which have all too often played havoc in traditional theology with the Christian thought of God.

One of these is the essentially pagan conception of the Divine impassibility, which has even gone so far as to suggest that God in His transcendent bliss could contemplate with equal dispassion either the redemption or the annihilation of the world. Could He, then, according to the love revealed in Christ? Must we not rather (again for want of better terms) urge the existence of emotion or feeling in God—of infinite yearning for fellowship with His creatures, of boundless compassion for their need and frailty, of pain unspeakable caused by the loss of a created child or his persistent rebellion and distrust? In view of Christ it is surely monstrous to suggest that God has no heart, and that it would be in any way untrue to His nature, or unworthy of Him, that in the presence of weak and erring mortals His love should assume the form of tender and merciful compassion. This, of course, is not to be glibly spoken of or taken lightly: it is the mercy of God, and therefore "a real capacity "[31] for righteous condemnation. But if we will remember this, and reflect how little mercy there would be in allowing the wicked to continue in wickedness, then surely it must appear how supremely worthy of God it is that it should be so ; and the path must open once more to the vital conjunction of mercy and righteousness.

Likewise excluded are philosophical conceptions of the

Divine self-sufficiency. Not that the necessity of the creation, and of its free responding love, make God dependent on men either for His existence as a loving God or for His blessedness as such: it is only because His love elects to flow outwards, and only because it is what it is, that these things are necessary—and this love is freely determined alike in outflow and in character by God alone. Thus faith will never countenance the suggestion that God and man are mutually dependent or that He would be any less God blessed for evermore had He never created the world. But it must also assert that, since His love has in fact called for free and responsible objects outside of Himself, He has not the self-sufficiency of a philosophical Absolute but, by the inner necessity of being true to His own loving nature, must create such objects, must seek to communicate His own blessedness to them, and cannot be indifferent to their response. And if the love of the Creator is wholly able also to *secure* that response and the fellowship it seeks, yet it is not by any mechanical or abstract means—be it the infusion of a quasi-physical grace, the mystical promotion of a substantial union, or the working-out of a rational principle—that it does so:—

" Its approach and method is that of so revealing itself constrainingly within the fields of concrete human life and personality that our trust, our responsive and grateful love, is addressed and persuaded in ethical modes, which call out the spontaneous consent of the free and conscious spirit. Thus men come most freely, being made willing by the grace which has appeared in Jesus." [32]

There is no term better calculated to express all this than the Bible term—grace. For grace " is love in its princely and sovereign form, love to the indifferent and the disloyal ",[33] flowing down in forgiveness to overcome their sin. Once more, this is not merely grace as such, but the grace of the pure and holy God: it cannot tolerate unworthiness, and far from its being at variance with judgment, holy Wrath at evil is a vital element in it—indeed, it is precisely because God is gracious to make Himself known to His people that He will surely visit their iniquities upon them.[34] Yet even as such it is the sovereign grace of God in Christ, creating worth where none was, answering Wrath with redemption, and stooping to triumph over sin.

(c) *The Sovereign Purpose of God.* In discussing the Divine sovereignty we shall best begin by emphasising that it is *God* we are speaking of, and no mere speculative Absolute: His is not bare sovereignty exercised merely for its own sake, but sovereignty with a *purpose*, and if we would avoid frigid and vacuous conceptions of it we shall do well to seek to understand it in that light. Yet it is inadvisable to follow the older dogmatic in taking God's purpose as simply the promotion of His own glory, for although that is patient of a good meaning, in itself it tends to suggest that God is concerned solely with the self-enclosed interest of His own life; whereas the purpose revealed in Christ has also a most important relation to the world and thus " in a certain sense is outside His own being, and involves the good of other beings than Himself ".[35] On the other hand, this must not suggest that it is in any way laid on Him from without, for it is, of course, freely determined by Himself alone: to this extent the end of all His action is indeed His own glory—but His glory is His love.

On the whole it will perhaps be best to interpret the sovereign purpose of God as meaning the establishing in time and perfecting in eternity of what Scripture calls His Kingdom: a perfect unity of body and soul, spirit and nature, a redeemed community in a redeemed world with God over all.[36] Here we see the uniquely biblical view of the sovereign eternity of God, for which time is no barren phantasmagoria but laden with significance and meaning: it is not only despite all the changes and chances of the temporal world, but even by means of them, that God is bringing in His eternal Kingdom. For prophets and apostles the Divine eternity "overshadows time, imparting to every moment of existence its own critical relation to God" and thereby its meaning, while faith here and now looks forward to the consummation when "at the completion of God's revealing work time will be replaced by eternity".[37]   And it is the peculiar glory of Christ our Saviour that He has established this eternal Kingdom once for all at a point within the temporal world.

God is apprehended in His sovereignty as possessing the attributes which underlie the possibility and the reality of such a Kingdom.   And if we would consider these, we come at once upon the concept of His *Omnipotence*.   This takes such a central place in all religion that it "might seem to rank as the Divine attribute *par excellence*".   And if as Christians "we justifiably take Holy Love as marking the very essence of God", it would be disastrous to suppose that omnipotence is now "merely casual or subordinate";[38] * for it is in fact vitally important—so much so, indeed, that one cannot even overlook the suggestiveness of the contention that it is "in a way a compendium of all the qualities in which the uniqueness of God becomes manifest".[39]   It not only forms the very foundation of Old Testament thought, but is also of vital importance in that of Jesus Himself.   For Him, as for the prophets, it means primarily that God is omnipotent *to save* (*cf.* Matt 19:25 f.), but also has a wider reference: He is the Creator and Sustainer of all that is, and as such He is not only able to act within the acknowledged regularity of the world,† but, because there is a glory in the

---

* So also Kaftan, *Dogmatik* [6], pp. 198, 206 : in so far as it has a place in all religion, "omnipotence is the Divine attribute *par excellence*" ; and if we give it second place because holy love "manifests God's very essence" whereas omnipotence expresses His relation to the world, it must on no account be concluded that "omnipotence is something unimportant or casual", for it is equally indispensable.

† This does not apply only, or even primarily, to the material world, but equally, and even more, to the "adamantine moral order" which ensures that men will reap as they sow.   This order, too, God can and

Father's might the world can never exhaust, He has also the power to intervene in ways we can only call miraculous, omnipotently wielding all things according to the purpose of His unspeakable grace.

As a definition, then, we may take this: " God is omnipotent in the sense that He is able to realise perfectly whatever He wills ".[40] That, of course, does not mean that He is literally " capable of anything ": there is a host of things He cannot do—die, sin, make twice two five, or contradict Himself in any way. But then, neither is it really thinkable that He should will them, for " the possible is determined by what God is, and only so "; [41] hence this is really covered by the definition given. Still, it may be as well to add expressly that the quality and direction of His will must be learnt from Jesus Christ. This, indeed, is vital. For our normal ideas of power are almost incurably physical and utilitarian, including moral considerations only as an afterthought, if at all: they can only lead to a conception of omnipotence as simply crushing all resistance out of hand, so that it cannot be too strongly emphasised that here too—as indeed everywhere— our thought of God must not be governed by any general human considerations, but solely by concrete relation to the revelation in Christ. It is also only from this point of view that there can be any hope of solving the age-old difficulty which cannot reconcile the existence of evil with the thought of an almighty God. For if we would see the true relation of God's omnipotence and human evil, we have only to look to the Cross of Christ, where the one perpetrates the greatest atrocity of all time and the other, in free grace, does not annihilate the resistance, but makes it serve the redemption of the world: " Neither the sin nor the transcendent purpose is unreal, but the sin is swept up into unconscious subservience

does perpetually use ; but His equally omnipotent intervention in forgiving grace to make all things new is the greatest—and commonest— miracle of all, and indeed the best (if not the only) starting-point for our conception of what miracle is. *Experience of Forgiveness*, pp. 182, 184.

to the purpose in whose realisation there can be no break-down ".[42]

Here we see that in His omnipotence, as in all else that He is, God is in a real sense *Immutable:* by nature He is constant, steadfast in His purposes and sure in all His ways. But this immutability is not " the changelessness of the Absolute, with its implicit denial that prayer is answered or that there can be such a thing as a Divine saving *act* ": it is rather " the infinite mobility of sovereign grace ".[43] Thus the omnipotence which meets us here is (as every Calvinist has rightly insisted) not the iron necessity of Fate, aimless, impersonal, utterly careless of the individual life ; but neither is it the sheer irresistible might of an Absolute Monarchy to which some of the representations of " hyper-Calvinism " come all too perilously near. It is the omnipotence of One who in Christ is the eternal, unchanging Lord and Father of us all and of each individual soul, almighty to create and therefore also to redeem—One whose might is that of *electing grace,* choosing men in eternity for fellowship with Himself, making Himself known in sovereign initiative, and enabling them freely to choose Him in answering faith. This, the everlasting glory of our Gospel, we must not and cannot hide.*

As sovereign Ruler of the world God is also *Omnipresent* and *Eternal.* The normal interpretation of these attributes has wavered between two lines of thought. The one begins by simply denying to God all spatial and temporal limits, and ends either in a virtual pantheism (in which omni-presence becomes simply identity and the Universe is eternal) or in making Him subject to space and time—to both of which positions faith must at once demur. The other, to pre-serve His absoluteness, so exalts Him above space and time

---

* The following four paragraphs are added here for greater complete-ness, and based on the Lecture Synopsis (read in the light of certain other passages). But it should be noted that the treatment there is not detailed, and that it belongs to a somewhat earlier period than the foregoing.

as to give Him what is really only a negative relation to them ; but that is to abandon the view of historical events as having a real meaning for God and a real place in the unfolding of His purpose, which is not only peculiar to biblical faith but vital to it. We must hold, then, that God is not subject to space and time but they to Him, and that He does not stand in a merely negative relation to them but in a truly positive one as their Creator and Lord. It should be made clear, however, that when theology speaks of the omnipresence and eternity of God, it does not intend to fix His metaphysical relations to space and time, so much as to bring out the truth that His relation to us does not alter with the vicissitudes of time and place.

That God is omnipresent means that "nowhere can we escape from Him and nothing can shut Him out of our lives (*cf.* Ps. 139)". Transcendent though He is, He "inhabits, pervades, moves, inspires the world . . . with a dynamic ubiquity involving a directly active relation to each part " [44]— a relation somewhat analogous to that of soul and body though by no means identical with it. This does not mean that the form of His presence is everywhere "immutably" the same. For He may be present in varying ways to the natural world, to the sinful and to the redeemed ; so that in a sense we may speak of degrees of Divine immanence— provided we recognise that God is never just partially present, but always fully so, only in a whole hierarchy of different forms, and provided we are not speaking on the basis of any general conception of immanence, but solely in view of the absolute and utterly unique presence of the fullness of God-head in Jesus Christ. Or again, He may withhold from us in one place the knowledge of His presence, and in another graciously reveal Himself to faith—as the Old Testament well knew. But for all that, the same God is everywhere, and the different forms of His presence are not imposed on Him by changes of place, but determined by His own free grace.

Similarly, that God is eternal means that "He abides in changeless fidelity to His revealed love, despite the transience of the world ".* Once more this does not mean that His relation to us is timelessly invariable. For it undergoes a change from condemnation to gracious acceptance when He forgives—a change which is real, and no mere subjective illusion as Ritschl sometimes tended to suggest.[45] Again, however, the change is not dictated by temporal circumstance, but due to the creative action in time of His own eternal redeeming grace.

Lastly, God is apprehended in His sovereignty as *Omniscient*. The faith called forth by Christ is at once convinced that God's complete knowledge of our heart—of all that we have and are—is the *prius* of our redemption (*cf.* I John 3 : 20) ; and from this assurance it moves on to the claim that nothing whatsoever (be it material or spiritual, past, present or future) which might promote or impede the realisation of His purpose can be unknown to Him. The method of His knowing we cannot tell: we can only say that it "acts as an intuitive and synchronous knowledge of all things ".[46] And in regard to the vexed question of its bearing on the freedom of the creature, we must simply insist that God's foreknowledge is no mere mechanical predetermination: whatever the intellectual difficulties, we must seek to balance together the two certainties that no future event can be unknown to God, and that no external necessity is thereby imposed upon it—after all, what we have here to do with is the omniscience of sovereign redeeming grace, bent upon the voluntary submission of a free world, and omnipotent to secure it.

(*d*) *The Triune God*.[47] Christian faith, as evoked by revelation, cannot be said to include a full Doctrine of the

---

* *Cf.* Ritschl's definition : " The eternity of God is apprehended in the fact that, amid all the changes of things, which denote at the same time the variation of His action, He remains in Himself the same and maintains the purpose and the plan in which He creates and guides the world ". *Unterricht*, § 14, *cf. Rechtfert. u. Versöhn.* ⁴, iii, 283.

Trinity among its immediate utterances. Yet it *is* immediately aware that God is the Father of our Lord Jesus Christ and our Father, who has created us and willed our redemption ; that the Christ who revealed Him and wrought that redemption is none other than the very Son of God incarnate ; and that the Power which brings home the revelation and sustains the new redeemed life is nothing in man—not even in redeemed man—but the Spirit of God, no less Divine than the Father Himself or than the Son who revealed Him in history. And it is also convinced beyond all shadow of doubt that there are not three separate Gods, but one only. Thus some real doctrine of the Trinity is at once implied in its immediate convictions—and implied in such a way that only a mere arbitrary refusal to think can prevent our seeking to bring it to expression.

For confirmation of this, we need only glance at the New Testament thought on the subject and at the reasons which led to the development of the full doctrine from it. No fresh and unbiased reader of the Gospels can seriously urge that, as Jesus sought in His life and teaching to reveal God to men, the primary thought in His mind and the one He most wished to impart was an articulated conception of God as Triune. And just as little can it be held that that was in the foreground of the apostles' thought. Yet they knew it was to Christ that they owed their redemption, and since God alone can redeem they recognised Him not only as their Redeemer, but as their Lord and their God ; while they could only ascribe the peculiar quality and ethical power of the new life to the Spirit, and because His working was indistinguishable from Christ in the heart they were convinced that He, too, is Divine. These assurances could be summed up in such a phrase as that " through Christ we have access by one Spirit unto the Father " (Eph. 2 : 18), but the New Testament thought on the subject is free and living throughout, not bound by any rigid forms or capable of being forced into literal harmony. Thus Paul can omit the Spirit from the

opening greeting of an epistle and close it with a threefold
blessing (II Cor. 1:1, 13:14), although it is the same God
he is thinking of in both cases ; or if we compare the thought
of different apostles, we find that for John it is the Father
who imparts the Spirit in response to the Son's request (14-16),
while Paul clearly holds that the Father is Lord, the Son is
Lord and the Spirit is Lord, yet just as clearly does not mean
that there are three Lords (Rom. 8).

In the New Testament, then, there is no sign of the Trinitarian doctrine as we know it : living convictions which were
to form its basis there are, but nothing more. Yet it was
inevitable that the demand for interpretation of these convictions should soon become urgent—the more so as their
very lack of rigidity left them specially open to misinterpretation. And thus when the early Church, in the process
of formulating her credal statements, " passed from God's
revelation to His nature " [48]—when, in other words, she
sought to answer the question Who and What the God is
who is revealed—she rightly saw herself compelled to build
on these same convictions an articulated doctrine of the
Trinity which would guard against false and unworthy interpretations of them. The interests which made it a matter not
of choice, but of necessity, would seem to be mainly three.
For the doctrine aims first and foremost at vindicating the
full and eternal Deity of Christ and of the Spirit ; and along
with that it is one sustained and determined attempt to
defend, against all such mechanical interpretations of the
New Testament as lead virtually to tritheism, the conviction
that Father, Son and Holy Spirit in their unity constitute
the God of our salvation ; while it is also concerned to assert
the finality and completeness of the Christian revelation.

The modern theologian has no option but to follow suit.
We cannot, it is true, force the rigid distinctions of later days
on the living and fluid language of the New Testament, or
hope to find in it a completely harmonious and theorised
doctrine merely waiting to be lifted ; yet the convictions of

faith to which our exposition must be true are the same now as ever they were, and if we would express all that Christian faith means by God, whether in the first century or in the twentieth, we cannot but say: Father, Son and Holy Spirit. On the other hand, we are not bound by the traditional doctrine: our task in relation to past doctrines, it will be remembered, is first to understand and then, if need be, to correct them. And thus we may well take exception to foreign or unworthy elements in the Church's Trinitarian thought—not least the way in which it soon lost its roots in the New Testament history and became an independent interest of philosophical speculation, or the stress which, in Protestant Orthodoxy, it finally put on the difference of the three at the expense of their unity. Yet whatever its short-comings, they must not blind us to the true and proper motives which went to its formulation, or prevent our letting our own construction be guided by them. For only as our thought, too, is governed by these same interests can it hope to give true expression to the fullest convictions of Christian faith.

What, then, are we to make of the doctrine? We have to choose first between two views—the economic or modal, and the immanent. Both agree that God is revealed in history in a threefold way: as the Father who created us in love, as the Son who came among us for our redemption, as the Spirit who abides with us for ever as the Giver of life. But there the advocates of the economic view would rest. God, they urge, has disclosed Himself in different phases or modes as Creator, Redeemer and Renewer, and no more questions are to be asked. We cannot go on to unverifiable speculations on the Divine nature in itself. We have no ground to project into God's being the distinctions which *our* minds, in artificially detaching different aspects of it, are compelled to make. We must be content to confess Him as known in history and experience, and there must be an end of the matter.

Now, the truth of the positive part of this theory is not to be denied. The terms Father, Son and Spirit do in fact refer primarily and properly to God Himself in relation to Christ or to His redeemed children, to the Jesus of the Gospels, and to the Spirit of Christ in the heart ; and only secondarily and inferentially to the Persons of the Trinity. Nor should we forget that the earliest forms of the doctrine—Tertullian's, for example—were of this economic kind, ascribing to the three Persons the several *oeconomiae* or dispensations of the creation of the universe (together with its conservation and government), the redemption of man, and the continuation of that redeeming work in regeneration and sanctification.

But it is otherwise with the negative part. For in the first place, however true the contention that history must be our starting-point, it is a very different matter when we are arbitrarily forbidden to go any further. Christian men will rightly refuse to let their minds be tied to the supremely practical language of the apostles, but will permit them to range beyond the bounds of what is immediately verifiable in experience, however many " trespassers will be prosecuted " notices the well-meaning theological positivist may erect ; and indeed, here as elsewhere, it is not only our right but our duty to seek the fullest possible elucidation of the convictions of faith, without being unduly troubled by the protests of positivist border police that we have strayed into the domain of metaphysic. But in the second place, and worse than that, if it be denied that the distinctions *we* are obliged to make must necessarily be carried over into the Divine nature, then that at least implies that for *us* God is Father, Son and Spirit but in Himself is really something else—and some modern exponents, calling upon the theory of the relativity of knowledge, have even gone so far as to say so expressly. We shall grant at once that we can only know God as He makes Himself known, and that faith can never fathom the full depths of His being or give an exhaustive description of Him as of any common object of observation. But if the knowledge He gives us is appearance only, while what He is in reality remains as a kind of fourth factor, unknown and unknowable in the transcendent background, how can we call that revelation at all, far less revelation of God? It is clear that such a suggestion, whether expressed or implied, goes to cancel the very conviction from which any doctrine on the subject must start: that God is *revealed* as Triune, that in Christ we have a full and final revelation of God as He is.

The economic view, then, is to be rejected, and we must hold firmly to the conviction that the Triunity of God is immanent in His nature. It will now be convenient to proceed by taking up a position towards the main objections to a doctrine of this kind.

One frequent objection is, that it is an effort to gain a new and deeper insight into the nature of God by abstracting from His relation to man and the world. But the effort cannot succeed, for God *is* in fact in such a relation, and to disregard it is to see Him " precisely as He is not, either in Himself or otherwise ".[49] In any case the New Testament revelation bears directly and solely on God's redemption of men and His final purpose with them, and to ignore that even for a moment is simply to become indifferent to history and to indulge in speculations for which faith can have neither the slightest justification nor any real concern.

It is clear—particularly from the reference to God's redemption and final purpose as the sum total of revelation— that it is still the positivist objections of the Ritschlians that Mackintosh has in mind. And here, as before, he grants the partial truth of their contentions. Thus he admits at once that to lift the Father-Son relationship to the eternal sphere adds nothing *new* to our knowledge of God, and that Trinitarian thought severed from its roots in the historic revelation at once enters the realm of irresponsible phantasy —as is illustrated by second-century discussions involving the Second Person as the Logos in the sense of a merely philosophical principle of cosmic reason.

But at the same time it is a real question whether the objectors have not been so short-sighted as to fail to see behind the vagaries of early Trinitarian thought its real basis in the determination to assert the full Godhead of Christ. For unless that Godhead be first denied, it is difficult to see how it can be contended that faith is neither concerned with the reality of an immanent Trinity nor justified in attaching importance to it. At any rate, if as Christians we are convinced that Christ is in truth the very Son of God, then we have surely a very real and vital interest in asserting that that relationship did not begin in the first century of our era, but existed from all eternity and before all worlds. For far from being indifferent to history, that is merely an assertion of the true Divinity of the historic Redeemer—" an attempt to set forth the absolute background of reality from which history derives its significance, and to exhibit the gift of Christ as flowing from the life of God ".[50]

The *life* of God—that is also supremely important in this connection. For what real meaning can be given to it apart from an immanent Trinity? * Yet it is a simple fact of experience that only the *living* God, and not a solitary monad or any of the creations of speculative philosophy, can be a real object of worship or fully satisfy the souls of men. And thus, since it is impossible to see how we can speak in a real sense of the living God apart from " active distinctions essential to His being ",[51] the very champions of experience are themselves flying in its face when they deny the importance of such distinctions.

Here, however, we must be careful to distance ourselves from certain modern writers who, regarding the doctrine of the Trinity as merely an attempt to describe in broken human terms the unfathomably rich and manifold nature of

* It is perhaps significant, although Mackintosh does not note the point, that all Ritschl makes of the phrase " the living God " is, that it means He is " opposed to nature " as " the spiritual, self-determining Will, which is supreme over its ends and its creatures, and consequently must be distinguished from them all " (*Rechtfert. u. Versöhn.* [4], iii, 471).

God, seek to commend it to the modern mind by pointing to the fact that life, as it rises in the scale of being, exhibits ever greater variety in ever more perfect unity—some even going on to suggest that in the complete unity of the perfect being of God there may be not only three distinct factors, but also others unknown to us. That such a view reflects imposing truths cannot be gainsayed, and we certainly " have a right to ask whether Deity can be an eternal life or can be thought as such, except on terms implying a varied wealth of inner content ".[52] But if we set out from Christ, and not from the observation of life in general, we cannot rest there : " What the revelation mediated in history denotes is no mere vague wealth of Divine existence, but eternal Fatherhood, eternal Sonship, moving within the eternal life of Spirit ".[53] And if we are convinced that that is a full and final revelation we shall have no interest in affirming the possibility of a future disclosure of yet more similar distinctions.

A second objection is aimed against the frequent argument that the knowledge and love of God, to be superior to time, must have an eternal object and that only in an immanent Trinity can that be found. Against this it is argued that the required object is simply the universe as a whole, while in any case the argument can prove no more than a duality in God.

The second part of this objection is perfectly true : there is, in fact, no speculative argument which can suggest " a third Divine distinction which is either ' Holy ' or ' Spirit ' "[54]— surely a salutary reminder that our starting-point is not philosophic thought but history and life. But the first half cannot be upheld. For the objectors are bound to admit that the physical universe cannot properly be loved at all, far less reciprocate love, while men at least are not eternal, but only recently began to be ; and though men may not be the only rational creatures, they are the only ones we know, so that it is simply arguing from ignorance to urge that there are others who are eternal.

If, however, the objection itself can thus be set aside, the argument it attacks is one which may be not altogether unfruitful in helping our minds to apprehend the distinctions faith asserts. For if God is eternal Fatherly Love, it is not unreasonable that that Love should have an equally eternal Object ; but if that is so, the Object can only be in God Himself, distinct as Object from Subject yet one as equally Divine. And thus the conviction that Fatherhood and Sonship " symbolise vital distinctions apart from which Godhead cannot be ",[55] is one in which reason may find its own. Nor is this all, but it is here, too, that the meaning of creation may become visible to our minds : for it is in the eternal love moving between Father and Son that the impulse to create potential sons has its rise, and the relations of God and man begin to be luminous only in the light of this interior Divine life. Again, however, Mackintosh seems to hear positivist murmurings in the gallery. And so it is emphasised once more that such reflections cannot be summarily dismissed as metaphysics—not, at least, until it is " proved that metaphysics, in this connection, is anything more than a name for persistent thinking ".[56] For, as has repeatedly been said, we are not here constructing a doctrine of the Trinity from rational presuppositions, but only seeking, as far as may be, to make luminous to the mind a Divinely-evoked " initial certitude of faith which no subsequent speculative procedure can impair ".[57]

A third, and final, objection is, that if in view of the Divine love we speak of eternal relations between Father, Son and Spirit, that amounts to asserting the existence of three Gods ; and at least such a " social " conception of God cannot properly be called orthodox.

Theology, it is true, has usually preferred to follow in one form or another the famous Trinitarian analogies of Augustine—"memory, understanding and will", or " the mind, self-knowledge and self-love "—arguing that these different aspects of the one human being are, like the Persons of the Trinity, each equal to each of the others and to the whole. It is clear that arguments which start from a single human self-consciousness can never lead to tritheism. But it is difficult to see what connection "understanding" or "self-knowledge" can have with the eternal Son who lived on earth as our Redeemer, and we shall do well to reject such analogies as compromising the basis of Trinitarian thought in historic revelation and belonging to realms "quite un-related, so far as can be seen, to the historic antecedents by which the doctrine must be judged and sanctioned ".[58] * On the other hand, the objectors have certainly a very strong position in so far as those whose doctrine is inspired by the analogy of love will be hard put to it not to compromise the unity of God.

Two things, however, must here be emphasised. Firstly, in speaking of God's love as between Divine *Persons*, we do not mean Personalities in the modern sense. That must indeed mean tritheism, but it is a sense in which the word Person in Trinitarian thought neither is nor ever has been employed: it is used simply for lack of better—"*non ut diceretur sed ne taceretur*", as Augustine put it [59]—to denote a mode of being which is the ground of real distinction of function, but not of separate conscious individuality or " essence ". And in the second place, if it is *God's* love we are speaking of, then it need not imply mutually exclusive personalities just because *in us* that is an essential condition of love. Perhaps it may also be helpful here to point to the simple fact that even among men love at its highest partially transcends individual differences and merges them in a cer-tain unity. For although we cannot conceive this as ever becoming a unity in which the real distinction between love's subject and its object is not one of separate individuality

* Elsewhere the ethnic analogies unearthed by comparative religion are likewise dismissed : they have nothing in common with the Triune God of faith but the number three, for " when not simply representative of natural processes personified, they spring out of philosophic theory manipulating abstract ideas " (*Originality of the Christian Message*, p. 31).

(just as we cannot even conceive " the vital unity of movement or of life "), yet might we not perhaps (as Bergson has
contended in this other case) somehow feel it so intuitively,
and thus " envisage faintly, under the form of idealised
human relationships " [60] something of the distinction without
division in God which faith asserts? * It is true that we can

---

* One is conscious of some difficulty here. It would seem that
Mackintosh wished to disown the familiar analogy of lover, beloved, and
love, along with the rest, first dismissing its third element as valueless
and then pointing to the tritheistic tendency of the doctrine it inspires.
And it must surely kill any possibility of such an analogy when he urges
that the Divine Persons are not Personalities, that God's love is not
subject to the conditions essential to ours, and (as he now goes on) that
this cannot possibly be apprehended either by thought or by feeling—
according to the (later) Lecture Synopsis, it cannot even be *imagined*—
but is known only of faith. In the midst of this, however, comes the
perplexing suggestion that the unity at least of Father and Son may be
faintly similar to an intuitively perceived ideal form of the comparative
unity of human beings in love—which makes it look for a moment as
if the ghost of the analogy has returned after all. Yet it is clear that,
whatever Mackintosh has in mind, it can hardly be an analogy of being.
For he always regarded the suggestion that human persons could
ever be one personal being as utterly absurd (*cf.* esp. *Aspects of Christian
Belief*, p. 43, *Apprehension of God*, pp. 195 f.) ; but in that case the ideal
unity, however it is to be apprehended, can only be some kind of perfect
harmony between distinct beings and it is difficult to see what analogy
that offers to the unity of " active distinctions " within the single being
of God. One feels, especially in view of the number of peradventures
and question-marks, that the suggestion is hardly meant to be taken at its
face value, but is rather made only (in Augustine's phrase) " for the sake
of not saying nothing ". Yet it is worth going on to notice a truth which
may be reflected here :—If by " idealised human relationships " we may
understand these relationships in their perfect form as revealed in Christ,
then an analogy does exist : the relationship of Father and Son is
indeed analogous to that of man and woman (as also, to take other examples, of soul and body, Christ and His Church, God and man).
It is an anology, however, not of *being*, but of *relation*—indeed, it is
precisely because they are between beings of such a totally different kind
that the relationships are only analogous (*i.e.* at once similar and completely different), not just the same. And there must never be any
suggestion that the relation of Father and Son, as revealed, can be seen
to be analogous to a human relation whose nature we already knew or
guessed : rather it is only in the light of that revelation that we can
know the true relation of man and woman at all.

never apprehend such a thing: it is a mystery which must elude us to the end, for we cannot project ourselves by thought or feeling into the transcendent being of God in order to view it from within. But if we will only refrain from pressing upon God's life the particularity of our own, such a mystery must always be less of a problem than the concept of a bare, unethical monad, capable of neither life nor love, and complete in loneliness.

Yet in the end, whatever avenues of speculation we may explore, and whatever the difficulties and dangers with which they are beset, " it is in the unity of God as known in Christ that our minds come finally to rest ".[61] For it is with the Divine nature as thus known that the doctrine of the Trinity is all along concerned, never with a problem of " ontology mixed with arithmetic ":[62] it is from God's saving revelation of Himself in history that it sets out, and it can only circle round and return to it again at last. " God as Holy Love we name the Father; this same eternal God, as making the sacrifice of love and appearing in one finite spirit for our redemption, we name the Son; God filling as new life the hearts to which His Son has become a revelation, we name the Spirit "; and in making this confession we bow in humble and adoring faith before the wonder and glory of the one God who " is never alone, but always the Father towards whom the Son has ever been looking in the Spirit of eternal love ".[63]

2. THE TRANSITIONAL CHARACTER OF THE DOCTRINE

The strange thing about this at first sight clear and unified doctrine of God is, that on a closer study it is seen to reflect two quite different lines of thought. It is well to say " reflect " rather than " reveal ", for neither is defined with perfect clarity. Indeed (in keeping with what we have said of the fluid character of Mackintosh's thought) it is rather like a reflection in moving water: two lines, which in fact have little in common, are here seen crossing and recrossing in such a way that it is not always easy to say precisely on which the train of thought is actually moving. Yet the picture is not distorted beyond recognition, and we are given a fair idea as to what, if it finally clarified, we should then see.

(a) *The Ritschlian Line of Thought.* On the one hand there is much of a decidedly Ritschlian character. True, if we confine our attention to Ritschl there is not such a great deal we can bring under this head. Completely in character, of course, are the opening objections to the traditional doctrine (though Ritschl was for rejecting the term absolute altogether), the reference to the Deistic and Pantheistic tendencies of its Aristotelian presuppositions, and the rejection of all mechanical ideas of grace, be they Roman, mystic or rationalist. Then there are other points at which, if in one way or another slightly removed from Ritschl, Mackintosh still stands in his immediate neighbourhood. Thus he objects to all theories of God's righteousness which are based on the analogy of an earthly state and would set it in opposition to His mercy; yet he also insists that the two attributes, if inseparable, are not identical, and that judgment has a real place. Likewise, he agrees that love must be the very heart of the Christian conception of God, but with the reservation that it cannot be regarded as His essence. Or again, he associated the Divine sovereignty directly with the purpose to found the Kingdom, from which he undertakes to derive the sovereign attributes; yet the very suddenness with which the concept of the Kingdom appears, and the somewhat loose relation in which even these attributes are after all set to it, are in marked contrast to its place in Ritschl's thought as (in effect if not altogether in intention) the very centre round which all else revolves. And if both writers seem to have shared the admiration which all the nineteenth-century champions of the Divine personality had for Lotze's argument, Mackintosh at least does not give it the same centrality, but assigns it to a few paragraphs in the course of what he clearly regarded as a very secondary part of the discussion. Finally, somewhat further off from Ritschl, yet still traceable to his influence in respect of its indebtedness to a debate occasioned by him, is the discussion of holiness in its relation to love.

That, however, is about all we can say from the point of view of Ritschl's own work, and if that were all, we might perhaps hesitate to speak of a very pronounced Ritschlian strain in Mackintosh's doctrine. But if we take into consideration also the teaching of Kaftan,[64] the matter begins to assume a different complexion. For at the very start the definition of God at once recalls Kaftan, and in the course of its exposition there are striking parallels, one or two of which we have already noted.

Kaftan begins with a similar, if more plaintive, criticism of the lamentable attempts of traditional theology to combine the Christian conception of God with the Absolute of ancient philosophy, followed by the same assertion that theology must construct its doctrine solely by reference to the scriptural revelation. And he likewise insists that in doing so we can add no new truth, but simply expound "according to faith's own inner logic" the knowledge believers already have, first of the being of God and then of His attributes as merely "a more precise definition of His being".[65] The first assertion of faith is, that God is the Absolute, in the sense of "the highest Good, above which there is none, and the highest Power, which prevails immutably—the eternal End and Ground of our existence and of all that is"; [66] and in this sense the use of the term is permissible in theology—but *only* as "the framework of the knowledge of God in all spiritual religions",[67] whose content can be derived solely from the concept of God held by the religion in question, *i.e.* in our case from the scriptural revelation. From that revelation we learn that God is "supramundane (*überweltlich*) personal Spirit" and that His "basic attributes are Love, Holiness and Omnipotence".[68]

The *Personality* of God is not made known to us by any speculative reflections, or on the ground of the analogy of our own life (though such analogy must inevitably be an element of our *thought* of God, and may even form its starting-point). Rather, we learn of it through the practical experience of personal fellowship with Him and the assurance therein given that this fellowship is to be perfected through the perfecting of personal character in the Kingdom which is our destiny. That He is "supramundane" means that He is inwardly independent of all spatial and temporal limitations—He is the *heavenly* Father, "exalted above the spatial world", and the *eternal* God, "in the sense that He stands above time, true to Himself and changeless in His purposes" [69]—and this not just as governing space and time, but as "in His inmost being removed (*entnommen*) from them"; [70] or, more precisely, it means that His being and life are completely "unentangled" (*unverworren*) in those of the world (by which is very plainly meant the *material* world). And our knowledge of this is similarly given in the conviction that our life in His Kingdom, of which we even now have a foretaste, is "supramundane" in this sense. But if it is thus never by speculation that our knowledge of these facts is reached, it has been well demonstrated by Ritschl's argument for the personality of God that subsequent reflection points the same way ; and although such argument can never *prove* the truth of faith's convictions, it has nevertheless a real defensive value against philosophical objections.

God's *Love* is likewise known in the experience of communion with Him, in which He imparts to us His Spirit and Life. Since it consists in self-impartation, it cannot be regarded as His essence, but presupposes the spiritual personality in the bestowal of which He proves His love—else we should have an endless circle: love is self-bestowal and the self thus bestowed is love. God, then, is in essence personal Spirit, whose characteristic mark or attribute is love ; yet what can and, for the sake of its further implications, must here be affirmed is only a logical priority, for the two —personality and love—are, in fact, inseparable, and form together the very heart of the Christian conception of God. From the analogy of human love we learn that God's love (unlike His goodness) is directed not on all creatures, but only on personal beings, *i.e.* men ; that it is constant and unchanging ; and that, since even the purest love, if totally disinterested, would be love no longer, it must find in its objects the satisfaction of its own interest (though that is not to make God dependent on the creation, for His love rests always on the self-determination of His own free will). Again, as the self-bestowal of a personal Spirit who is completely free from the material world, it has as its end perfect fellowship with similarly free personal spirits. But since we are clearly not independent of the world, it is simply an inner necessity of the case that the Divine love should *train* us to such fully independent personal character ; and since that can only be done through moral discipline—the mortification of the flesh and the love of the brethren—we recognise it as a *holy* love. Finally, in the presence of the sinful this love takes the form of longsuffering, faithfulness, mercy, grace : grace, indeed, is but a more precise term for a love which is directed on the unworthy and undeserving, and which not even their recalcitrance can change.

In recognising that, as we have just seen, the necessity of moral discipline is grounded in the very being of God, we become aware that He is a *Holy* God. Holiness, however, is not to be understood in its Old Testament sense, but means simply absolute goodness or moral perfection, and is used in preference to any other term because it well denotes precisely these qualities as they are in the God who is completely exalted over the (material) world. From the knowledge of God's holiness, in turn, comes that of His *Righteousness*. And we are later told [71] that this attribute, in virtue of which He creates and maintains the moral order of the universe, issues inevitably in the punishment of evil wherever it appears—a fact which is simply due to God's own holiness, and is the foundation of all human penal law.* Yet our human views of this penal aspect must vary according to our inner relation to God ; and thus, while His enemies can see it only as His judgment upon them, to the eye of Christian faith it is but the disciplinary action of His love.

Omnipotence is the third basic attribute ; and if we rightly subordinate it to holy love, it is nevertheless equally essential to the full Christian conception of God.† Like holy love, it is the attribute of a personal Spirit, and it therefore cannot mean in any vague or physical sense that God can do all He wills. For faith knows very well the direction and content of His will, and thus gives to that otherwise vague definition the concrete meaning that as sovereign Lord of the universe He has full and complete control of all means to the realisation of His purpose of holy love. In this conviction is contained again the further certainty that He is *Omniscient*, as perfectly aware of all the circumstances in which He acts, *Omnipresent* in the sense that He is personally present in all He does, and *All-wise* as invariably choosing the appropriate means to His end. But if we would here guard ourselves from the error and vanity of idle speculation on the relations of Spirit and Nature, we must never lose sight of the facts that all these are the attributes of a personal Will, and that while we can be certain of their reality, we cannot and need not have any clear knowledge of their working in detail.

Such, briefly, is Kaftan's doctrine of God ; and the similarities with Mackintosh's are too obvious to call for further mention. But the question which here arises is, what is particularly *Divine* about such a God? This exalted Being, not indeed fully comprehensible, yet so very analogous

---

* *Cf.* p. 130, *supra.*   † *Cf.* p. 138, *supra.*

to ourselves—is He not perhaps too human to be Divine? For if He is merely a personal Spirit, free from the irksome limits of space and time and endowed with the most perfect conceivable form of omnipotent holy love, then is He not after all a Being we can recognise only too well as a perfected version of ourselves, or (as Feuerbach liked to have it) God made in the image of man, the human spirit as it longs to be? It is, of course, insisted that it is only by revelation that we can know Him and learn how like ourselves He is. Yet one may still ask whether " revelation " has not perhaps been used as a sort of imposing clothes-line on which to hang well-worn themes carefully patched with ethical silk ; and how far such a Being, even if " revealed ", is really other than the old arch-enemy, the " magnified non-natural man ".

If, again, love is not God's essential nature, but the active attribute of a spiritual Personality which stands behind it, is He not after all only a motionless Spirit, an abstract philosophical idea? Indeed, if He loves, not for loving's sake, but to fulfil a higher interest by imparting to us our highest ethical Good, or Himself as that Good—if, to put it bluntly, His chief end, to attain which He wields all things in His sovereign power, is our release from the trials of the flesh and the limitations of temporal life—then can even the adroitest mental acrobatics dispose of the old gibe that He is simply the projection of our desires (this time our ethical desires) upon the clouds?

Or yet again, is this " supramundane " Spirit, so carefully purged of all that can be called Nature, really to be equated with God the Father almighty, Creator of heaven and earth? Is it not rather only one more philosophical conception of the heaven He created—the spiritual element to which philosophers for centuries have ascribed the dominance over the material element, and a highly ethicised form of the Absolute Spirit of Hegel himself ? One wonders what has become of the Divine aseity which orthodoxy, for all its shortcomings, never lost from sight ; and whether, if the older theology obscured God's love in its anxiety to throw His absoluteness into sharpest relief, the latter has not simply reversed the error, focusing upon the immediate foreground, and leaving the picture more blurred than before.

These are questions to which there is really no answer in Ritschl and Kaftan ; and it cannot be denied that they also arise on occasion where Mackintosh's doctrine appears to reflect their thought. Yet it must surely be equally obvious that " reflection " is all we can speak of here, and that his presentation as a whole is so much less vulnerable at these vital points as to cast considerable doubt on the extent of any thoroughgoing agreement with theirs.

Thus if it be asked whether he considered the personal being of God to be analogous to ours, we seem to have at least one definite statement: " Let the line of ethical self-hood on which we are placed be prolonged, and at some incalculably higher point we must think the selfhood of God as existing with ineffable perfectness ".[72] * And in view of this we may incline to regard more doubtful cases, such as the frequent remark that our terms must have an " expanded " sense, as but dimmer reflections of the same idea.

Yet we can hardly fail to notice that very many of these cases *are* doubtful and in themselves *could* have another meaning, whereas the example cited is one of a very few unambiguous cases (all occurring in somewhat philosophical contexts) and belongs to a part of the discussion explicitly announced as secondary. Not only so, but it is clear that, whatever his thought on the subject, Mackintosh certainly does not make so much of such analogies as Kaftan. Rather, the persistently recurring theme is, that the qualities which in their unity make up God's personal being are not only unlike what they are in us, but such as we could not even imagine. Thus we do not have to look far before the question arises whether it is with a completely representative statement that we have here to do.

* *Cf.* p. 125, *supra.*

Or again, like Kaftan, and likewise on a human analogy, he argues that love is not the essence of God but His primary attribute.* And in view of this we may perhaps wonder if, in spite of all assurances that revelation alone must be our guide, the later argument† which sees in the Divine love the ground of our creation and of God's relation to us is after all based on a similar general analogy, as from its phrasing it could conceivably be and as the argument of Kaftan it recalls expressly is ; and whether the undefined " blessedness of His own life " which God in love confers upon His created children is also to be understood in Kaftan's sense.

Only, if the argument in Kaftan's case is not likely to occasion surprise, we certainly raise an eyebrow on finding it in Mackintosh: *this* is something we were hardly led to expect, and as we read on we find nothing to mitigate the sharpness of our feeling that it is somehow out of place. Elsewhere we were always given to understand that the contrary is the case: thus, to take only three clear examples, it was laid down but a few pages previously that holiness and love are " intrinsically constitutive " of God,[73] while we read in a much earlier work of " the holy love which makes His essence ",[74] and in an almost contemporary one that " His very nature is sacrificial love ".[75] Again, an argument so clearly based on our experience of human love accords very ill with the repeated statement on succeeding pages that our conceptions of the Divine love must not be taken from such experience. And yet again, if even God's love presupposes personality because " it takes two to love and to be loved ", must not Father and Son be two Personalities before there can be love between them? Or if, as we are told in this connection,[76] the demand of " our divisive and spatialised logic " that it should be so does not alter the fact that it is not, must the " logical priority " demanded here be decisive? Nor is even this all: for not only does the argument thus appear inconsistent with the rest of Mackintosh's thought, but it

* *Cf.* p. 133, *supra.*   † *Cf.* pp. 135 ff., *supra.*

is also difficult to see what purpose it serves. With Kaftan it was otherwise: he used it as the basis for certain corrections of Ritschl's teaching as to the source of our knowledge of God's love and the nature of His Kingdom, which need not detain us here.[77] But Mackintosh draws no conclusions from it, and indeed never refers to it again: it stands only to puzzle the reader and to raise the question whether it truly represents his position and calls for the reinterpretation of other statements, or whether the truth is rather that somehow or other a red herring has here been drawn across the track.

Often enough, too, he speaks of God as a transcendent Spirit, and no doubt most of what he says could be taken without much difficulty in Kaftan's sense. Yet only his seeming general bias in Kaftan's direction could incline us to do so. For his language in itself is not conclusive: there is neither a single statement on the spiritual being of God which could be referred without hesitation simply to pure, incorporeal Spirit as opposed to Nature, nor any on His transcendence which must inevitably put in place of the Divine aseity what is ultimately only the transcendence of the spiritual over the material world. Thus here above all, the question of agreement with Kaftan remains open from the start.

All along the line, then, there is room for considerable doubt as to how far he really saw eye to eye with Kaftan at all. That is the very least we can say. But in fact we can say a great deal more. For the truth of the matter is, that a closer examination seems to indicate that, in spite of the frequent use of arguments strikingly similar to Kaftan's and sometimes even identical with them, he was in actual fact on another and very different track, whose nature was becoming clearer as time went on and which was to lead him in the end to a very definitely non-Ritschlian position.

(b) *The Biblical Line of Thought.* Mackintosh begins his real argument for the personality of God by saying that it is immediately implied in faith's fundamental conviction of redemption into fellowship with Him in Christ. And if there is so far little apparent difference from Kaftan, yet we find in the sequel * an identification of the "personal" God with the "living" God of the Bible, which must ultimately set the two writers poles apart.

True, the definition given is not in itself altogether promising. An "infinitely rich and mobile spiritual form of being that inwardly enjoys its own blessedness and ponders its own vast purpose, and, outwardly, reacts with sensitive awareness on human life in mercy and judgment" *could* easily enough be simply a perfected version of the human spirit, all too thinkable without any particular revelation and all too clearly analogous to ourselves. Again, since (although "infinitely mobile") it is not explicitly said to act in any other sense than that it reacts on men, it *could* be the itself motionless Absolute Spirit of a dozen faiths and philosophies as much as the living God of the Bible; while if the mainspring of its action is "sensitive awareness" of the moral struggles of mankind, it could very well be only a postulate of our own moral experience. And since there is no express indication that it has also a Nature of its own and is not "pure" Spirit as opposed to Nature, it *could* be simply identical with the higher spiritual element of the universe, or Spirit as we commonly think of it—endowed this time with a highly ethical character, yet still incapable of real existence in its own right since higher and lower, Spirit and Nature, are essentially related and have only abstract existence in themselves. Yet all this, plausible as it may be, would surely be a complete misinterpretation. For there are certainly hints—and often more than hints—of something very different.

Having laid down that the "personal" God is merely another name for the "living" God, Mackintosh goes on at once to say that it is in His mighty works, and as the Doer of them, that He is known to be such. Here we may pause for a moment to recall the fundamental tenet that God as

* *Cf.* pp. 126 f., *supra.*

revealed is God as He is in Himself, which in this context must mean that, although He certainly exists not only in His works but also in Himself apart altogether from His relation to the world, yet if He is there revealed as One who *acts,* then in Himself also He is active. In other words, if revelation is our guide, then it is impossible to come above or behind the active God to an inactive God: in Him being and doing are one, and He is active not just sometimes or accidentally, but essentially and always. We may remember that this is no mere general activity, but that of a self-conscious and self-impelled life which is uniquely—or, as it is once put,[78] "most absolutely and incommunicably "— God's own. If we now read on, we find that it is as our Father that the living God is made known, through the revelation in Christ as made luminous by the Spirit—which may well recall the original proviso that it is only in the light of the doctrine of the Trinity that the term personality as applied to God can receive its full interpretation. And if we follow these pointers to the doctrine in question, we come on a fact which is the most profoundly significant of all because, once it is brought out, it provides the key to the whole: it is *only* as essentially Triune that He is the living (personal) God at all.*

This at once determines the direction of our next step. For the self-impelled activity of the Triune Divine life is defined here as a very particular one: it is a life, Mackintosh tells us, of "neither loveless thought, nor abstract thought, nor mere boundless energy ",[79] but of eternal love moving between the Father and the Son in the Spirit. But if that is so, then there can surely be no talk of personality resting, as it were, behind an active attribute of love: if the personal God is the living God and as such also the loving God, then love must belong to His essence as much as personality and life. He is not a static something which, when He acts, acts lovingly, but the living Trinity, always and essentially active, always and essentially

* *Cf.* p. 148, *supra.*

loving; and if His love is self-bestowal, yet the Self thus bestowed cannot be abstract Personality or morally perfect Spirit or anything else but Father, Son and Holy Ghost in eternal fellowship of love. In a word, love *is* God's essence— not in the abstract and general sense in which Ritschl affirmed and Kaftan denied it, but in the concrete and very particular sense that the living Triune God is revealed in Jesus Christ as One whose essence it is to love. This, indeed, is not made explicitly plain; yet it seems to be plainly enough implied. And here, surely, the repeated references to love as God's essence may come to their own. For it is surely better to read them in this light, in which they can be given their full value, than to take them as loose or exagger- ated statements to be revised in the light of an argument which appears once only and which, we have seen, is suspect not only because it disagrees with them, but on other counts as well.

But if love is God's essence in this sense, then just as it is impossible to reach an inactive God beyond or above the active God, so also we cannot come beyond or above His loving to a higher Good which is other than His love. In that case the undefined blessedness of God's own life must be taken to be, not that of moral perfection and freedom from the world, but simply that of the loving fellowship which as Triune He has in Himself. And its communication to us must mean our inclusion in that fellowship, not for the sake of any higher end (since there can be none) but simply for its own sake. If thereby God's glory is manifested and our salvation secured, His Kingdom established and our broken relationships restored, yet it is not because He realises these ends or for the sake of their realisation that He loves: it is because He loves that He realises them. But He loves also even before He realises them, and He loves eternally in Him- self apart from the created world altogether: He loves simply for loving's sake and because it is His essence to do so.

Again, this is not made explicit, yet seems to be clearly

enough implied. It *is* made plain, at any rate, that it is in the eternal love of the Father to the Son—it would scarcely be an unfair interpretation to say, in its overflow—that the creation has its ground, and in its light that the relations of God and man are to be understood.[80] So that although Mackintosh could speak of these things elsewhere in a manner reminiscent of Kaftan, we may nevertheless be well justified in seeing the relation to Kaftan as little more than formal and holding that it is still the revealed love of the Triune God and not love in general that he has in mind ; and it will then not be unreasonable to see against the same background the references in the sequel to God's blessedness and His communication of it to us.   Moreover, we may recall in this context the repeated insistence on the point that what the Christian seeks, and what is conferred on him in Christ, is fellowship with God, not for the sake of any other end—not even the highest moral ends—but in and for itself ; while far from ever suggesting that God's love is to be inferred from benefits conferred or ends realised, Mackintosh tells us* that He would still be the loving God had He never created the world at all (*i.e.* apart from all such ends and benefits), and that it is His love which is the guarantee of all the blessings we enjoy and because He has given Himself to us in Christ that He will give all else besides.   In view of all this we shall surely not be far wrong in believing that for Him God's blessedness is simply that of His love ; and that just as he held that this love, as peculiarly *God's* love, is its own ground, freely directed on the ungodly and itself creating the worth it cannot presuppose, so also he was aware that it is its own end, including all other ends in itself.

But now, further, this Triune God, essentially active and essentially loving, is also transcendent, " holy ", sublime. And if it be asked what precisely is meant by these terms, it soon appears that there is much more in them than meets the eye. To begin with, they are applied to a spiritual Being

* *Cf.* pp. 134 ff., *supra*.

who appears to be more than just Spirit as distinct from Nature. God, Mackintosh tells us, is the God of the *whole* man ; and he protests frequently against the failure of so much theological thought to recognise that body and soul are one indissoluble person and in their unity " make up the world which God has created and will redeem ".[81] Elsewhere he is at pains to emphasise the biblical writers' unique and unwavering hostility towards abstraction, as witnessed by " their profound sense of the vital conjunction and co-operation of nature and spirit "; [82] while he calls attention to the fact that the doctrine of the Trinity is grounded upon the same insight as gave rise to the Johannine protest against the " hyperspiritualising tendency "—the insight, namely, that in Jesus Christ we have to do, not with some kind of Spirit or Aeon but with very God incarnate.[83] And perhaps most significant of all, in the discussion of the biblical conception of God which immediately precedes his own reconstruction, he insists that Scripture's many ascriptions to Him of passions and bodily parts are not to be explained away at the behest of any metaphysic, but are " of vital importance " for the thought of a living God who enters into intimate relations with men.*

All this makes it most unlikely that he thought of God as " pure " Spirit, which he saw to be nothing but an abstract idea and therefore unable to love, create, redeem, sanctify or act in any sense at all. We shall surely be nearer the truth if we hold that in asserting that God is Spirit, he was still

* *Apprehension of God*, p. 111. He adds, " What the conception of God may become when once the life-blood of anthropomorphism has been drained out, we see in the God of Mohammed . . . ' like the desert, monotonous and barren, an unfigured surface, an unresponsive immensity ' ". And he speaks later (p. 114) of the allegorisation of anthropomorphisms in Hellenistic Judaism as resulting inevitably in loss of the concreteness and vitality of the prophetic vision of God, in a sense of the suspension of living revelation, and in " a view of the Divine nature characterised by excessive blankness and (as it were) thinness of internal life, remotely supreme, and severed from the world by a wide gulf ".

thinking of the God who as Father, Son and Holy Ghost
has *also* a " Nature " of His own,* but who is rightly called
Spirit because His Nature is but the medium of His Spirit's
action, because His acts have not the contingent and
mechanical quality of natural events but are the acts of a
free self-conscious Spirit—in a word, because He is a Person,
in whom the unity of Spirit and Nature is not one of equality,
but one of irreversible supremacy and subservience. If this
is the interpretation which is to be put on Mackintosh's
assertions that God is Spirit—and at the very least it is one
to which he leaves the door wide open—then they are surely
unexceptionable. This God, however, is One whose Spirit
must be as different from Spirit in general as His Nature is
from Nature as we know it ; so that His " transcendent
otherness " must hold good of His relation not only to the
natural world but to the spiritual as well. And this, too,
Mackintosh apparently knew, for he writes that God " ineffably transcends both earth and heaven ", in a context in
which it is clear that " heaven " means the world-soul or the
spiritual world.†

   * Although careful to point out that Fatherhood and Sonship are
symbols, he is nevertheless equally emphatic that they are not *mere*
symbols from which a higher philosophy will release us, but have a real
meaning.   Nor was it by the simple expedient of thinking away their
natural associations that he sought that meaning (what real meaning
could be attached to them on such terms, or what would such a process
of abstraction be but obedience to the dictates of a spiritualistic philosophy ?) but by relation to the revelation in Jesus Christ. And if
according to that revelation they have a real meaning which they alone
can express, must that not be because there is something in the God
there revealed which, though not, of course, like Nature as we know it,
nevertheless cannot be described except in natural terms ? For the
same reason we are also at liberty to speak (as Mackintosh freely did)
of the face of God, His eyes and ears, His arms, hands, feet, His right
hand, etc. For these, too, surely have their place and have a real
meaning which cannot be otherwise expressed and is not to be arbitrarily
interpreted in terms of pure, abstract Spirit.
   † *Cf.* p. 122, *supra*. Here is an excellent example of a statement
which has a formal parallel in Kaftan, but a very different meaning.
Kaftan, too, could speak of God as transcending both earth and heaven

So far so good. Yet if the most we can say of God is, that He is " transcendently other " than the world (even including the spiritual world), then despite our best endeavour we shall inevitably find ourselves using language which is more properly applicable to a philosophic Absolute than to the God of the Bible—and which ultimately implies, either that the world and its history are unreal (since God, the real, is what is other than the world), or that God is not Absolute after all (since the world, too, is real and is necessary to Him at least in so far as it is the " other " which it is His essence to transcend). Mackintosh was well on his guard against the former error, and perhaps for that very reason sometimes came dangerously near the other. But for the most part he just managed to steer clear of it also. Thus when he speaks of the creation of the world as necessary to God and sub-jecting Him to conditions, he is careful to add that the necessity is grounded in His own will and the conditions " freely chosen ". Or when he goes on to say that in creating it God does " what from our human standpoint we have no option but to describe as taking risks, for He ventures the possibility that men may refuse the love He seeks ",[84] then we must surely allow for a strong emphasis of the spoken word on the phrase " from our human standpoint " ; for he was well enough aware, too, that the love which is omnipo-tent to create is omnipotent also to redeem, and that in its designs there can be no breakdown. Indeed, his normal practice is to avoid both errors by simply bringing the two points of view together, setting the absoluteness of God and the reality of the world, the freedom of the creature and the omnipotence of grace side by side as an " antinomy " which reason cannot penetrate and only faith can resolve.

If we would account for the felicity with which he so often keeps his equilibrium, perhaps we shall not be far

—but with the significant addition, " if heaven is conceived as a place in space " (*Dogmatik*[6], p. 192). That He also transcends the whole spiritual world is a fact Kaftan never makes clear.

wrong in tracing it to a conception of the transcendent "holiness" of God by which is meant His true Divinity or Aseity, and not just His otherness in relation to the world. In other words, he seems to have realised that the Triune God of the Bible is *a se*, existing absolutely in His own right. He does not rise from non-existence to existence or even develop out of Himself, and there is no necessity of any kind laid on Him, not even the necessity of being what He is: He simply *is*, possessing in Himself everything which (did He not already have it as Father, Son and Holy Spirit) would be necessary for His existence, and it is nothing else but the mere fact of His existence which puts out of the question any possibility of His non-existence or of His being other than He is. Nor is He bound even by His own absoluteness: He does not *have to* remain absolutely alone in His Triune blessedness, but can create a real world of free creatures over against Himself, can make Himself known to it, can enter into the most intimate relations with it and rule sovereignly over it, can even Himself stoop to become a creature in it, without the slightest detriment either to His own absoluteness or to the freedom of the created world.

Precisely *this* is what is specifically *Divine* about Him. And it is only as we keep our eyes open to this fact of His aseity—to the primary or positive absoluteness, majesty, transcendence, freedom, holiness, otherness (or whatever term we prefer) which He has in Himself—that we can be enabled to use these terms in their secondary and negative sense of His relation to the world without merely echoing the dicta of philosophy and neglecting one side or the other of the antinomies which result for our thought. Against this background, indeed, no such antinomy can be a pure paradox or complete contradiction after all, but rather the holding together of two elements in mutual explanation and control. For then, because this God has in fact created the world and entered into a Covenant with it, we shall be compelled to speak first and foremost of grace, relation, nearness, and add

judgment, absoluteness, sublimity, by way of further definition. We must begin with the Holy One *of Israel*, binding
men to Himself as the heirs of His promise and the people
of His choice, and only then and as such One before whose
unconditional demands and burning wrath they have to
tremble in fear and awe ; we must set out from unique and
most intimate immanence, in order to say that it is one not
of identity, but of the transcendently Other ; we must
remember that it is in the nearness, weakness and humility
of human flesh that we first meet the omnipotent and
sovereign Son of God.

These things cannot, of course, be read directly out of
Mackintosh's work, yet it would seem that what we have
now outlined, or something like it, forms a true part of the
background of his thought. And if it never came to full
expression or attained the prominence one could wish, there
are nevertheless signs enough that he was aware of it. For
he maintains that the Triune God " is *causa sui* " in the
sense that He " owes reality to Himself alone ",[85] insists (as
we have seen) that God would be no more and no less God
whether or not there were a world, and repeatedly denounces
the conception of a God who " once was not ", or develops
in any way, or has to make terms with anything whatsoever
before, above or beyond Himself ; [86] while he urges that for
biblical faith God simply *is*, " not because it happens to be
so, but because it cannot be otherwise ",[87] and that this alone
determines what is possible.[88] Here, too, we may recall the
contention already noticed that the creation is due solely
to the free overflow of His love, together with a whole string
of passages which might be summed up by saying that, once
the world is created, the glory of God's sovereignty can never
be exhausted within it but, precisely because He is *God*, He
not only sustains its continuity and its regularity alike, but
can also both rule the exception and break the rule—all without any surrender of His own absolute sovereignty or any
denial of either freedom or law, but rather in the fullest

confirmation of the reality of all three. And whatever is to be said of the formal arrangement of his topics (to this we must presently recur), he does make plain that when we learn of the repelling nature of the holiness of God it is with an *underlying* conviction of His grace, while his thought of transcendence in fact developed, not in and for itself but in correction of false theories of immanence, and his whole doctrine is one sustained attempt to read the glory of God nowhere else but in the face of the incarnate Christ.

We cannot here go on to trace this line of thought further in detail, yet we can surely see already that all along the line, whatever else is to be said of Him, *this* God could neither be described as analogous to ourselves nor be imagined easily enough apart from revelation altogether as simply our own human ideal. Right at the start it is difficult to see how a Person in whom being and doing are uniquely and essentially one could be analogous to persons in whom they are inevitably two. And it is just as difficult to see how we could ever think of such a Person: for our thought, being can surely only be an abstract state of material or spiritual existence, and activity only a series of changes from one such state to another or of relations between different beings, so that any concrete unity of the two must be simply inconceivable—or if by some feat of thought or feeling we could imagine something of the kind, it could still never be the Person faith adores.* Again, the personal being of God is essentially Triune. As such, Mackintosh insists, it is definitely not analogous to that of man ; and as such, he goes on, it remains

* Mackintosh was inclined to agree with Bergson that movement cannot be thought at all, but only intuitively perceived—although he later felt it impossible to make such a complete separation between conception and intuition. But he makes it plain that, though there may be formal parallels between Bergsonian "intuition" and Christian faith, the two are by no means the same ; and that whatever the unity of movement which is Bergson's God may be, it is not what Christians mean by the living God (*cf. Person of Jesus Christ*, p. 525, *Aspects of Christian Belief*, pp. 252 ff.).

a mystery which must ever baffle thought and feeling alike, and which faith alone can know. When we come to the question of the Divine aseity, it is the same. God is not just a personification of Spirit as we know it, but a Person who exists and lives in His own right with a positively free self-consciousness and self-determination exercised not only within the created universe, but also above and beyond it ; whereas we can never be personal in our own right, but only in union with our Creator,[89] and are self-conscious and self-determined only in the negative sense that within the created world we can assert ourselves in a manner relatively free from external causation or random impulse. In that case it is not easy to see how He can be of one class with ourselves—or even, since the antithesis of the created world between chance and necessity, freedom and law, must surely be ultimate for our thought, how we could conceive Him at all.*

From this point of view many of the apparent analogies between God and man assume a rather different aspect. Now, for example, the repeated contention that self-consciousness and self-determination, activity, knowledge, feeling, will, and whatever else is to be predicated of the personal being of God, are not the same in Him as in man may be taken to mean not that they are nevertheless similar, but that they are totally different ; or the acknowledgment that we are persons only in a secondary sense will mean not that our personality is like God's only less perfect, but that we are persons of a completely different kind. And thus in place of an analogy of being we have simply a formal identity of terms : we have no option but to apply to God the terms used of ourselves (there being no others at our disposal), but they receive from His self-revelation a totally different

* Mackintosh repeatedly insists that reason can never get beyond this antithesis. And once he indicates that if by intellect or "intuition" we would " cast down the idol Determinism ", it can only be to enthrone the goddess Chance ; whereas the God who acts sovereignly not only in both, but also " beneath and over all " can be known only as He reveals Himself to faith (*Aspects of Christian Belief*, p. 255).

content—an "expanded meaning"—which they are not adequate to bear. In other words, God is indeed Triune, personal, loving, holy and all the rest, but (and here we see that the initial warning against a method of general induction* is to be taken in deadly earnest) this statement cannot be reversed: neither the Triune, nor the Personal, nor Love, nor Holiness, nor any combination of them, is in itself God. And if this be the God of whom Mackintosh speaks, then He is indeed no "magnified non-natural man" whose personal being is only too clearly analogous to our own, but One whom we could not even imagine and who in the fullest sense of the term must reveal Himself creatively to faith if we are to know Him at all.

It is the same with the other questions: here they simply cannot arise. To the extent that the outline just given truly represents Mackintosh's real thought of God, it is merely ludicrous to suggest that he has put one more unmoved Mover in the place of the essentially active Triune God of Christian faith. To that extent, too, his God cannot be only the projection upon the clouds of our own desire for a means to attain the blessings for which we long ; for apart from all else, if *the* blessing which God confers, and the one which leads in all others by the hand, is our inclusion in that loving fellowship which as Triune He has in Himself, then it is one we could never desire, for the simple reason that of ourselves we could have no knowledge of it. And if we have correctly interpreted his conception of God as Spirit and of the Divine transcendence, then there can surely be no suggestion that he has after all presented but another form of the Absolute Spirit of philosophy, or was oblivious of the aseity of God.

(c) *Signs of Transition.* This line of thought, which can be traced further without much difficulty through the discussion of the Divine attributes, is in fundamental agreement with Barth.[90] It would, of course, be absurd to attempt to

---

* *Cf.* p. 120, *supra.*

foist on to Mackintosh Barth's doctrine in all its detail. And just as little can we pretend that the line we have now begun to trace is perfectly clear and well-defined: it most obviously is not, but requires considerable care to detect—indeed, at first it may scarcely be detected at all. Yet if we will hear him to the end and then listen once more, then amid all the light and shade, themes and counterthemes of his work we seem to perceive as underlying ground-motif the thought of a God who in essence is Triune and as such at once both loving and *a se*, absolute in a positive sense or (to use Barth's word) free. Sometimes it is clear, sometimes distorted almost beyond recognition, yet always it is there—or if at times it may seem to disappear altogether for a moment, it soon asserts itself again. At the end it is much more noticeable than at the beginning ; and it can hardly be doubted that this is largely due to the influence of Barth, and that, if he had lived to read Barth's doctrine of God, he must have found himself as much in agreement with it as with the *Prolegomena*. It now remains to notice some of the indications of affinity with Barth, and some of the signs of transition from a more predominantly Ritschlian conception of God to a more predominantly biblical one.

It is plainly in the doctrine of the Trinity that the heart of the matter lies. Here, although Mackintosh's doctrine is certainly not worked out with the same tenacity as Barth's,[91] or in anything like the same detail, yet it is in fundamental agreement so far as it goes—particularly in the statement of the problem, the contention against the Ritschlians that no short-sighted concern with the vagaries of the doctrine's history must be allowed to estrange us from its true intention and meaning,[92] and the repudiation of all analogies to the Triune Being of God in the created world—so that it can hardly surprise us to find him finally expressing his highest approval of Barth's presentation.[93]

Yet just as crucial as the doctrine itself is the place given to it ; and here certain signs of development begin to appear.

It is true that Mackintosh did not set it in the fore-front of his work.* He did, however, make plain from the beginning that he had no doubts as to its importance, but wished only to separate the *fact* of an immanent Trinity from the extraordinarily difficult task of its dogmatic presentation. That God *is* essentially Triune, whatever articulated dogma that may imply, he regarded as the most vital and fundamental element of Christian faith and the one which removes it at a bound from every other,[94] while in a sermon preached on the occasion of the 1929 Union, and later published with the title, " What the Church lives to Proclaim ",[95] he urged that the constitutive elements of the Christian message are simply these three: the Fatherhood of God, the Redemption wrought once for all in Christ, and the Power of the Spirit. But such a clear-cut distinction between the fact and its presentation in the doctrine could hardly be maintained in practice ; and thus his own doctrine, although the formal attempt to construct it was left to the end, actually seems to have been the real background of his thought all along. No doubt it was because he was not always fully conscious of this that he could sometimes employ arguments which it must have ruled out of court ; yet always it was there— and there in such a way that, as we have seen, it is only when set in its light that his thought can be properly understood. Presently it forced its way forward with the express indication (of which the earlier Lecture Synopsis shows no trace) that if the discussion of God's Personality is to precede that of His Triunity, then it must be left to further review from that quarter. Later still, we find him beginning an essay on " Things most certainly Believed "[96] with the statement that,

---

* It so happens that it appeared in his first book (*Person of Jesus Christ*)—and that in a form which, except in point of clarity, seemingly underwent little subsequent change. But this, however fortunate from the point of view of anyone reading his works in chronological order, can only be a happy chance after all ; for its place in his Lectures was, after the fashion initiated by Schleiermacher, at the very end of the course.

strictly, one thing only is believed, namely, " God, the Creator, Reconciler and Redeemer ", and that all else can only be an exposition of this—a statement in which we can hardly fail to mark the use of Barth's phrase in place of the usual " Creator, Redeemer and Sanctifier ". And in the end he apparently agreed with Barth's contention that the theologian must take the doctrine of the Trinity as his startingpoint, not as a kind of solemn conclusion to the whole.

Roughly parallel to the movement just described is the one towards final and even more definite clarity on the question of analogy between the being of God and that of man. At the beginning, and for long, Mackintosh seems to have been more or less content to walk in step here with the nineteenth century in general, and perhaps the philosophy of Pringle-Pattison in particular, in reviewing whose Gifford Lectures he noted (at that time apparently with approval) that " the position that man at his noblest is the index of God may be described as Professor Pringle-Pattison's fundamental article of faith " [97]—though it should be added that the issue may have been somewhat confused by the fact that both for him and for his teacher " man at his noblest " means the Man Jesus Christ. Yet the philosophical element in his thought, and with it the unambiguous suggestions of analogy which occur only in its context, receded more and more into the background. This can be most clearly illustrated if we take as an example the Lotzian argument for the Divine person-ality which is one of the chief sources of perplexity here. In the Lecture Synopsis it seems to form an integral part of the argument, but by 1929 (as we have seen) it is relegated very definitely to a subsidiary place, while only two years earlier, in the purely theological context of forgiveness, the philo-sophical objections to the personality of God could be dismissed altogether with the comment: " I can tell from the start that our arguments and counter-arguments will never meet. They move in different planes ; they have no common and decisive major premise ; and unless we both are out for purely logical exercise, the debate might just as well be called off." [98] *

On the other hand, even when following the older tradition, he can never have been wholly content with it. For alongside the clear, but less and less representative, suggestions that there is an analogy, we find right from the beginning not only a number of cases where none *need* be implied, but also increasingly unmistakable indications that none is possible. And his last work puts it beyond all reasonable doubt that in the end it was for this position that he decisively declared. For here there is no suggestion that God

---

* This is surely the better insight, for it is difficult to see how the philosophical argument can prove its point : on the premises—first, that God is absolute or infinite Spirit, a highest Being or highest human Good, analysable and definable by human reason, and second, that " person " properly means " self-conscious and self-determined human Ego "—the objectors are surely irrefutable. In the first place, it cannot then be proved that we are persons in a secondary sense : for by definition we are persons proper. Nor, again, does it help to say that personality is a mark of being at its highest and therefore to be predicated of God in some expanded sense as One who stands at some infinitely higher point on the line we ourselves occupy. For that, intentionally or not, is to accept the premise that God is simply the highest Being we can think ; but to call such a being personal is in fact absurd, because a being we can think remains a being ultimately determined by our thought, not One who in addition to being infinite is also really self-conscious and self-determined and therefore liable to confront us in sovereign ways which we can neither anticipate nor comprehend. And even supposing, thirdly, that by some manner of means it could be proved to the opponent's satisfaction that this Absolute Being is personal, there remains the insuperable difficulty that, whatever it is, it is not the Christian God—of whom, consequently, nothing has been proved after all. If, on the other hand, we are speaking not as philosophers but as theologians, and mean by God the God revealed in Christ, then we shall certainly hold that He is the sovereign, unanticipated God, that He alone is truly and properly personal and we are not, that His Personality is such as our ordinary term is not adequate to describe and such as we can never fully think out or visualise. But then we have abandoned not only the premises of the objectors, but the whole complex of ideas which goes with them ; so that there can scarcely be an argument. For a full discussion of the question *cf.* Barth, *Kirchl. Dogmatik*, II/I, pp. 323-334.

is some highest Being whom we can or could recognise as summing up in Himself all that we value most (and therefore inevitably analogous to ourselves). Rather, he maintains that He is "the sovereign unanticipated God", whose self-revelation shatters our whole sense of values and creates it anew ; he urges against one writer after another the neglect of His "transcendent otherness" ; he speaks with the highest approval of the way Barth "exposes all attempts" to "say 'God' by saying 'Man' in a loud voice" ; and he likewise commends Barth's insistence that to suggest merely some kind of quantitative difference between God and man instead of making an illimitable qualitative one is "in theology the unpardonable sin ".[99]

If we now turn to the argument that love is not God's essence but His primary attribute, it soon appears as if here also it is with a relic of former times that we have to do. For the Lecture Synopses show that at one time Mackintosh undertook to derive *all* the attributes from God's purpose to found His Kingdom ; and although it would seem that even then he had rather lost sight of this by the time he came to the Divine love, and that in any case his thought of the Kingdom had more in common with the first question of the Shorter Catechism than with Ritschl and Kaftan, yet we can see that this is a context in which the repetition of Kaftan's argument would be more in place. But in a doctrine from which the concept of the Kingdom has so far receded as to touch only the fringes of the discussion of the sovereign attributes, such an argument rather resembles some sea-creature left high and dry by the tide as a sign of what once had been.

No doubt the tide has not long turned, and lingering traces of life and attractiveness are still provided by a shallow pool in the form of the deceptive abstract noun "love". For love in an abstract sense can clearly only be the attribute of a personal being ; so that Kaftan's correction of Ritschl here seemed only logical. And on the basis of this correction

Kaftan was able to put the source of our knowledge of God apparently in God Himself rather than in man and the world: for Ritschl, God is a Power who is recognised to be love because He seeks above all things our highest end (unity with our fellows and mastery of the world) and then personal because we know that love acts with the conscious purpose of spiritual and personal will, whereas for Kaftan He is a personal Spirit whose primary attribute is recognised to be love because in self-bestowal He confers our highest Good (a share in His life of moral perfection and freedom from the world). It is therefore not difficult to see why Kaftan's argument against Ritschl should have appealed to Mackintosh for a time: it seemed both more logical and less humanitarian. Yet once he had detected their common error in conceiving love abstractly, and realised—as sooner or later on his own principles he must surely have done—that to say "God is love" means concretely that the Triune God is *loving*, or that He *loves*, then it can only have appeared to him as, so to speak, a pretty creature cut off from the means of life and one feels it must soon have shrivelled up and disappeared.

In the case of the Divine aseity the question of development is a little more difficult—not because there are no signs of change, but because from the beginning it is doubtful just how much Mackintosh's references to God as transcendent Spirit had in common with Kaftan beyond a certain verbal similarity, while on the other hand the movement towards a fully decisive expression of the positive meaning of transcendence was never completed. There are, however, indications that this concept, too, was pushing its way to the fore.

There is, firstly, a notable change in the definition of God. In its earliest form it ran: "God is the personal Spirit in whom Love, Holiness and Power are perfect and perfectly united ",[100] which is at least verbally very near to Kaftan. It might perhaps be a sign of dissatisfaction with the inadequate term Spirit that it is later dropped in the Lecture Synopsis, although the new expression " infinite Personality " (in which the adjective presumably refers to the contention that personality can be infinite as well as finite) is probably little more than a variation on the same theme. Now, however, in the form of the definition we have had before us, comes a more significant change to " absolute Personality " where, although the term absolute cries out for more explanation than is given in the passing references, none is forthcoming and one is forced to ask what it means.

Any philosophical interpretation is ruled out at once by the early insistence that the word may only be used with a specifically Christian meaning. But neither can it easily be (as for Kaftan) a general term for the highest ethical Good endowed with complete power to assert itself, which Christianity shares with all other religions and which receives from revelation a somewhat higher meaning than elsewhere. For the conclusion of Mackintosh's own previous comparison of the Christian conception of God with others was, in effect, not that it is simply the highest of a series, but that it has practically nothing in common with the rest except its terms ; while at this stage he was already beginning to contend that revelation involves the complete revision of all our ethical categories, and indeed makes reasonably plain that he wishes " absoluteness " to denote that which is " more than ethical " in God.[101] In fact, if a definition of the term be sought in the light of its use elsewhere, it soon appears to mean generally that God is not subject to anything else whatsoever, but exists and acts unconditionally in His own right ; while there are some passages in which it seems to refer particularly to the uniqueness and " otherness " of this God, and a number of others where it is virtually the equivalent of His omnipotence, probably with the particular connotation that He exercises it in Himself above and beyond the world as the sovereign Creator of all things. If this be so, then the introduction of the term absolute here surely represents a move towards recognition of the Divine aseity, requiring for its completion only an explicit definition in terms already lurking in the not-too-distant background ; and the description of God as " the absolute Personality " will not be merely one more variation on the previous theme, but rather another form of the ancient credal " God the Father almighty, Maker of heaven and earth ".

A second point which must concern us here is the Divine holiness in its " primary " sense. From the beginning Mackintosh insisted that " holy " is not a purely ethical term ; but the Lecture Synopsis indicates that at first he was more or less content to note that in the Old Testament it refers also to the unapproachable " otherness " of God, and then go on to speak of the Divine holiness mainly (but not solely) as the exaltedness of " the moral law alive ", consequently antagonistic to sin, yet expressing itself in forgiveness as much as in judgment. Later, however, there seems to be a change of emphasis. Instead of ethical (but also more) we find unapproachably sublime (but not merely so), and the " wholly other " sublimity of God is given a full section to itself, traced in the New Testament as well as the Old, and immediately balanced by a new section on His nearness.*

* One thinks at once of Otto here, yet it was not from him that Mackintosh learnt of this, but from A. B. Davidson in his College days long before, while it was probably Titius who first called his attention to the New Testament recognition of it (*cf.* esp. *Jesu Lehre vom Reiche Gottes*, pp. 104 ff., also *Der Paulinismus unter dem Gesichtspunkt der Seligkeit*, pp. 33 ff.). Moreover, although he acknowledges indebtedness to Otto for calling fresh attention to the point, he could not be blind to the fact that the Holy God is not *the* Holy, the Numinous, the *mysterium tremendum* (neuter !) of religion in general, but is removed from it at once as a Person who, not just in spite of His unapproachable majesty but *because* of it, can and does enter into the most intimate relations with men. He had already called attention in these terms to the gulf which separates Old Testament from ethnic conceptions of holiness (*Originality of the Christian Message*, p. 42), and he finds Otto's failure to emphasise this very point the chief vitiating feature of his work (*cf.* Review of Otto's *Aufsätze das Numinose betreffend* in Expository Times, XXXV (1923-24), p. 555). No doubt at this stage he sometimes comes nearer to Otto than he meant, for he has a tendency to use phrases which (in isolation and given a little ill-will) could well be referred to the Numinous as such.

Here, then, is particularly clear evidence that Mackintosh has taken a decisive step away from a purely ethical conception of God,* with which he had never been wholly content and whose inadequacy he had always felt most acutely at this point.

He does so, however, in such a way as to raise new difficulties which both make plain that this can only be a first step and indicate the direction of the next. For one soon feels that a discussion of the sublimity of God in these terms does not properly belong just here. No doubt the earlier position had prepared a natural and almost inevitable opening for it. And no doubt, too, in view of its immediate purpose it was well that it should be introduced here—to prevent the possibility that holiness defined as " purity and goodness " should be taken as merely an ethical conception. Only, that purpose is already served once it is made plain that " purity " and " goodness " here are not the abstract terms of moral philosophy, but refer to qualities which are wholly real only in God and whose revelation entails the revision of all previous ethical standards ; while on the long view it causes some confusion to have " holy " used with two more or less distinct meanings. Moreover, if the holiness of God in this primary sense is virtually His Divinity, then surely it does not belong to the " attributes ", but to the fundamental definition of His being—where indeed a place has already been prepared for it by the introduction of the term absolute. One feels that, sooner or later, when a definition of absoluteness was given, sublimity must have been taken up into it,

Yet he never had the slightest intention of suggesting that men already knew of the unapproachable majesty of God, and Christ's part was to reveal the astounding fact of His nearness and love : rather, he wished to make plain that both His sublimity and His love are known for the first time in Christ.

* In this connection it is also worth noting that now for the first time he urges against Idealistic Pantheism the transcendence of the Creator over both the material and the spiritual world, whereas before he had been content to point to its implied denial of the reality of moral values (cf. p. 122, supra).

leaving to holiness the " second " sense (not altogether unlike
Barth's) which is surely the true biblical one: the purity
and goodness of God, in virtue of which He chooses men for
fellowship with Himself, confronts them in their perverse
opposition with the terrible and awe-inspiring fire of His
wrath, and overcomes their perversity in redemption—in
which sense it becomes a further definition of His grace.*

This brings us already to a final point: the signs of transition in the general structure and treatment of the doctrine.
The fact is, that at this stage it simply defies any attempt to
reduce it to a clear and unified system ; and this is so unlike
Mackintosh that we are driven to the conclusion that he is
in process of reformulating the whole. His troops, so to say,
are on the move from a weaker position to a stronger one, but
en route there are signs of disorder in the ranks. They have
already come a good distance, and there are hints enough
as to where they are going ; but in the meantime they have
reached only temporary billets on the way, in which some are
well-placed and comfortable and others decidedly the reverse.

In plain language, the original structure of the doctrine
(as found in the Lecture Synopses) was simple and straight-
forward, if somewhat one-sided. God was defined as the
infinite Personality, whose attributes are to be derived from His
revealed purpose to found the Kingdom. Kingdom at once
suggests power, and thus the first set of attributes is Omnipotence (announced as the basis of the conception of which
love is the crown, and qualified as the might of an ethically

* There is perhaps some value in the reflection that " the absolute
Personality " is the definition adopted by Haering, to whom Mackintosh
is now drawing near at some important points—particularly in the new
discussion of God's love as specifically that of the Holy One (p. 134,
supra). Haering, however, though aware that " holy " could also be
given the sense of " sublime ", prefers to avoid the confusion of the
dual meaning by keeping it for the stringent and subduing character
of God's love and using " absolute " to denote His sublimity. Thus
if Mackintosh, with his somewhat different conception of the terms
involved, were presently to adopt the same plan, he would at least
have a precedent of which he was certainly aware.

holy God), Omnipresence and Eternity, Omniscience. Then comes the second set: Holiness (in relation to love), Righteousness (also in relation to love), and finally the long-awaited and much-anticipated crown, Love (with the note that the best name for it is grace). One decided weakness of this construction was, that it unduly emphasises the truth that all that God is, He is in relation to the world, and tends to obscure the other and equally important one: that all that He is in relation to the world, He is also absolutely in Himself. This, of course, was not Mackintosh's intention, and in actual fact he breaks through his scheme every here and there at least to glimpse the other side of the matter. Yet such a formal arrangement could not but wreak its revenge on the content again and again. For example, if (as we were told) "even God's omnipotence implies relations to beings other than Himself", if omnipresence and eternity are essentially definitions of His relation to us, or if righteousness is simply "the moral perfection attaching to His government of the world", then is it only in relation to the world that He possesses these qualities, while in Himself He is something else after all? Now, however, in the form of the doctrine we have had before us, there is very much less room for such questionings: the prospect opens to an omnipotence exercised beyond and above the world as well as in it, while (whatever would now be said of omnipresence) it is the eternity of God before and after all worlds which alone gives meaning to the events of time, and His righteousness is also the self-consistency and worthiness of *all* His ways.

The new construction of the doctrine, indeed, alike in form and in treatment, witnesses to a new, or at least more fully conscious, awareness of this second aspect of the truth. Mackintosh still starts, of course, with relation—rightly, since it is there that God is made known. But from beginning to end his thought now swings constantly between God in that relation and God in Himself. God is the absolute Personality. He is known as personal in a relation of personal fellowship—but also as the sovereign Initiator and Sustainer of that relation ; and again (after the philosophic digression), He is revealed in Christ as unique and incomparable—but also as One whose dealings with us are in a true sense those of a Person. His " attributes " or, as Mackintosh now prefers to call them, " characteristics " are to be discussed under the heads, first of holy love, and then of power. Under the first head the vital interrelation of sublimity with nearness and love, holiness with grace, righteousness with mercy, is more carefully (though not yet fully) worked out—particularly from the side of love. The second head is altered in the end to " sovereignty with a purpose " and a new section on this theme introduced, in which the swing back and forth is particularly marked. God is sovereign—but with a purpose ; the purpose involves the world—but is His own absolute choice ; it is therefore His glory—but His glory is His love. And again, the purpose is to establish the Kingdom in time—and to perfect it in eternity ; thus the Divine eternity has a positive relation to temporal events—in which it uses them to serve an eternal end ; eternity gives time its reality and meaning—while time looks forward to its final replacement by eternity ; and finally the two points of view are brought together, as it were, in the thought of the glory of Christ in whom the eternal God has once for all entered time for the redemption of the world. Similarly with the revised treatment of omnipotence. It is omnipotence *to save*—but also has a wider reference. And from here we are given a brief glimpse of the Divine " immutability "—qualified as that of sovereign grace.

Yet in spite of all this general evidence of Mackintosh's new approach, his doctrine appears neither altogether unified nor altogether complete when looked at in detail. The confusion is more evident with the characteristics of God's love, the lack of completeness more obvious with those of His sovereignty ; but in both cases something at least of the answer is already indicated.

In the first case, the chapters on holiness and love are each clearly divided into three sections, and a general indication is given that some sort of correspondence is intended. Yet in the end the correspondence is only very rough. This is partly due to a certain lack of precision in the use of terms: on the one hand it is never very clear in which of its two senses the word holiness is being used and the distinction is not always preserved between " pure " holiness and righteousness, while on the other hand there is a tendency to employ love, grace and mercy interchangeably. But this is not the only source of confusion. For if the distinctions indicated by Mackintosh himself be preserved (as has been attempted in our summary as far as possible), the balance is still upset by the fact that it takes the first two sections on love (nearness and love) to answer to holiness in its primary sense, while the third section falls into two halves (mercy and grace) which answer respectively to the third and second sections on holiness—and even then there is considerable overlapping. The source of the trouble here is surely the inclusion of elements which are not properly " characteristics " at all—sublime holiness and love in so far as it is distinct from mercy and grace. But when these are removed to the primary definition, one by the joining of sublimity with absoluteness or aseity, and the other through the recognition that love is in fact the essence of God—both steps which, as we have seen, are already quite near—then the way lies open to secure the balance which Mackintosh sought.

The only question then remaining is that of order. At the present stage, although the characteristics of love have rightly been put before those of sovereignty, the former arrangement which put holiness before love still remains unchanged. Yet three things are already noticeable: Mackintosh has now begun to open the way from love back to holiness, he urges that the pure holiness of God is known with an *underlying* conviction of His grace, and above all, he announces this set of attributes as those of " holy love ", where holiness is clearly

a qualification of love. Here again, then, it is surely but a
short step to the further improvement of beginning with
grace and mercy and then adding the holiness and righteousness which form the further definition of them.

With the sovereign attributes the incompleteness is apparent at once: omnipotence is announced as the "starting-
point", and yet, apart from a momentary glance in the
direction of "immutability", nothing else follows. What,
one may ask, has become of the rest—in particular, the
former omniscience, omnipresence and eternity? They
belong, presumably, to the more technical and difficult
points which, according to his Preface, Mackintosh felt it
advisable to omit in the presence of a largely non-theological
audience. This in itself suggests that he now thought of
them somewhat differently, for as they are treated in the
Synopsis there does not seem to be much grave difficulty
attaching to them. But at any rate, since he clearly held
them to be essential to a complete doctrine, the question
remains: how would he deal with them now, or presently?

Here we must of necessity be somewhat vague—and yet
not entirely so, for we are given two valuable hints. First,
the fact that the prospect opens momentarily from the omnipotence with which God executes His loving purpose to the
"immutability" of His sovereignty, suggests that these
attributes are also to go in pairs. And secondly, eternity and
omnipresence, formerly taken together in the traditional
manner, have now apparently fallen apart—it was almost
inevitable that they should, for the only bracket holding
them together in orthodox theology was a philosophical conception of the Divine infinity (which they expressed in two
relations, one to time and the other to space), and since
Mackintosh had abandoned this from the beginning their
separation could hardly be long delayed. Now a clear place
is made for eternity on the side of the Divine sovereignty, and
although the concept is given only a few sentences they are
enough to show that it is somewhat nearer to Scripture than

before ; while if it be asked what would correspond to it on the side of loving purpose, then in view of its apparent, and surely also scriptural, association more than once with the term glory (unexplained apart from the single remark that God's glory is His love), we may hazard a guess that it might well be this. Omnipresence, on the other hand, is not here discussed at all. But from the biblical point of view its earlier discussion,* in which it clearly belongs to the side of loving purpose, would scarcely require much alteration except perhaps by way of expansion ; while if it means the whole presence of the same God in different forms, and does not imply partition or division in Him, that suggests that the concept of His unity might reasonably answer it from the other side. As for omniscience, we can only suggest that, if it is because God is omniscient that He can do all He wills while on the other hand it is because His sovereign grace is omnipotent that He knows all things without subjecting them to mechanical necessity, then there could at least be no objection to Barth's contention that omniscience and omnipotence belong together under one head in so far as the omnipotent action of God's love is that of a Person who both knows and wills.

Mackintosh, then, is approaching a position in which God would be defined as the absolute Personality who is sublime (" holy ") Love ; or since His personality will hardly require such a special place in the foreground once the fires of the controversy on the subject have passed (as they are already doing), He might be described simply as the absolute or sublime (personal) Lover. Because the love which He is in Himself as Triune overflows to demand also external objects, He creates the world and reveals Himself to it in a relation of personal communion and most intimate immanence ; but because He is absolute in Himself, He is revealed also as One who in that relation remains its sole Author and Sustainer, independent of the world, incomparable with it, ruling

* Cf. p. 141, *supra.*

transcendently over it. And now He makes known in that relation also the further "characteristics" or "attributes" of His love and sublimity. He reveals not only His love, but also His grace and mercy; and because His love is *sublime* these must be defined in vital conjunction with His holiness and righteousness. And again, in His sublimity or sovereignty He is known as "immutable", eternal, undivided; but because this is sovereignty with a loving *purpose,* in His "immutability" He is almighty (and all-knowing), in His eternity glorious, in His unity omnipresent.

It is almost too obvious to call for special mention how very near this is to Barth. Indeed, it would require only the addition of a third pair of attributes under the head of love —the traditional long-suffering and wisdom, which Mackintosh for some mysterious reason completely overlooks—to make Barth's scheme complete. Whether, given longer years, Mackintosh would of himself have come to such a position is, of course, an unanswerable question. But this much is certain: he was already so near to it that he must have recognised both in the framework of Barth's doctrine and in his treatment as a whole a further point, and one with a clearer and wider outlook, on the road he himself was travelling towards a truly biblical doctrine of God.

CHAPTER IV

CONCLUSION

BY way of conclusion we may now look back to the six characteristic features of Ritschlianism enumerated in our first chapter, which were the main source of its attraction for Mackintosh.

1. The first was its thoroughly practical conception of the Christian faith as the final answer to man's moral needs and thus inseparably bound up with morality. It is easy to see how that would appeal to a Scot brought up in a Calvinist tradition—the more so as it appeared to vindicate the reality of moral values over against their denial by materialism and the doubts cast by its idealist counterpart in Hegel. Yet it was precisely here that he first laid the finger of criticism upon Ritschl's work. For he protested from the beginning that whatever needs true religion may satisfy, it is essentially communion with God for His own sake and to make it anything else is to put man and his ideals at its centre instead of God.* Not only so, but for all his interest in morality, he also insisted that God is " more than moral "—so much so that mere moral values, however important, can never be the primary interest of faith. And it was surely this which led him in the end to reject Ritschl's theology as a thoroughly rationalistic moralism. Ritschl, it is true, might have felt that he had forestalled such a criticism ; for he had declared that morality was not his sole concern and had likened

* In itself, of course, this need not imply very grave difference from Ritschl, for it was a correction insisted upon by such disciples as Kaftan and Herrmann. But in Kaftan's case, as we have seen, the God who is to be sought for His own sake is after all only a human ideal—a reflection of the human spirit at its ethical best. So that man and his ideals are still at the centre, and the improvement is more apparent than real. In Herrmann's case, too, much the same would have to be said in the end.

Christianity to an ellipse—with a religious focus (the "redemption and justification through Christ") alongside the moral one (the "universal moral Kingdom of God").[1] But while Mackintosh recognises this, he sees equally clearly that the celebrated figure remained only a figure: in actual fact Ritschl's thought was not elliptical but circular, and morality was the centre of the circle.

This, Mackintosh finds, had disastrous consequences both for his views of God and for his understanding of the Christian life. For even the concept of God was drastically pruned until it fitted his moralistic prepossessions. Thus God the Father Almighty ultimately becomes only a means to our ethical ends, whose function is "to stand surety for the attainment of human purposes".[2] The living Lord Jesus Christ has His being and function prescribed for Him by a fixed ethical system which lays down "the boundaries of moral being which He must not pass".[3] The Holy Spirit is relegated, almost casually, to the background, and seems to stand for little more than a lingering influence of the long-dead Christ upon the mind of the believer and the Church.

At the human level it is much the same. Christianity becomes merely the best means towards spiritual independence of the natural world, and thus cannot be radically distinguished from other religions—or even from civilisation, which is "also in its own way the conquest of nature and the realisation of man's free sway over the world".[4] Faith loses both its venturousness and its God-given certainty by being made essentially submission of the will to One who has for us the value of God, acceptance of His purposes because we can see their value for our lives. Most surprising of all perhaps, faith and practice are subtly prised apart again in the end. For in Ritschl's own words, "Good works do not follow directly from faith in so far as faith experiences reconciliation with God", and "Justification has no immediate bearing upon right action":[5] the moral inspiration of the believer's life is supplied not by faith, but by his own independent resolve to adopt the ethical tasks of the Kingdom—" a point in theology, and a central one, at which Ritschl barely gets beyond Pharisaism ".[6] In a word, his whole system is vitiated by the fact that from first to last " life for him revolves round the moral man " ;[7] and thus his main weapon against materialism and idealism recoils disastrously upon himself.

It is true that, as Mackintosh points out, the younger Ritschlians were freely critical of their master's work and did much to strengthen its more obviously vulnerable points. Yet it requires only a little care to detect that their fundamental principles remain practically the same, whereas Mackintosh's standpoint is radically different. It would seem, indeed, as if the Calvinist upbringing, whose practical emphasis helped to lay him open to Ritschlian influences, itself provided the antidote. At any rate, it is reasonably clear that his practical interest, whatever its outward similarity to Ritschl's, has a fundamentally different ground. For his concern is not with man's activity merely in itself, but in its relation to the aseity or sovereign freedom of God. Not that he was satisfied with late orthodoxy's treatment of the Divine aseity : he felt that too often it tended to speak as if God is and does everything, man nothing. Yet neither was he able to fly with the Ritschlians to the other extreme of making man practically everything and God whatever man's sense of values will allow. Rather, he wished to make it plain that in very truth God is and does everything, and precisely for that reason man can be and do something too.[8] It is the believer's communion with *this* God which is for him the heart of the Christian faith. And it is this which gives his thought the twofold centre, outwardly so similar to Ritschl's ellipse. If he speaks of God, it is the God who in Christ addresses His sovereign revealing Word to man ; if he speaks of the activities of the believer's life, it is the life of the man who is enabled by the Holy Spirit to hear and answer that Word in faith. It must then be equally possible, as he saw, to start either with the older theology from the

13

revealing Word, or with Schleiermacher and other modern writers from the faith of man—whether that be interpreted primarily in terms of thought, "feeling", "moral will", or more generally "experience".[9] For the crucial question is not which starting-point is adopted. It is whether in the one case the Word is truly Divine, or simply an echo of man's own words ; and whether in the other case it is a Divine Spirit which calls forth and sustains man's faith, or merely a reflection of his own spirit on the clouds.

It must be obvious that this type of thought is fundamentally trinitarian. And one of the earliest significant indications of Mackintosh's difference from the Ritschlians is that he was determined to take seriously the doctrine of the Trinity, precisely in order to maintain the full Divinity of Christ the Word and of the Spirit.[10] Not only so, but it becomes increasingly plain that by "Divine" he does not merely mean "ethically perfect": he means rather free, absolute, sublime, a se. No doubt many of his early utterances were somewhat ambiguous. For we have seen how heavily his whole concept of God was overburdened at the start with Ritschlian elements which gave it much of the appearance of a perfected ethical human spirit. Yet it was formed against the background of a vitally important doctrine of the Trinity, and with an underlying awareness of the Divine aseity which made its presence felt chiefly in regard to the concept of holiness. Nor was it long before these began to push their way into their rightful place in the forefront, thereby causing more and more of the foreign elements to be discarded until finally the firm outlines of a fully biblical concept of God are clearly seen.

Human life, when set in its relation to this God, turns out to be a very different thing from what the Ritschlians made of it. And although Mackintosh discusses the same activities, often in practically the same terms, the difference can hardly be long overlooked. Thus, as we have seen, he took over much of their discussion of religion. Yet his starting-point was no general conception of ethical religion: it was the question what the Christian believer, engaged in the God-given task of evangelism, is to make of the outwardly similar beliefs and practices of other faiths. Hence he knew with ever greater clarity how to make a distinction the Ritschlians could never make between Christianity and all other religions. The distinction is not a foregone conclusion, as orthodoxy seemed to suggest ; for it is not to be made in principle, but in fact. In principle, all faiths could be true, because God has always provided the necessary conditions for true religion. But in fact man has used these very conditions to rebel against God by manufacturing a religion for himself. And this factual difference is so complete that the Gospel message, far from ushering in the final stage in man's religious development, must rather lay bare the full wicked-ness of even the best (*i.e.* outwardly most similar) things in all " ignorant worships ", and call for their abandonment in favour of the one true worship of God in Christ. Again, we have seen how deeply influenced he was by the Ritschlian conception of religious knowledge as given in the form of value-judgments, yet confined his discussion to the know-ledge of Christian faith—well aware that that faith is created and sustained solely by the sovereign revelation of God in Christ. And this awareness led him to make plain in the end that the standard of value is not merely ethical (as the Ritschlians held) but transcendent ; it is not part of the stock-in-trade of man, not even of Christian man, but is known only as it is continually revealed in Christ and apprehended in the power of the Spirit. For that very reason believing conviction is both a tremendous venture and an utter, un-paralleled certainty. Again and again the believer makes what may well be called a leap in the dark, abandoning every ground on which man normally seeks to verify the truth—and finds himself not in the dark but in the hand of God, with all his standards of value transformed from top to bottom, and with such an assurance of the truth as the world can neither give nor take away because it rests not on the shifting sand of mere human ideals, but on the rock of Christ. Here, too, in the act of faith in which man recognises and commits himself to God in Christ, Mackintosh found the mainspring of the Christian ethic. And if he welcomed Ritschl's emphasis on the new moral life of the Christian he felt himself all the more bound to insist that that new life has no independent source, but flows directly from faith's new relation to God: "reconciliation with God *ipso facto* brings power to do God's will ".[11] Not only so, but the new moral life is new also in this, that its keynote is no longer merely duty and obedience, but rather love and thankfulness.[12] For the recognition of God's love must kindle ours, and the knowledge of what He has done for us must awake the desire to do something for Him, "not as price, but in gratitude ".[13] Here the Law is no longer an imposition, but rather a welcome sign-post, obedience is no mere duty but a privilege, and we "walk the way of God's commandments " not because we " must ", but because there is really no other way for a thankful child of God to walk.

2. In the Ritschlian undertaking to bind faith and theology solely to the historical revelation in Jesus Christ, Mackintosh found a valuable curb to the speculative excesses of Hegelianism, and also the hope of giving their true significance to the events of the time-series. But although he welcomed it for these reasons, he soon found that Ritschl had gone much too far. It is good to bind theology to historical revelation, but it is too much of a good thing also to bind the revelation to history—namely, the historical life of Jesus (outward or inward) between Bethlehem and Calvary. For this, in itself, is but a human life—extraordinary, no doubt, yet definitely human. It is also good to let the events of the time-series be given their true meaning by revelation, but it is not at all good first to make the tacit assumption that they already have it and that it is they which have to give revelation *its* true meaning. For that can only result in trimming

the concept of God to fit particular historical presuppositions. Yet these are precisely the things that Ritschl did. And the more clearly Mackintosh realised this, the more definite became his second main criticism of Ritschlian thought: when his historism has done its work, the pre-existence of Christ becomes little more than a meaningless symbol, His present sovereignty merely a posthumous influence, and we are ultimately left with One who can only be either an exceptionally perfect moral man or else an absolute ethical ideal which has somehow got imprisoned in history. Neither of these conceptions seems to have much advantage over Hegel's " Christ-idea ". And thus Mackintosh finds it is the same with Ritschl's historism as with his moralism: it was his chief strength against Idealism, but also the source of his greatest weakness.[14] Or if we may put it so, he used it to demolish the " Christ-idea ", but the smoke from the explosion need not hide from us the fact that he was " hoist with his own petard ".

Mackintosh, on the other hand, though glad to follow Ritschl in insisting that the Word was made *flesh,* was also well enough aware that the flesh could profit nothing if it were not the *Word* that became flesh. Hence the vital importance he attached to the pre-existence and the present sovereignty of Christ. For him the historical revelation which is the ground of faith and theology is not given merely in Jesus' earthly life: it is the work of the Lord who came into history from the bosom of the Father, and is now present in His risen power " all days unto the end ". No doubt there are some early passages which have a decidedly Ritschlian tone, as if particular events of Jesus' life themselves constituted a revelation of God to His followers. Yet even then he seems to have realised that it was not the events themselves, but the power of God working in them. At any rate, he was soon emphatic enough that unless *God* is in past events, they reveal nothing to anyone, and unless He is present now to bring home their import, they reveal nothing to us.[15] Thus the pre-existence and the present sovereignty of Christ are things which neither the believer nor the theologian can afford to underrate, far less ignore: they are supremely important, since apart from them there could be no true revelation at all, and therefore neither authentic faith nor good theology. They are also an integral part of what is revealed; and it is for this reason that history must be interpreted by revelation, not *vice versa*. For history in itself has really no ascertainable meaning: it is the movement of a sinful world, and that movement is a chaos—or would be but for its relation to the sovereignty of Christ and the long-promised new age now present in Him. It is this critical relation, and it alone, which imparts to each historical event its true significance.[16] But it is a relation which is not yet plain for all to see. It can be known only as it is revealed to faith; and hence revelation is the only key to the real meaning of the events of time.

3. Ritschl conceived of the Kingdom of God as a universal moral Kingdom being realised in and through the events of the every-day world, and thus he appeared to do away with orthodoxy's seemingly rigid and arbitrary distinction between the sacred and the secular. While his corresponding conception of faith as essentially a free act of the moral will seemed to avoid the sacrifice of human freedom involved in the old idea that it is primarily the acceptance of traditional dogma. Such views might therefore be expected to arouse Mackintosh's sympathies, and no doubt did for a time. Yet he could not overlook the fact that the advantages were gained through an over-simplification of the problem, and involved a dreadful impoverishment of the Gospel message. For the Divine Kingdom, so conceived, is " hardly more than (as with Kant) a realm of moral ends, a purely present and mundane commonwealth ".[17] And the life of its members is concentrated almost entirely on the task of promoting the human race's independence of natural circumstance and its unification in love—an aim which may well inspire moral

triumphs, but is scarcely likely to stimulate much "joy unspeakable and full of glory". It must be obvious that a moral faith is sufficient to recognise such a Kingdom and enter upon its life ; but it is equally clear that such a faith is a decidedly sober affair and singularly devoid of the rapture of the New Testament. For all that Ritschl has done in the end is to exchange an apparently rigid dualism for a bare ethical monism, to substitute a purely moral faith for a largely intellectual one, and thereby to miss even more completely than orthodoxy the true wonder and glory of God.

In Mackintosh's own pages we find a very different state of affairs. Here the Kingdom of God is no purely mundane realm of moral ends, but a transcendent eschatological reality embracing both the spiritual and the natural order—the complete and final sovereignty of the Father over all creation which is to be manifested at the last but is even now a present fact for faith.[18] The life of its members is not just a struggle to dominate nature at the behest of an ethical ideal: it is the triumphant life (spiritual *and* natural) of those who are the sons of God through Jesus Christ, guided and inspired by the indwelling power of the Holy Spirit.[19] The faith in which its presence is discerned and its life lived involves more than the simple exercise of the moral will: it is a Divinely-evoked act in which man recognises the promises and claims of God in Christ and in humble trust and adoration commits his whole being to Him. In all this the recognition of the Divine aseity precludes both barely monistic and rigidly dualistic views of God and His world. There can be no mere monism. For although God in His sovereignty is absolute, it is an absoluteness in which the creation can have completely real existence over against Him.[20] And although within the created world there is a final and perfect unity, it is one in which the natural order is not negated in favour of the spiritual, but makes its distinct positive contribution to the unity of both. Yet neither can there be any complete dualism. For although God and the world are distinct, the creation is no purely separate reality, but can exist only in direct relation to its Creator.[21] And although there is a real distinction between the world of faith and blessedness and "this present world" of sin and death, yet there is no rigid division but the "powers of the age to come" are already present everywhere transforming and superseding the old. It is part of the wonder of the Gospel that these things are so. And their truth is discerned neither by moral earnestness nor by intellectual credulity, but by the biblical faith which sees all things under the judgment and the grace of God revealed in Jesus Christ.

4. Mackintosh found Ritschl to be wholly justified in contending that we can know God solely in Christ and natural theology must be rejected. True, the chief ground of this contention would seem to be his objection to the use of general ideas which have no roots in history and no bearing upon morality.[22] But if to that extent the argument rests on the somewhat precarious basis of his own philosophical pragmatism, the contention itself is valid enough. The only pity is, that Ritschl did not obey his own rule: his system is Christo-centric in name rather than in reality.[23] For in actual fact he sought to control Christ according to historical and ethical principles as naturally discernible as any others. And thus he could well be charged with putting a natural theology of the conscience in place of one of the intellect, producing in the end a Supreme Moral Being which has no more in common with the God of Christian faith than has the Supreme Rational Being, First Cause and Final End of traditional theism.

For his own part, Mackintosh, as we have repeatedly seen, made a much more determined and considerably more successful attempt to base his thought in Christ alone. In the present context this means that although he rejected natural theology as emphatically as Ritschl did, its rejection (like that of natural religion) could never be simply a foregone conclusion. For it was not at the dictates of any philosophical theory that he rejected it. It was because he recognised that for sinners there is no true knowledge of God, and therefore no true theology, except through an unveiling of Divine grace in which their sin is taken away.[24] And since it is a simple fact that no such unveiling takes place apart from the revelation in Christ, that revelation is for us the sole ground of faith and doctrine. That, however, is not to say that God Himself is bound to any one method of self-disclosure: on the contrary, He has also "the power to reveal Himself through Nature if He should will this, and in so far as He wills it ".[25] Hence the fact that He does not do so must not be erected into a principle, as though He could not. And a claim to have found Him there, or a natural theology built upon it, cannot simply be rejected in principle, but strictly only when critical examination has established the fact that this is not the same God as is revealed in Christ. In this argument some confusion was doubtless caused by Mackintosh's early assertion of a general revelation in Nature, history and conscience—as if he wished to provide a basis for some sort of natural theology after all. But we have seen that this was apparently not his purpose: what he wished to assert was rather the fact that God is present and knowable in all these spheres—so that the sinner is culpably responsible for his failure to see Him there.[26] This, too, must be recognised by those who find God in Christ. And there need have been little difficulty but for the early use of the term "revelation" which, in this connection, he ultimately abandoned.

5. The Ritschlians' separation of theology and philosophy was one of the chief attractions which their teaching had for Mackintosh, particularly in view of the havoc caused in theological thought by its subordination to the philosophy of Hegel. Yet it soon transpired that by "philosophy" they meant simply speculative thought as such, and that they objected to this merely because they took their stand on what Kant called the practical, as distinct from the pure reason.

That in itself need cause no undue concern, for it is simply the rejection of one kind of philosophy at the behest of another. But the trouble started when they went on to reject, for the same reason, all theological doctrines of a speculative character. For this, he found, was not to free theology from philosophical bondage: it was really only to subject it to Kant instead of Hegel.[27]

This was a procedure with which Mackintosh could never find himself in agreement. For his own objection to philosophy did not depend on whether it uses one particular faculty or another: he objected to it because in either case it works with its own *a priori* principles, whereas theology is based solely on the Word of God in Christ and must therefore sit light to any established principles of human thought, whether theoretic or practical. That does not mean that from the theologian's point of view philosophy is simply worthless. For there is a type of argument which is philosophical rather than theological, and to which he was prepared—at least at first—to assign a subordinate rôle in the task of countering philosophical objections to the faith. It was for this reason, for example, that he undertook the translation of such works as Wendland's *Miracles and Christianity:* miracle, he knew, lay at the heart of the Gospel —indeed he considered the whole Christian life to be a miracle from start to finish—and he felt that this book would be more helpful than any which had yet appeared in English to those who were being shaken by the contemporary output of anti-miracle literature.[28] And it was for the same reason that he occasionally included a philosophical argument such as we found in his discussion of the personality of God. Yet he insisted that apologetic of this kind is in no sense a necessary task, but a purely optional one.[29] One might ask if it is not also inadvisable—thinking, for example, of the confusion which the argument for the Divine personality caused in his doctrine of God. But he probably soon realised himself the danger of the theologian's thus stepping aside from his

proper path : such translations as the one mentioned are confined to his earliest period, and we have seen how the
philosophical element in the doctrine of God was soon
rigorously subordinated and later dropped out altogether.[30]
At any rate, as far as the task of theology proper is concerned,
he was determined to free himself from all philosophical
dictation and to exclude any use of the reason, " pure " and
" practical " alike, which is based on preconceived principles.
At the same time he recognised that in revelation God does
not speak past the speculative reason to the conscience, but
transforms both faculties and demands the service of both.
And therefore he set himself with equal determination to the
task of thinking out in the obedience of faith whatever
" speculative " doctrines the service of Christ requires.

6. In the case of mysticism Mackintosh again felt that
Ritschl's opposition was amply justified—yet only up to a
point. Mysticism in general must certainly be rejected. But
the opposition has carried Ritschl too far if it blinds him to
that other mysticism known to the Scriptures, which is distinguished from all else by the fact that it is the mystical
union of *Christ* with *His people*.[31] This relation is not, as
elsewhere, " a preliminary step to union with God ",[32] but
is itself union with God in Christ. It is not one for which
sin becomes an illusion, but one in which sin, with all its
terrible meaning, is taken away. It is not a relationship in
which the individual loses himself in God, but the union of
Christ with His Church, analogous to that of Father and
Son,[33] in which each individual comes to his own place of
honour. This is a mysticism which a scriptural theology
cannot afford to overlook, as Ritschl and so many others do,
for it is really only in virtue of it that theology can exist
at all.[34]

Looking back over the whole, we can see how near
Mackintosh stood to the Ritschlians—and how far from
them. His thought is often Ritschlian in outward form ; yet

it is thoroughly biblical in its foundations. And if, like the great cathedral of which he spoke,[35] the structure he built upon these foundations was never finished, yet it came near enough to completion for us to see that it is not a Ritschlian one. No doubt many of the windows look the same from the outside, but when we view them from within we find a richness and a glory of which Ritschl could never have dreamed.

It must be clear, too, that our description of his thought as a Theology of Transition was not unjustified. At the beginning he stood within the nineteenth century—near its outermost border, no doubt, yet within it. For his mode of thought was deeply coloured by it, and his terms of expression (whatever his dissatisfaction with them) were its terms. But by the end he had reached a point where the view was very different, and where he found himself standing side by side with Barth. In many ways the new position was one more of promise than of attainment, for he was never able to complete the revision and clarification of his earlier teaching which it must entail. But the outlook at least was perfectly clear. If we may use a scriptural analogy, he might be compared to Moses on the journey of promise. For guided by the Word of God, he sought to lead towards true biblical doctrine a theological generation which still hungered for the flesh-pots of the Enlightenment; and if at times he may have succumbed to temptations by the way, yet in the end he stood like Moses on the Mount and was allowed to survey the promised land.

REFERENCES

Contractions : ACB = *Some Aspects of Christian Belief.*
               CAG = *The Christian Apprehension of God* (paging of 4th edition).
               CEF = *The Christian Experience of Forgiveness.*
               JC = *The Doctrine of the Person of Jesus Christ.*
               LS = Lecture Synopses (unpublished).
               OCM = *The Originality of the Christian Message.*
               TMT = *Types of Modern Theology.*
               ERE = *Encyclopedia of Religion and Ethics.*
               RuV = *Rechtfertigung und Versöhnung* [4].

CHAPTER I

[1] *Religion in Geschichte und Gegenwart*, II, iv, p. 1499.
[2] C. C. J. Webb, *Religious Thought in England from* 1850, pp. 100 f.
[3] Stirling, *The Secret of Hegel*, p. xxii.
[4] JC, pp. 262, 263 n., *cf.* TMT, p. 130.   [5] TMT, p. 102.   [6] Pp. 113 f.
[7] P. 115.   [8] P. 104.   [9] P. 105.   [10] *Ibid.*   [11] JC, p. 257.
[12] TMT, p. 108.   [13] P.110.   [14] P. 116.   [15] P. 115.
[16] P. 103.   [17] P. 104.   [18] Pp. 116 f.   [19] *Cf.* TMT, p. 115.
[20] *Cf.* OCM, p. 34.   [21] S. Pringle-Pattison, *Hegelianism and Personality.*
[22] JC, p. 264.   [23] TMT, p. 133.   [24] *Ibid.*   [25] ACB, p. 263.
[26] P. 271.   [27] TMT, p. 112.   [28] CAG, pp. 57 f.   [29] *Cf.* TMT, p. 134.
[30] ACB, p. 28.   [31] TMT, p. 131, *cf.* ACB, p. 30.   [32] ACB, p. 30.
[33] P. 26.   [34] P. 24.   [35] JC, p. 503.   [36] CAG, p. 184.   [37] Pp. 183 f.
[38] *Cf.* TMT, p. 295.   [39] CAG, p. 184.   [40] TMT, p. 108.
[41] ACB, pp. 19 f.   [42] P. 15, *cf.* CAG, p. 215.   [43] ACB, pp. 19 f.
[44] TMT, p. 110, *cf.* ACB, pp. 3 ff.
[45] *Cf.* ACB, pp. 5 f., CAG, pp. 100, 215, TMT, p. 110.
[46] *Cf.* ACB, p. 175, TMT, p. 180.   [47] ACB, p. 167, *cf.* CAG, p. 54.
[48] *American Journal of Theology*, Jan., 1899.   [49] ACB, p. 121.

CHAPTER II

[1] LS: " Subject-matter and Function of Dogmatic ".   [2] *Ibid.*
[3] CAG, p. 12.   [4] *Cf.* pp. 95 ff., *infra.*   [5] CAG, p. 13.   [6] P. 127.
[7] JC, p. viii.   [8] P. 316.   [9] P. 248.   [10] CAG, p. 59.
[11] LS: " The Specific Nature of Believing Knowledge ".   [12] JC, p. 301.
[13] TMT, p. 148, *Cf.* Art. " Dogmatic Theology : Its Nature and Function ", *Expositor*, 6th series, vol. X (1910), p. 428.   [14] CAG, p. 77.
[15] P. 78, *cf.* JC, p. 514, TMT, pp. 240, 242.   [16] JC, p. 300.

[17] ACB, p. 176.   [18] *Cf.* pp. 23 f., *supra*.   [19] ACB, p. 35.
[20] Pp. 35 f., *cf.* OCM, p. 39, CAG, pp. 119 f.   [21] CAG, p. 48.
[22] ACB, p. 37.   [23] TMT, p. 62.   [24] CAG, pp. 91 f.
[25] LS: " Christian Experience as a Medium of Doctrine ".
[26] *Cf.* JC, p. 352 n.   [27] CEF, p. 108.
[28] Review of Stephan's *Glaubenslehre*[2] in *Expository Times*, vol. XL (1928-29), p. 471.
[29] Review of Wobbermin's *Richtlinien evangelischer Theologie, ibid.* vol. XLI (1929-30), p. 378.
[30] " Dogmatic Theology: Its Nature and Function " (Inaugural Lecture to the Chair of Systematic Theology in New College), *Expositor*, 6th series, vol. X (1904), pp. 413 ff.   [31] TMT, pp. 147 f.
[32] Kaftan, *Dogmatik* [6], § 1.   [33] *Ibid.*, §§ 2-5.   [34] TMT, p. 173.
[35] CAG, p. 15.   [36] P. 18.   [37] RuV, III, p. 185.   [38] CAG, p. 19.
[39] RuV, III, p. 187.   [40] *Ibid.*   [41] CAG, p. 21.   [42] Pp. 21 ff.
[43] P. 86.   [44] *Cf.* RuV, III, p. 192.   [45] CAG, pp. 31, 35.
[46] P. 25.   [47] P. 26.   [48] P. 23.   [49] P. 42.   [50] P. 32.   [51] P. 29.
[52] RuV, III, p. 189.   [53] CAG, p. 30.   [54] P. 36, *cf.* pp. 22 f.
[55] P. 37.   [56] P. 38.   [57] *Ibid.*   [58] RuV, III, p. 188.
[59] *Ibid.*   [60] *Ibid.*   [61] OCM, pp. 1 f.   [62] TMT, p. 150.
[63] CAG, p. 16.   [64] Pp. 75 f.   [65] Pp. 197 f.
[66] CEF, p. 18, *cf.* p. 82.   [67] TMT, p. 278.
[68] P. 205. He is no doubt thinking of Barth, *Christliche Dogmatik*, I, § 18, *cf.* also *Kirchliche Dogmatik* I/2, pp. 328 ff.
[69] Schleiermacher, *Kurze Darstellung*, § 22. This is fully discussed in *Glaubenslehre:* §§ 3-6 and *Reden*, II-IV.
[70] *Cf. Glaubenslehre*, §§ 7-10, *Reden*, V.   [71] *Glaubenslehre*, § 11.
[72] *Cf. Kurze Darstellung*, §§ 73, 78-80.   [73] *Cf. Glaubenslehre*, § 13, 1.
[74] § 94, 2.   [75] § 100, 2.   [76] TMT, p. 177.
[77] Note on *Ages of the World* (Christian) in ERE, I, p. 190 n.
[78] OCM, p. 27.   [79] CAG, p. 37.   [80] *Kurze Darstellung*, § 33.
[81] CAG, p. 97.   [82] *Ibid.*   [83] P. 75.
[84] For the revelation in Nature, Acts XIV, 17, Rom. I, 19, in History, Acts XVII, 26 f. For that in conscience he gives no special ground. It is sometimes expressly included under " History " (CAG, p. 96), sometimes omitted altogether (pp. 37 f.). With the following paragraph, *cf.* Barth's exegesis of the passages concerned in *Kirchliche Dogmatik*, I/2, p. 332 ff.
[85] *Institutio*, I/ii, 1.   [86] I/iii, 1.   [87] I/iii, 3.   [88] I/ii, 1.   [89] I/iii, 1.
[90] I/iii, 2.   [91] I/iv, 1.   [92] *Ibid.*   [93] *Ibid.*   [94] I/iv. 4.
[95] *Ibid.*   [96] I/ii, 2.   [97] I/v, 1-10.   [98] I/v, 11-15.   [99] CAG, p. 75.
[100] OCM, p. 27.   [101] CAG, p. 38.   [102] TMT, p. 241.
[103] OCM, p. 191.   [104] CAG, pp. 39 f.   [105] P. 40.   [106] *Ibid.*
[107] P. 41.   [108] Pp. 45 f.   [109] P. 60.   [110] *Cf.* RuV, III, p. 194.
[111] CAG, pp. 48 f.   [112] P. 49.   [113] P. 50.   [114] P. 44.   [115] P. 53.
[116] P. 58.   [117] *Cf.* pp. 56 ff.; *Sermons*, pp. 115 f.   [118] CAG, p. 60.
[119] RuV, III, pp. 4 ff.   [120] *Sermons*, p. 118, *cf.* CAG, p. 59, TMT, p. 154.

[121] CAG, p. 60, *cf.* JC, p. 352 n.   [122] *Sermons*, p. 119, OCM, p. 190.

[123] CAG, p. 54, *cf.* TMT, p. 154.   [124] CAG, p. 55.   [125] P. 23.

[126] P. 61.   [127] ACB, pp. 125, 146.   [128] CAG, pp. 63 f., TMT, p. 144.

[129] CAG, P. 64.   [130] P. 65.   [131] P. 66, *cf.* p. 159.

[132] Pp. 67 f.   [133] RuV, III, p. 189.   [134] Edn.¹, 1874, p. 174.

[135] *Theologie und Metaphysik*, p. 11.   [136] ACB, p. 136.

[137] Art. "Feuerbach and Illusionism", in *Expository Times*, XLIII (1931-32), p. 203.   [138] CEF, pp. 34, 82 (*cf.* p. 18), CAG, p. 198.

[139] TMT, pp. 192 f., *cf.* Barth, *Kirchliche Dogmatik*, I/1, p. 201.

[140] TMT, pp. 174 f.   [141] P. 155.

[142] *Cf. Kirchliche Dogmatik*, I/1, pp. 219 ff.   [143] CEF, p. 35.

[144] *Cf.* Art. "The Unio Mystica as a Theological Conception" in *Expositor*, 7th series, vol. VII (1909), ACB, pp. 99 ff., JC, pp. 110 ff., 333 ff.   [145] ACB, pp. 109 ff.   [146] P. 118.

[147] LS: "The Specific Nature of Believing Knowledge".

[148] Art. "The Name of Jesus", *Expository Times*, vol. XXVI (1914-15), p. 153.   [149] CEF, p. 248.   [150] pp. 250 f.   [151] ACB, pp. 112, 215.

[152] Pp. 225 f.   [153] P. 153.   [154] JC, p. 311.

[155] RuV, III, pp. 581, 198 ff.   [156] Pp. 211 ff.

[157] Herrmann, *Die Metaphysik in der Theologie*, pp. 16 f.

[158] *Cf.* CAG, p. 64.   [159] ACB, 161 f., TMT, p. 142 f.

[160] JC, p. 299, *cf.* pp. 514, 522.   [161] P. 344.

[162] Art. "Implicit Faith", in ERE, VII, 180.

[163] *Immortality and the Future*, p. 235.   [164] P. 195.   [165] JC, p. 344.

[166] *Dogmatik*, § 23.   [167] *Verkehr des Christen*⁵, p. 9.

[168] *Der christliche Glaube*, pp. 429, 449 ff.

[169] JC, pp. 456 f., 459, *cf.* pp. 316, 319.

[170] *Cf.* JC, p. 300, TMT, p. 256.   [171] ACB, p. 169.

[172] *Cf.* Art. "Principal Denney as a Theologian" in *Expository Times*, vol. XXVIII (1916-17), p. 488.   [173] *Cf.* CAG, pp. 45 f., 55, 140, 246.

[174] JC, p. 304.   [175] P. viii.

[176] RuV, III, pp. 16 ff, *Theologie und Metaphysik* ² (1887), pp. 8 f.

[177] ACB, pp. 127 f.

[178] TMT, p. 143. Mackintosh is no doubt thinking of Barth, *Kirchliche Dogmatik*, I/1, p. 297.   [179] TMT, p. 143.

[180] Art. "The Reformers' Doctrine of Scripture", in Gore, *Doctrine of the Infallible Book*, p. 55.   [181] OCM, p. 53.

[182] *Cf.* JC, p. 514, LS: "Scripture as the Source of Doctrine" (2).

[183] *Cf.* CAG, pp. 81, 83.   [184] *Doctrine of the Infallible Book*, p. 56.

[185] *Ibid.*   [186] JC, p. 319.   [187] P. 311, ACB, p. 14.   [188] *Ibid.*

[189] JC, p. 314.   [190] Pp. 316 f., *cf.* CAG, p. 89.

[191] *Cf.* JC, pp. 8, 15 n., 27, 40, 107.   [192] P. 54.   [193] P. 318.

[194] P. 319.   [195] P. 374.   [196] *Cf.* esp. *Ethik* ⁵, pp. 100, 125.

[197] *Cf.* esp. Art. *Christlich-protestantische Dogmatik*, pp. 612 ff.

[198] *Ethik* ⁵, pp. 109, 112, 114.   [199] TMT, p. 157.   [200] P. 164.

[201] RuV, III, p. 378.   [202] TMT, p. 158.

[203] P. 179 (slightly abbreviated).   [204] P. 157.   [205] JC, p. 292.
[206] *Immortality and the Future*, p. 128.
[207] JC, p. 230, Art. " Dogmatic Theology: Its Nature and Function ",
Expositor, 6th series, vol. X (1904), p. 429.

CHAPTER III

[1] The following outline attempts to give the doctrine in its latest
available form, and follows in the main Chapters V-VIII of *The
Christian Apprehension of God*.   But the original character of this book as a
series of lectures to a general audience imposed certain limitations on the
discussion, and other writings have also been called upon here and there
—notably, *The Originality of the Christian Message*, pp. 38-57, the Articles
on " Grace " and " Mercy " in *Encyclopedia of Religion and Ethics*, VI,
364 ff., VIII, 556 ff., and the Synopses of the college lectures on
*The Idea of God in Traditional Theology, The Personality of God, The Nature
and Attributes of God* (1-3).   [2] CAG, p. 156.   [3] P. 131.   [4] P. 132.
[5] P. 137.   [6] P. 138.   [7] P. 139.   [8] *Die christliche Glaubenslehre*, i, p. 504.
[9] *Mikrokosmos*, iii, pp. 565 ff.   [10] CAG, p. 147.   [11] P. 150.   [12] P. 151.
[13] P. 153.   [14] LS: " The Personality of God ".   [15] CAG, p. 161.
[16] RuV, III, p. 260, *cf.* II, pp. 89, 101.   [17] CAG, p. 168.
[18] In reference to McLeod Campbell, *Nature of the Atonement* [6], p. 26.
[19] CAG, p. 170.   [20] P. 171.   [21] P. 177.   [22] *Ibid.*
[23] In reference to A. B. Davidson, *Theology of the Old Testament*, p. 144.
[24] CAG, p. 181.   [25] P. 191.   [26] *The Idea of God*, p. 289.
[27] CAG, p. 196.   Similarly also Kaftan, *Dogmatik* [6], p. 200.
[28] This, too, constantly recurs, *cf.* esp. CEF, pp. 25, 158, 215, *Highway
of God*, pp. 44, 115.   [29] CAG, p. 203.   [30] P. 205.
[31] Art. " Mercy ", in ERE, VIII, p. 556.   [32] CAG, p. 211.   [33] P. 212.
[34] OCM, p. 42, in special reference to Amos III, 2, *cf.* also Art. " Grace ",
in ERE, VI, pp. 364 ff.   [35] CAG, p. 214.
[36] OCM, pp. 55, 57, CEF, p. 173, ACB, pp. 251 f.
[37] TMT, p. 287.   Though much later, this seems to be only a sharper
formulation of what was already being expressed here.   [38] CAG, p. 216.
[39] P. 218, *cf.* Titius, *Jesu Lehre vom Reiche Gottes*, p. 106.   Barth makes
an illuminating comment in this respect, *Kirchliche Dogmatik*, II/1,
pp. 587, 613.   [40] CAG, p. 220.   [41] P. 221.   [42] P. 227.
[43] JC, pp. 472 f.   [44] P. 432.   [45] *Cf.* CEF, p. 178.   [46] JC, p. 477.
[47] JC, pp. 508 ff., OCM, pp. 29 ff., CAG, pp. 116, 156 f., LS: " History
of the Doctrine of the Trinity (1-2) ", " The Triune God ".
[48] LS: " History of the Doctrine of the Trinity (1) ".   [49] JC, p. 515.
[50] P. 517.   [51] P. 518.   [52] *Ibid.*   [53] *Ibid.*   [54] P. 519.
[55] P. 521.   [56] P. 522.   [57] *Ibid.*   [58] P. 523.
[59] De Trinitate, v. 10.   [60] JC, p. 525.   [61] P. 526.   [62] *Ibid.*
[63] *Ibid.*   [64] *Dogmatik* [6], §§ 13-18.   [65] *Ibid*, pp. 178, 199.
P. 181.   [67] P. 183.   [68] Pp. 185, 198.   [69] P. 192.   [70] P. 195.

[71] § 36.   [72] CAG, p. 150.   [73] P. 168.   [74] JC, p. 437.
[75] CEF, p. 185.   [76] JC, p. 525.   [77] Dogmatik [6], p. 201.
[78] CAG, p. 139.   [79] JC, p. 521.   [80] Ibid, cf. p. 150 supra.
[81] CEF, p. 89, cf. p. 27, Highway of God, p. 7.   [82] ACB, p. 6.
[83] JC, p. 519 n.   [84] CAG, p. 205.   [85] JC, p. 524.
[86] P. 517, OCM, p. 45, ACB, p. 254, CAG, pp. 135, 167.
[87] CAG, p. 103.   [88] P. 139 supra.
[89] Cf. JC, p. 150, Art. " Grace ", in ERE, VI, p. 365, CEF, pp. 181 f.
[90] Cf. Kirchliche Dogmatik, II/1, §§ 28 ff.
[91] Kirchliche Dogmatik, I/1, §§ 8 ff.
[92] Kirchliche Dogmatik, I/1, pp. 396, cf. pp. 145, 148 f. supra.
[93] TMT, pp. 299 f.   [94] Cf. esp. OCM. p. 30.
[95] Highway of God, Sermon II.
[96] Expository Times, XLVI (1934-35), p. 246.   [97] ACB, p. 262.
[98] CEF, p. 175.   [99] TMT, pp. 114, 155, 175, 196, 271, etc.
[100] OCM, p. 38.   [101] CAG, pp. 158 f.

CHAPTER IV

[1] RuV, III, pp. 10 f.   [2] TMT, p. 151.   [3] P. 175.   [4] P. 151.
[5] RuV, III, p. 522.   [6] TMT, p. 177.   [7] P. 173.   [8] Cf. p. 44 supra.
[9] Cf. pp. 38, 44 supra.   [10] Cf. p. 144 supra.   [11] TMT, p. 177, cf. p. 151.
[12] Cf. Highway of God, p. 43.   [13] CEF, p. 108.   [14] TMT, p. 179.
[15] Ibid.   [16] Cf. pp. 63, 138 supra.   [17] TMT, p. 152.
[18] Cf. TMT, p. 151, Art. on Ages of the World (Christian), in ERE I, p. 190 n.
[19] TMT, p. 176.   [20] Cf. p. 170 supra.   [21] Cf. p. 45 supra.
[22] Cf. TMT, p. 145.   [23] Cf. TMT, p. 161.   [24] Cf p. 59 supra.
[25] TMT, p. 147.   [26] Cf. pp. 66 ff. supra.   [27] Cf. p. 98 supra.
[28] Cf. op. cit. Translator's Preface.   [29] Cf. p. 21 supra.
[30] Cf. pp. 177 f. supra.   [31] Cf. ACB, p. 114.   [32] JC, p. 338.
[33] p. 111.   [34] Cf. p. 90 supra.   [35] Cf. p. 41 supra.

BIBLIOGRAPHY

A. Writings of H. R. Mackintosh

A. Ritschl : *Justification and Reconciliation* (vol. III of third German edition: *The Positive Development of the Doctrine*. English translation ed. by H. R. Mackintosh and A. B. Macaulay). T. & T. Clark, 1900.

F. Loofs: *Anti-Haeckel* (English translation). 1903.

Selections from the Literature of Theism (ed. by H. R. Mackintosh and Alfred Caldecott). 1904.

Life on God's Plan: Sermons. Hodder & Stoughton, 1909.

J. Wendland: *Miracles and Christianity* (English translation). 1911.

The Person of Jesus Christ. S.C.M., 1912.

The Doctrine of the Person of Jesus Christ. T. & T. Clark, 1912.

Immortality and the Future. Hodder & Stoughton, 1915.

The Originality of the Christian Message. Duckworth, 1920.

The Divine Initiative. S.C.M., 1921.

Some Aspects of Christian Belief (Essays, 1899-1921, collected and revised). Hodder & Stoughton, 1923.

The Christian Experience of Forgiveness. Nisbet, 1927, fourth edition, 1934.

F. Schleiermacher: *The Christian Faith* (English translation of second German edition ed. by H. R. Mackintosh and J. S. Stewart). T. & T. Clark, 1928.

The Christian Apprehension of God. 1929. Fourth (cheap) edition, S.C.M., 1934.

The Highway of God: Sermons. T. & T. Clark, 1931.

Types of Modern Theology. Nisbet, 1937.

Sermons, with a Memoir by A. B. Macaulay. Scribner, 1938.

Pamphlets

The Heart of the Gospel and the Preacher. Drummond Tracts, 1913.

Studies in Christian Truth, 1913.

Who is Jesus Christ? U.F. Church Series: The Church and the War, No. 15, 1917.

Articles, etc.

John Laidlaw: *Studies in the Parables and other Sermons*, with a Memoir by H. R. Mackintosh (pp. 1-47). 1907.

Charles Gore: *The Doctrine of the Infallible Book*, with a section on the Reformers' View of Scripture by H. R. Mackintosh (pp. 55 ff.). S.C.M., 1924.

Hastings' Encyclopedia of Religion and Ethics (1910-20): Note on " Ages of the World " (Christian) I, 190, and Articles on " Grace " VI, 364, " Implicit Faith " VII, 180, " Mercy " VIII, 556, " Sin " XI, 538.

Religion in Geschichte und Gegenwart [2]: Notes on F. H. Bradley, Bruce, Ed. Caird, John Caird, McLeod Campbell, Denney, Erskine, Fairbairn, T. H. Green, Sir William Hamilton, Inge, Jowett, Lodge, Moberly, Mozley, Oman, W. P. Patterson, Pringle-Pattison, Rashdall, Sorley, Streeter, Temple, Tennant, Joseph Ward, Webb.

Expositor, 6th Series.

VII (1903) pp. 180 ff. " The Objective Aspect of the Lord's Supper."

X   (1904) pp. 413 ff. " Dogmatic Theology: Its Nature and Function."

Expositor, 7th Series.

I   (1906) pp. 404 ff. " The Theology of Albrecht Ritschl."

IV   (1907) pp. 208 ff. " Christian Theology and Comparative Religion."

IX   (1910) pp. 417 ff. " Miracles and the Modern Christian Mind."

Expositor, 8th Series.

VII-VIII (1914) " Studies in Christian Eschatology."

    1. " The Christian Hope " (VII, pp. 111 ff.)

    2. Objections on the Threshold (VII, pp. 213 ff.).

    3. " The Return of Christ " (VII, pp. 298 ff.)

    4. " Death and the Sequel " (VII, pp. 427 ff.).

    5. " Immortality " (VII, pp. 538 ff.).

    6. " Future Judgment " (VIII, pp. 47 ff.).

    7. " Universal Restoration " (VIII, pp. 128 ff.).

    8. " Conditionalism " (VIII, pp. 242 ff.).

    9. "The life Everlasting" (VIII, pp. 315 ff.)

X   (1915) pp. 47 ff. " Eschatology in the Old Testament and Judaism.

pp. 97 ff. " The Eschatology of Jesus."

pp. 234 ff. " Eschatology in the Apostolic Age."

XII   (1916) pp. 300 ff. " Concerning Prayer."

XIII   (1917) pp. 193 ff. "Thoughts on Infant Baptism."

XX   (1920) pp. 31 ff. " Jesus Christ and Prayer."

pp. 371 ff. " The Vital Interest of the Church in Pure Doctrine."

XXIV (1922) pp. 60 ff. "The Knowledge of God Mediated by Forgiveness."

Expositor, 9th Series.
I   (1924) pp. 146 ff. "Review of Dr. Raven's *Apollinarianism.*"
        pp. 206 ff. "Jesus' Forgiveness of the Sinful."
II   (1924) pp. 64 ff. "Review of Gore's *Holy Spirit and the Church.*"
        pp. 406 ff. "The Ten Best Books on Miracle."
III   (1925) pp. 377 ff. "The Grouping of German Theologians."

Expository Times.
XXVI   (1914-15) pp. 151 ff. "The Name of Jesus."
XXVII (1915-16) pp. 346 ff. "The Revelation of God in Christ."
XXVIII (1916-17) pp. 488 ff. "Principal Denney as a Theologian."
XXXI   (1919-20) pp. 74 ff. "Christ and God."
        pp. 312 ff. "The Practice of the Spiritual Life."
XXXII (1920-21) pp. 343 ff. "The Minister's Message for To-day as Inspired by the New Testament."
XXXIV (1922-23) pp. 104 ff. "James Hastings."
XXIX   (1927-28) pp. 536 ff. "Leaders of Theological Thought: Karl Barth."
XL   (1928-29) pp. 311 ff. "Books that have influenced our Epoch: Herrmann's *Communion with God.*"
XLI   (1929-30) pp. 15 ff. "The Great Church Union in Scotland."
XLII   (1930-31) pp. 247 ff. "Christian Religious Doubts and how to deal with them."
XLIII (1931-32) pp. 197 ff. "Feuerbach and Illusionism."
XLVI   (1934-35) pp. 246 ff. "Things most certainly believed."
Reviews of Foreign Theology in each of vols. XXXIII-XLI.

B. OTHER WRITERS

T. K. Abbott: *Kant's Theory of Ethics* [6] (English translation of Kant's Ethical Writings). Longmans, 1909.
Karl Barth: *Christliche Dogmatik*, I. 1927.
  Kirchliche Dogmatik. Zurich, 1932 ff.
  Die protestantische Theologie im 19. Jahrhundert. Zurich, 1947.
  Die Theologie und die Kirche. Munich, 1928.

A. W. Benn: *The History of English Rationalism in the Nineteenth Century.*
2 vols. Longmans, 1906.
J. Calvin: *Institutio Christianae Religionis* (Opera Selecta, ed. P. Barth and
W. Niesel, Munich, 1928).
Th. Haering: *Der christliche Glaube.* Stuttgart, 1906.
W. Herrmann: *Ethik* [5]. Tübingen, 1913.
  Der Verkehr des Christen mit Gott [5],[6]. 1908.
  Systematische Theologie (Dogmatik). 1925.
  Art. " Christlich-protestantische Dogmatik " in *Kultur der Gegen-
  wart,* I, IV, 583-632.
M. Kähler: *Der sog. historische Jesus und der geschichtl. bibl. Christus* [2].
  1896.
  Angewandte Dogmen. Leipzig, 1908.
  Das Kreuz Grund und Mass für die Christologie. Gütersloh, 1911.
J. Kaftan: *Dogmatik* [5],[6]. Tübingen, 1909.
H. A. A. Kennedy: *St. Paul and the Mystery Religions.* 1913.
  The Theology of the Epistles. 1919.
A. S. Pringle-Pattison: *Hegelianism and Personality.* 1887.
  The Idea of God in the Light of Recent Theology. 1899.
A. Ritschl: *Rechtfertigung und Versöhnung* [4]. Bonn, 1895.
  Theologie und Metaphysik [2]. 1887.
  Unterricht in der christlichen Religion. Bonn, 1875.
F. Schleiermacher: *Reden uber die Religion* [4]. Berlin, 1831.
  Der christliche Glaube [2].
  Kurze Darstellung des theol. Studiums. Berlin, 1830.
J. W. Scott: Article—" Neo-Hegelianism ", ERE, IX, 300.
A. Titius: *Jesu Lehre vom Reiche Gottes.* Leipzig, 1895.
  Der Paulinismus unter dem Gesichtspunkt der Seligkeit. Tübingen, 1900.
W. Vollrath: *Theologie der Gegenwart in Grossbritannien.* Gütersloh, 1928.
C. C. J. Webb: *Religious Thought in England from* 1850. Clarendon Press,
  1933.

INDEX